Nations Out of Empires

Also by Harry G. Gelber

AUSTRALIA, BRITAIN AND THE EEC, 1961–1963

NATIONAL POWER, SECURITY AND ECONOMIC UNCERTAINTY

NUCLEAR WEAPONS AND CHINESE POLICY

PROBLEMS OF AUSTRALIAN DEFENCE (*editor*)

SOVEREIGNTY THROUGH INTERDEPENDENCE

TECHNOLOGY, DEFENSE AND EXTERNAL RELATIONS IN CHINA, 1975–1978

THE AUSTRALIAN–AMERICAN ALLIANCE

THE COMING OF THE SECOND WORLD WAR

THE ROLE AND FUNCTION OF UNIVERSITIES

THE STRATEGIC BALANCE (*editor*)

Nations Out of Empires

European Nationalism and the Transformation of Asia

Harry G. Gelber
Visiting Research Fellow
Asia Research Centre
London School of Economics and Political Science

First published 2001 by
PALGRAVE
Houndmills, Basingstoke, Hampshire RG21 6XS and
175 Fifth Avenue, New York, N. Y. 10010
Companies and representatives throughout the world

PALGRAVE is the new global academic imprint of
St. Martin's Press LLC Scholarly and Reference Division and
Palgrave Publishers Ltd (formerly Macmillan Press Ltd).

ISBN 0–333–92149–6

This book is printed on paper suitable for recycling and made from fully managed and sustained forest sources.

A catalogue record for this book is available from the British Library.

Library of Congress Cataloging-in-Publication Data
Gelber, Harry Gregor.
    Nations out of empires : European nationalism and
    the transformation of Asia / Harry G. Gelber.
        p. cm.
    Includes bibliographical references (p.) and index.
    ISBN 0–333–92149–6 (cloth)
    1. Asia—History. 2. Nationalism—Europe—History.
    3. Nationalism—Asia—History. 4. Europe—History–
    –1492– 5. Asia—Relations—Europe. 6. Europe—Relations–
    –Asia. I. Title.

    DS33.7 .G45 2001
    303.48'2504—dc21
                                                    00–069470

10   9   8   7   6   5   4   3   2   1
10   09   08   07   06   05   04   03   02   01

Printed and bound in Great Britain by
Antony Rowe Ltd, Chippenham, Wiltshire

This is for
Alexander, Charlotte, Sebastian,
James, Henrietta and Rebecca

Contents

Preface

The story of European colonialism in Asia is nothing if not a well-ploughed field. If I have ventured to try my hand, it is in the hope that there may still be room for a general perspective, and one which emphasizes the role of European nationalist ideas and construction in the story of both colonies and metropoles. It is not, however, a perspective which tries to cover all of the colonial efforts of Europe or the West: that seemed to me too large a canvas, too complex a story to be dealt with in a single volume except at a level of generality verging on the banal. Nor does it deal with all of Europe's colonial powers, or with all parts of Asia. Instead, this book confines itself to a tale, and a thesis, that concentrates on Britain, France and the Netherlands in Europe, and on India, Vietnam, Indonesia, China and Japan in Asia. Nor could it claim to be based on fresh research in primary sources. It relies, instead, on the rich store of secondary material. Beyond that, this book flows from my general interest in nationalism, not merely as a set – perhaps kaleidoscope – of ideas but as a pattern for socio-political construction.

Like anyone working in such a field, I owe much to many people. First and foremost, to the London School of Economics, which has once again offered me the academic hospitality without which the work would not have been possible. In the School, my primary debts are to the Asia Research Centre, to the chairman of its Research Committee, Professor Lord Desai, and to its director, Professor Michael Leifer, both of whom have saved me from a number of errors. I have also had invaluable advice and help from Professors Christopher Andrew and David Fromkin, Mr Christopher Gelber and Professors Fred Halliday, Christopher Hill, Donald Horowitz, James Mayall, Tony Milner, Robert O'Neill, Sir Robert Wade-Gery, Professor Wang Gungwu and Donald Cameron Watt. At Palgrave, Ms Josie Dixon and her colleagues have been helpfulness itself. It is surely unnecessary to add that any errors of omission or commission that remain are mine alone.

HARRY G. GELBER

Introduction

The story of European colonialism occupies a deceptively neat period of modern history. It begins with the first Portuguese voyages into the Indian Ocean at the start of the sixteenth century, and ends with the breakup of the British, French, Dutch and other empires (including the Soviet one) five centuries later, during the twentieth. That neat framework is, however, debatable. There were Western Christian colonies in the Holy Land, and Portuguese and Italian voyages to Africa, long before Bartolomeo Diaz rounded the Cape of Good Hope. And five hundred years later, a globalizing international scene is in many ways dominated by political and financial institutions in which, former colonies sometimes complain, they are the objects and the former colonialists the subjects. Nevertheless, European and, more broadly, Western colonialism looks like a reasonably closed historical epoch and it is possible to discuss not only its details but the larger trends which made it an important and fascinating phenomenon.

There was, of course, no single cause for the long centuries of Western expansion. Much European exploration stemmed from simple curiosity or adventurism. In its early stages, Europeans wanted to find out what was there; whether there really was an edge to the world, so that if you went too far you would fall off. There were resource pressures, not to mention simple greed, which encouraged the search for wealth and, as part of that, profitable and secure trade. There was the simple lust for war and conquest among Europeans accustomed to conflict. In addition, the states of Europe sought security, whether in the fifteenth and sixteenth centuries against Islam or, in the nineteenth, against each other in the scramble for Africa. Not least, there was the desire for settlement: Siberia was occupied for just this reason, and the United States is the child of English, Scots, Irish and German

1

settlers' as are Canada, Australia and New Zealand. The same is true of the Spaniards who settled in Latin America or the French who made their homes in North Africa and parts of the Pacific.

Of particular interest are the great maritime empires created by Western Europe, especially those of the British, French and Dutch in East, South and Southeast Asia. They are quite distinct from the land-based empires of the Ottomans, the Russians, or the Austro-Hungarians and passed, in general terms, through five stages. The first lasted from the fifteenth to the end of the seventeenth century. In this, with the exception of Spain, the Europeans deferred to local empires, and inter-course with local societies was between cultural (though not religious) equals. The European presence in the East Indies – 'East of Suez'? – was almost entirely commercial, confined to tiny coastal settlements where soldiers and traders huddled together under the guns of Western war-ships, but in truth were dependent on the goodwill of their hosts. For the major empires of India and China, or Japan's Tokugawa shoguns, they were politically and strategically quite marginal.

By the early eighteenth century a second stage opened. The political and military organization, technologies and skills developed in Europe – partly as a result of an endless series of wars – started to make pene-tration into the Asian interior possible. Native authorities could now be dealt with from a position of some superiority. The Europeans found they could defeat larger – in some cases very much larger – native armies and dictate advantageous and even exploitative treaties to local rulers. It was the start of a kind of hegemony, but without direct control. European positions depended on the ability to overawe or manipulate local elites and rulers.

The situation was promoted by revolutionary changes in Europe. Starting in the seventeenth and eighteenth centuries, the development of nationalism, especially in Britain and France but also in Holland, Spain and Russia, played a decisive role in the evolution of Europe's states, and therefore also in their colonial expansion. This was much more than the ideas about ethnic and religious separateness by which men have always identified themselves. It was not confined to philoso-phies, or even political or cultural or ethnic passions. It combined several elements whose conjunction not merely fuelled the growth of Europe's empires but provided much of the driving force of modern national and international history. One was a set of political ideas which implied an historically novel basis for political and state legit-imacy and therefore action. Here was a changed conception, brought about by the three great Western revolutions which span the eighteenth century, of the very sources of legitimate political sovereignty. Ever since, the nation-state has meant a sovereign community not only self-consciously separate in history, language, culture and, almost always, ethnicity, but one whose internal loyalties, cohesion and capacity for common action are actively promoted. That has also brought the development of novel systems of social organization, including the administrative expansion and centralization of the state and the promotion of a common language and educational system. Without these conjunctions, nationalism could not have triumphed within Europe. But once it did, it produced social energies and efficiencies which helped to energize not only Europe's own wars but its overseas expansion.

One would not expect such changes to occur quickly or easily; and their precise combination and timing naturally varied a good deal, both between the Europeans themselves and in their impact on other societies which they influenced or dominated. In Britain and France the establishment of national and secular political principles, and the forms of social organization those principles made possible, took at least a century to develop. As they did, they also helped to fuel the industrial revolution and the financial networks which accompanied it. They provided much of the impetus for the change from merely commercial activities to the expanding imperial state. And they underpinned the belief in Europe's 'right to rule'.

These developments overlapped with the third stage, roughly from the end of the eighteenth century to the latter part of the nineteenth. It saw the advance of direct European rule, and was made possible by much more than the new ideas and social structures. It depended heavily on the industrialization of Europe and North America and on their rapid technological advances. And the technical advances rested on the scientific rationalism of the previous two centuries, not on national principles. Yet their exploitation depended heavily on the financial, administrative and especially industrial developments which the new state structures encouraged. So, now, steamships could bring very large numbers of people to the colonies and help to explore river systems. Railways opened up continents and made mass transport of people and goods possible. Medical science opened up still more land, as it overcame scourges like yellow fever and malaria. Breech-loading and later quick-firing guns confirmed the West's military superiority. The result was a degree of European (and, for that matter, American) dominance which seemed entirely beyond challenge. It was accepted by almost all the colonial peoples, as proof of the superiority not just of the technology and prowess but of the culture of the colonial power. The white man, whether in law, in administration or on the battlefield, had demonstrated his natural superiority and therefore clearly had a right to rule. Nor was it by any means simply a matter of oppression. European law and government brought hitherto unknown security, stability, health and, at times, education.

A fourth stage in the colonial story came towards the end of the nineteenth century. It had two parallel elements. One was the debate within Europe itself about the moral justification of empire, beyond simple assertions of imperial pride or even of strategic need. That began a dispute between liberal imperialists, who justified and celebrated empire as bringing civilization to the dark corners of the earth, and liberal humanists, for whom empire violated the very principles of liberty, equality or social justice which Western societies claimed as their own. Together with that came other critiques, whether from socialists implacably opposed to the bourgeois state and all its works, or Christian groups emphasizing the brotherhood of man or the new trade unions that saw empires as costly in money and men.

At the same time came politically effective nationalist assertions in the Asian colonies themselves, moving through three broad phases. First came attempts at conservative revival. This was followed by a search for assimilation and co-optation in governance. Only then came the forced development, whether in India or Vietnam or Japan, of socio-economic developments which recognizably followed European examples. It was rising local assertion in modern nationalist forms, by groups or parties organized along national rather than regional or sectional lines, which could then express demands for political independence.

A fifth, relatively brief, stage came in the two or three decades ending around the 1960s. It saw the collapse of Western empires in the Asian-Pacific area, whether for reasons of political principle, psychological exhaustion and economic weakness in the colonial metropoles or the growing power of nationalist assertion in the colonies themselves.

In dealing with so large a field, the account offered in this book is limited in various ways. It is not an account of Asian modernization. Modernization is, in any case, a question-begging concept, since it can only mean movement in the direction of the modern, i.e. contemporary and 'advanced', world. It is not easy to see what social factors, whether domestic or international, can be excluded from that.

Nor does it try to deal with the entire colonial experience. It is confined to some aspects of the British, French and Dutch efforts at colonization in India, Vietnam, Indonesia, China and Japan. It focuses strongly on the particular importance of European-style nationalism and the growth of the nation-state, and its role in the story of colonization and decolonization and the changing role of the individual from subject to citizen; since the subject of a monarchy has different rights and functions from those of 'citizenship [which] is by definition national'.[1]

The book also assumes that somewhat different interpretations might apply in, say, Latin America or Africa, or in dealing with the latter-day empires of the United States or Japan. It is therefore not a comprehensive account of Europe's total influence on Asia, still less of the important and sometimes subtle ways in which Asia has influenced Europe. It underlines Europe's political, military and administrative genius, which is a different thing from virtue. And it tackles the story in a conventionally chronological way, which can easily confuse sequence with cause and give excessive importance to events which can be dated.

One other word of caution. No attempt to highlight one theme can do full justice to the confusing, contradictory and invariably messy empirical detail. Nor can nationalism, or the development of the nation-state, be usefully seen as a separate or even clearly delineated phenomena. Emphasis on them may, nevertheless, be heuristically useful and offer revised avenues of interpretation.

1
The Asian Order

The Asian-Pacific region is vast and immensely varied in geography, topography and climate. The Pacific Ocean alone covers a third of the earth's surface and is twice as large as its nearest rival, the Atlantic. On its shores lie the steamy islands of Southeast Asia, the mountains of Japan, and in China harsh northern plains as well as the hot, rainy regions of the south which are the region's best agricultural land. It was in these fertile valleys, capable of producing rice, that early populations grew. By AD 1 around 53 million people lived in China, or 86 per cent of all the peoples bordering the Pacific. At about the same time, settlers from Korea and China introduced Japan to wet rice cultivation. Major population increases in the region only began around the eleventh or twelfth centuries, with the spread of rice strains yielding two harvests a year. By the thirteenth century the population had reached 100 million and went on growing. By the end of the fifteenth century China alone probably had 100 million people and two hundred years later India had also passed the 100 million mark. The standard diet was vegetarian: almost 98 per cent of calories consumed came from vegetables, very little from meat or fish. Raising cattle for meat is a waste, since they consume more calories than they yield as food.

If geography and climate are varied, so are peoples and civilizations. For a thousand years before the arrival of the Europeans, they were shaped by contrasting trends. There was a constant movement of war and conquest, and an often lively network of communication and commerce. The Asian order was not only large, but sophisticated and interdependent in trade and ideas, coupled with much underlying stability in the major cultures and religions.

The states and empires of South and East Asia were constantly threatened by tribal raiders from their north, often driven by population pressures on the steppes. China, especially, went through repeated periods of this kind of insecurity. India was similarly threatened. But Turks, Turcomans, Mongols and Kirghiz were no mere scourges. In the three centuries before AD 1500, they dominated the entire known world with the exception of Western and Central Europe. Turkish and Mongol rulers governed India, China, Persia, Egypt, North Africa, Mesopotamia, the Balkans, Russia and the Hungarian plain.

The greatest of these rulers, whose very name is still a byword for terror, was Genghis Khan. Cruelty may have been part of his genius, but he was a great captain; brave, tenacious, shrewd, patient. He also encouraged able administrators, adopted a code of law and practised religious toleration – if only for the political purpose of ruling many different peoples – and was learned in the arts and traditions of China. He created and ruled what may well be the greatest empire the world has ever seen. Earlier wars against the Hunnish empire of Kin had given the Mongols excellent military training, even in the arts of Kin's Chinese allies. But it was Genghis who organized the Mongol tribes and began to create a military state in which every male between the ages of fifteen and seventy served as a soldier, thus producing great armies, largely of mounted archers and bound by iron discipline. Mongol commanders planned meticulously, paid close attention to logistics and supply; their strategy, tactics and, not least, political and tactical intelligence were almost always vastly superior to those of their opponents. In a series of remarkable campaigns Genghis launched these armies westwards against Central Asia as well as southwards, against China. He attacked there in 1211 and by the early 1220s held most of China's north. Further west he took major cities like Bokhara and Samarkand. By the time he died in 1227, Genghis ruled the lands from the coast of the Pacific to the Black Sea, and from the forests of Siberia to the Persian Gulf.

After his death the empire grew further. A mere fourteen years later, the Mongols had moved further westwards. They overran Poland and seized the Hungarian plain. They plundered India's northwest, including the Punjab, though they did not establish governance there. Other Mongol armies invaded Persia and Syria. They captured Baghdad in 1258 and crushed the Abbasid caliphate which had dominated Mesopotamia for five centuries.[1] They moved further into China too, occupying all of north China by 1234 and, after more conquests by Ghengis's grandson Kublai, the Sung empire in the south as well. In the meantime, other Mongol armies had reached Tonkin and Annam in what is now Vietnam. The Mongols even attempted, around 1280, to invade Japan, which was only saved when a *kamikaze*[2] storm destroyed Kublai Khan's navy. At its greatest extent, the empire ran from the mouth of the Amur river to Hungary and from Siberia to north India, Burma and even Java.

In all these campaigns the ruthlessness of the Mongols – and of their successors – became proverbial. Echoes of the Mongol terror persist to this day, as in the word 'Tartar'. Ghengis and his successors regularly adopted a policy of terror and selective massacre. They sacked Bokhara. Herat was destroyed, leaving a million dead. A series of Russian towns were destroyed and their inhabitants massacred. Kiev was left without a single inhabitant, the surrounding steppe strewn with skulls. The terror continued, even when Tamerlane captured Delhi in 1398. Each of these conquests was a catastrophe. From Korea to Hungary, vanquished armies were simply obliterated. In whole regions the Mongols were apt to leave peasants in their fields, to sow and raise crops, only to slaughter them afterwards anyway. Millions were killed and many more enslaved.

The Mongol empire quickly became too large and varied to be governed from one tent-city. So Persia, Central Asia, China and Russia came to be dominated by different branches of the ruling family. But family unity gave way to competition and some Mongols 'went native'. The wealth and culture of China, especially, undermined Mongol cohesion and military enthusiasm. Their rulers took the Chinese name Yuan and retained Chinese institutions, including the civil service and tax system. That encouraged a Chinese reaction against the Mongols and brought the properly Chinese Ming dynasty to power. It governed from 1368 and expanded Chinese power, for example over Korea and into Annam.

The political patterns of early modern Asia developed from the disintegration of this Mongol empire, beginning with the death of Kublai Khan in 1294. The empire quickly broke into three major and several minor fragments. The three were the Chinese empire, a Persian one and the rule of the Kipchaks in Russia. But matters were complicated by the spread of Islam. Islamic hegemony had by then passed from its original Arab base to the Persians, and from there to the Ottoman Turks. The Ottomans had risen to dominance in the Islamic world even before the Mongol conquests and now, roughly from 1300 to 1500, Islamic expansion resumed under their leadership. They moved into India as well as the Balkans, defeating the Slav forces at Kosovo in

1389.[3] They went on to destroy the remnants of the Eastern Orthodox Byzantine empire and, in one of the major landmarks of European history, to occupy Constantinople in 1453. Seventy years later, under Suleiman the Magnificent, they reached the gates of Vienna. By the fifteenth century, then, the Asian coastal scene was dominated by four great empires. In the west were the Ottomans, whose empire stretched from the Danube to the Red Sea. Further east lay the Safavids of Persia; but they lacked the kind of bureaucracy, and system of military service, which underpinned Turkish power. Further east again, and the pivot of Asia's seaborne trade, was India, soon to be dominated by the Mogul empire. It was Indian Hindus who had also colonized Southeast Asia. Finally, eastwards from India, and dominating the East Asian coastline, lay the majestic bulk of China.

These empires and principalities were far from inward looking or ignorant of the outside world. Japan had from ancient times been regularly affected, and in some respects even formed, by influences from Korea and especially China. Travellers – a cultural invasion of sorts – reached Japan from far-away Indonesia. Indo-China was repeatedly invaded. Before 1300 the Mongol court even sent an emissary to Europe in a vain attempt to create an anti-Arab alliance. He was Rabban Sauma, a Nestorian Christian and the first Chinese known to have visited Europe. He was received by the Byzantine emperor, the Pope and both Philip IV of France and Edward I of England. Franciscan friars reached the Mongol court in 1245 and 1253 and reported back, as did others a century later. But the most famous of the Western travellers was Marco Polo, whose journey appears to have lasted from 1271 to 1295, and who served for a time at the court of Kublai Khan. There were other occasional contacts with Westerners including, much later, Jesuit priests. Moreover, China regularly received tribute from surrounding societies and tended to dominate parts of Southeast Asia.

From early days, too, there was a system of strategic and commercial relations across oceans and deserts. Some Indian writings from 600 BC suggest that even then there was trade with Java and Sumatra. The Phoenicians traded from Cornwall to India. When Hannibal crossed the Alps around 210 BC in his struggle with Rome, he had Indian mahouts in charge of his elephants. By the twelfth century AD, Chinese junks traded fairly regularly with Indonesia, India, even the Persian Gulf. The Mongols launched huge naval expeditions; in 1274 and again in 1281 they invaded Japan, the second time with 170 000 soldiers and 4 500 ships – almost as many vessels as the Anglo-American navies deployed in the 1944 invasion of Normandy. In the early 1290s they sent 1000 ships and 20 000 men on an unsuccessful expedition to Java. By the fourteenth century Moslems controlled the carrying trade in the Indian Ocean and Moslem clerics dominated seaports in Java, Borneo and the Malay peninsula. Meanwhile Japanese pirates were harrying the Chinese coast.

Long before 1500, then, there was a sophisticated and what would now be called entirely multi-cultural network of merchants, sailors, officials and cut-throats in ports and settlements from China to mainland Southeast Asia, to Java, India, and to the coasts of Arabia and East Africa. As early as the thirteenth century, the Mongol empire and its *pax tatarica* gave relative security to travellers between the China coast and the Black Sea, down to the Gulf and even into what was to become Russia.[4] Much of Asia was therefore opened to European merchants and missionaries. Colonies of Italian merchants were established at Constantinople and at Trebizond, the terminus of the 'silk road' leading either via Samarkand to China or else to Ormuz on the Gulf. Indeed, Ormuz became a chief entrepot for the spice trade from the Malay archipelago through India and Ceylon to the Middle East and Europe; while Malacca became the main port for spice shipments from the islands either east to China or westwards to India, whence Arab or Persian traders brought them to Ormuz.

Combined with trade came a brief but brilliant period of Chinese trans-oceanic assertion. Between 1405 and 1433 Chinese fleets, commanded by legendary admirals like Cheng Ho, sailed the seas to display China's power to the barbarians, to assert power, to receive tribute, to collect information and to trade.[5] Cheng Ho made seven voyages to Java, Ceylon and East Africa, and gave Chinese to places like Mombasa. His fleets had up to 37 000 men and 300 or more ships. His treasure ships were probably the largest ships ever seen up to then, each longer than a modern football field and with advanced marine technologies. They were multi-decked, with watertight bulkheads, bamboo fenders, axial rudders and navigational compasses. Some were built for luxury, but the fleet also had warships, and troop and horse transports. By some estimates, between 1404 and 1407 the Chinese built, or refitted, some 1680 ships.

Long before the wave of European exploration began, therefore, Levantine merchants and Venice grew rich on the westward sectors of this inter-continental trade. They concentrated on the sectors which connected Italy with Alexandria and the regions beyond. But Genoese and Venetian traders could also use the trans-Asian land routes made safe by the '*Pax tatarica*' to travel to China in search of silks. Chinese traders, too, set up colonies in Novgorod and Moscow, while Chinese engineers worked on irrigation problems in Mesopotamia. Of course, all these connections and probes had their limits. Most of the peoples and states from the Mediterranean to China, had little concept of the extent of the southern or eastern seas, or the wider implications of that geography.

In contrast to these links of trade and conquest, in both India and China social and religious structures were highly resistant to quick change, conferring much stability and continuity. This meant that adapting to new circumstances was hard and change, once compelled, was apt to cause turmoil. In China, systems of Taoism and Buddhism took hold, together with a Confucianism whose logic emphasized personal moral obligations to others. In India, neither Hindus nor Buddhists questioned the principles of a permanent and harmonious order of the universe; while the caste system was critical in forming a collective identity which made non-Hindus irrevocably, and by definition, outsiders. Neither in India nor China nor Japan nor Cambodia was the individual conceived of as ultimately autonomous. Still less did society focus on individual liberties.

Yet stability and continuity are relative concepts. Asian societies developed a patchwork of languages, religions and social customs; and, with them, different ways of thinking and social norms. Ancient varieties of animism, astrology and geomancy remained omnipresent, especially in rural areas where pantheism made for a good deal of religious tolerance. In China, reverence for ancestors and the gods of nature, dating from at least a thousand years before the Christian era, were largely amalgamated into the newer thinking. In most areas ancient religious systems were linked to equally hardy social structures: caste systems in India, social hierarchies and family networks in China.[6] By the thirteenth century, the parts of Southeast Asia affiliated with India were dominated by Hinduism-Buddhism, and only towards the end of the fifteenth century did this start to give way in Malaya and parts of Indonesia to an Islam brought by Arabs.[7] In spite of Islam's 'modern' appeal – freeing people from the injustices of caste, making Brahmins equal to outcasts – its progress was slow and subtle.[8] It tended to adapt to cultures it conquered and its establishment therefore often included non-Islamic or pre-Islamic elements.

These cultures were not accustomed to separate social and political affairs from faith or belief. In most parts of the Far East such distinctions made no sense; and make no sense in the twenty-first century either. Belief systems are involved in all aspects of human life: in the state and politics, in philosophy and social or family relations. Confucianism, for example, is notably both an effort to explain the world in rational terms, and a system of political, social and personal ethics. It establishes a rule of life which tends strongly to maintain social order and hierarchy. That has existed side by side with Taoism, Buddhism and, for that matter, Marxism. There have been few religious wars in China or Japan akin to those in Europe.

In India, a mediaeval Hindu civilization was followed by an Islamic-Hindu one, imposed by the conquering Moslems from the thirteenth to the eighteenth centuries. The Islamic firestorm of the seventh and eighth centuries had tended to isolate the Indian world. Moslem arms expanded into Central Asia, while Moslem dominance at sea sharply reduced seaborne contact between India and the lands to the east and south. The result was a Moslem barrier between India and China. Hindu opposition to Islam hardened; while Hindu revival was accompanied by the resurgence of immemorial village superstitions, belief in magic, and later even some elements of Catholicism. Northern India, in particular, became the scene of political confusion and chronic warfare, even while cities and cultures flourished. Then Moslem arms occupied Northern India. Following a Turkish invasion, the Sultanate of Delhi was established in 1206. It came to dominate Northern India, strongly governed, and cemented by the continuing Mongol threat from the north. In 1220 Genghis himself invaded and the threat was not dispelled until the fourteenth century, when the Sultanate grew stronger with the annexation of Gujerat and further expansion southwards into the Deccan. Here was an autocratic state with a largely self-contained economy. It was dominated by its military aristocracy and army, and its rulers governed by terror and cruelty. Hindu temples were destroyed to make way for mosques. There were forced conversions. But in 1398 came another Mongol invasion, under Tamerlane, which sacked and destroyed Delhi itself. The Sultanate never recovered.

In 1526 Sultan Ibrahim Lodi lost the battle of Panipat against yet another Central Asian chief, a Turkoman named Baber. His army won with the aid of matchlocks, and artillery serviced by Ottoman Turks. He occupied Delhi and Agra and established rule of the Moguls (meaning Mongols) in India. He was a broadly civilized man, an accomplished poet and master of Turkish prose, as well as a remarkable warrior. He was interested in architecture, lovely gardens and music, and possessed a sense of humour. He encouraged religious toleration and his conquests extended as far as Bengal. By the time of his grandson, the great emperor Akbar, the Moguls ruled most of India. Akbar, even more than his grandfather, is a pivotal figure. He not only conquered, he organized; and, in organizing, changed India for good. He encouraged commerce and reformed the tax system. He abolished slavery. He did more. He encouraged the arts and promoted science and literature. The architecture of his time produced a synthesis of Hindu and Islamic traditions. In religion he was eclectic: he even had long discussions with missionaries from the newly founded Jesuit order, though he found them unconvincing. Not surprisingly, the masses loved him. His instinct for a synthesis of the varied groups and peoples he ruled may have created the first glimmerings of the idea of a common interest for the sub-continent.

In the Southeast Asian archipelago, the last great empire of Hindu culture was Majapahit. This commercial empire flourished after the Mongol invasion attempt of the 1290s was repulsed, and lasted until the beginning of the sixteenth century. In the fourteenth, it controlled the spice trade and the seas of the archipelago. In the meantime, traders from India and Southwest Asia had brought Islam to the region. When Marco Polo arrived in Sumatra the 1290s as the ambassador of the Mongol Khan, he found numbers of Moslems.[9] Then, or shortly afterwards, there were Moslem principalities, too. Almost at the same time came the first Catholic missionaries and small Chinese settlements by pirates or shipwrecked sailors. But it was the new Islamic religion that spread to Java from Sumatra as well as from the commercial entrepot of Malacca. It had grown, often under the protection of China, which sometimes sent armed ships to enforce its authority on Southeast Asian trade routes. By the sixteenth century Moslem princes had gained power in most of Indonesia. Islam also extended through Malaya, then a patchwork of small states, to Borneo and the spice islands; and spread from there to the Philippines, where its advance was only stemmed by Christianity following Spain's seizure of Manila in 1571. Naturally, faith was everywhere also a lever of secular power. In any event, by 1500 the broad political patterns of Southeast Asia were recognizably akin to those of the modern era.

The imperial monarchy in China continued to look mainly inwards. Between 750 and 1100 its population seems to have doubled and by the start of the sixteenth century China, with its 100 million people, already had the largest number of people of any state in the world.[10] But in 1368 the properly Chinese Ming, having defeated Kublai Khan's heirs, assumed the imperial throne. They presided over a cultural flowering and developed the arts, sciences and even various technologies to a high level. Early in the fifteenth century, they also moved the capital northwards from Nanjing to Beijing, an 800-mile transfer which involved vast expense for new palaces and walls, as well as for transport.

For all the cultural development, however, there was much governmental ossification. For Europeans, time was linear. For the Chinese, it was cyclical. Europe tended towards a rule of law. Its despotisms were mitigated by law, custom and privileges, the political rights and charters of towns. China developed centralized and bureaucratic methods of government. A mandarin class evolved, small in number, selected by rigorous examination based on the classics, strong on traditional styles and thought, and dedicated to state administration. Its powers were very great and its standards of administration often high. The mandarins were custodians of a peaceful and stable order, defining doctrine, judging behaviour and even thought.

But innovation and dissent were stifled and, with that, technological progress, people often being treated as objects.[11] From early days China had coal, coke and textiles, most of the elements that, centuries later, produced the industrial revolution in Europe. But it failed to develop them. Though China had many inventions, there was little follow-up. Nor did China have, then or now, property rights comparable to those of Europe; or encouragement for private enterprise; or an independent judiciary. Instead, there was emphasis on mutual and collective responsibility at local and district levels. There were rules, regulations and customs governing everything, qualified but also reinforced by stress on consensus.

This imperial order was at once human and religious: two sides of the same coin. The emperor was both spiritual and temporal ruler, guardian of the peace and prosperity of his people, himself the model of morality and justice. Whoever was emperor ruled by the 'mandate of heaven'. As sovereign in both domains he appointed officials, decided on the temple hierarchy and presided over the ritual start of farm work. If the mandate of heaven shifted, it was because the emperor and his family had fallen from proper standards of virtue and it was consequently time for someone else to become the virtuous ruler. Floods, disasters of all kinds, especially peasant rebellions, resulted from a lack of virtue in the ruler, hence were a fundamental breach of the contract between ruler and ruled. Between 1627 and 1636 crop failures and peasant rebellions from Fujian to the far northwest heralded the intervention of the Manchus in 1644. As late as 1975–6 earthquakes and floods were signs to the common people that the rule of Mao Zedong was coming to an end. So it was. He died. In the words of an ancient proverb: 'Heaven sees with the eyes of the people.' It was a sentiment echoed, in different words, by the American Founding Fathers.

This empire saw itself as the centre of the civilized universe. The Chinese scholar-bureaucrat did not think of a 'China' or of a 'Chinese civilization' in the modern sense at all. For him there were the Han people and, beyond that, only barbarism. Whatever was not civilized was, by definition, barbaric. Civilization was an empire without neighbours, since the concept of 'neighbour' means someone else who is also civilized. China therefore did not resemble a modern 'state'. 'China' was simply that entity which administered civilized society.

Consequently the emperor could not be merely one ruler among many, governing one state among many. That idea was not only foreign, it was irrational. The emperor was the apex of human civilization, the mediator between heaven and earth in a system where the Western division between temporal and spiritual had no meaning. Western rulers might think of themselves as political figures both temporal and local. In contrast, and by definition, the Chinese emperor had universal significance. It followed that no one could imagine such a thing as a treaty between sovereign states. It was rather that, since non-Chinese peoples were by definition barbarians, they were incapable of virtue and could only be kept in line by a system of rewards and punishments. Foreigners might appear from time to time from unknown regions to admire Chinese civilization and buy its products, but they could hardly be of much concern to the Celestial Empire. All that the Emperor and his officials asked was that such folk should not disturb the harmonious order of the Chinese realm. Beyond that, all barbarians owed tribute and homage to the emperor of China. All foreign relations were simply tributary relations, with barbarians carrying tribute to the emperor.

Moreover, since all other societies were mere tributaries of China and its civilization, tribute to the emperor meant not merely propitiating a superior but, much more importantly, the acknowledgment of a proper global order. It was tribute not so much to China as to civilization itself, embodied in the emperor. Refusal to pay tribute was not only an insult to the emperor's person, but a discordant note in the universal and harmonious scheme of things. It was an unnatural act which the emperor could not tolerate, it being his duty to maintain harmony

under heaven. Universal justice and order positively required acknowledgment of the centrality and superiority of the Chinese empire. More
pragmatically, too, China was ancient, insulated and great. Before the
seventeenth century the Chinese had never met any civilization that
was mightier, let alone more sophisticated. Even powerful raiders from
the steppes had been mere barbarians. Their incursions had always
been temporary and where they were not, the barbarians had been
absorbed and civilized in time. Naturally, this vision of China's role in
the world which, to modern eyes, defines inequality between states,
was in time to cause great difficulties. It had no room for 'international
relations' as commonly understood in the West.

Nevertheless, the Chinese empire, anti-cosmopolitan at home, could
hardly avoid external relations. It pragmatically established a tributary
system for relations with surrounding principalities. That sustained the
notion of China as the centre of civilization, emphasized cultural
imperialism and stabilized the Far Eastern international order. It also
secured peace along China's borders. In the words of a Ming document
of 1436: 'Since our empire owns the world, there is no country on this
or the far side of the seas which does not submit to us. The sage
Emperors who followed one another had the same regard and uniform
benevolence for all countries far and near.' China would not only not
interfere in the internal affairs of other states but would make tributary
status attractive and profitable for the tribute bearer. Consequently the
system, which indeed proved profitable for Korea, Annam, Manchuria
and others, produced generally peaceful and orderly results until the
sixteenth century, with its fresh Mongol incursions as well as piracy on
the coasts. It was that growing governmental weakness which led to
the rise of the Manchus on the northeastern frontiers.

One of the lesser but constant imperial preoccupations was Indo-
China. Its peoples had long fought among themselves and against
Chinese domination. Yet eleven centuries of that domination imbued
them with the religious attitudes and civilization of the Chinese
empire. They commonly date the beginning of their national independence only from AD 939 when, after the fall of the T'ang dynasty in
China, they decisively defeated a Chinese army. They foiled Chinese
attempts at reconquest in the eleventh and thirteenth centuries. 'The
more the Chinese labored to deprive this people of its ethnic identity,
the faster they promoted the development of a Vietnamese national
consciousness ... it is the story of Vietnam under Chinese domination
that contains the explanation of the ethnic durability and the irre-
pressible national vitality of the Vietnamese.'[12]

Then, in the thirteenth century, Indo-China was overrun by the Mongols (who also briefly organized north and central Burma [now Myanmar]). With the end of Mongol power came Vietnamese reassertion. Then the Chinese briefly recaptured control in Vietnam in the early fifteenth century and expanded their influence beyond. Yet Vietnam remained a centralized state, headed by a monarch whose absolute powers also rested on a mandate of heaven. The Le dynasty essentially kept the throne for three and a half centuries to 1788.

Vietnam clearly derived great benefit from its contacts with China, not only politically but by the influence of Confucianism. The Confucian ruler was expected to stick to established rules of behaviour, yet there was also an implied right of revolution against a ruler who did not do so. A number of Confucian practices were introduced to legitimize the monarchy, centralize state and monarchical power and improve efficiency. To this system the concept of a division of powers was completely alien and remained so for all of precolonial Vietnam. Confucianism became the official doctrine under the Emperor Le Thanh Tong (1460–97) and administration was structured, and the legal code regularized, on the Chinese pattern. Mandarins were recruited by civil service examination. As in China, this meant a professional bureaucracy selected by merit which implied a certain social fluidity. However, this officialdom, too, looked only to the past. 'They were opposed to any innovation, not only technical and economic but also spiritual, and their hostility to change hardened precisely when the survival of an independent Vietnam required a systematic modernization of the country.'[13] This encouraged efficient but rigid administration, a rational social hierarchy and a social ethic based on hard work, personal honour, and community service. The down-side was not only a rigid official conservatism but some official arrogance and self-seeking. Not surprisingly, for 900 years prior to French rule, the country's economy was static. It remained exclusively agricultural; trade was insignificant.

Beyond the eastern sea, Japan remained primitive from its earliest origins until the sixth century BC when Chinese civilization made its first major impact. But even in that primitive early Japan, archaeologists have traced links to Korea, Manchuria and even Siberia. Around the third or second centuries BC new invasions came from south China and the Indonesian archipelago. A political and religious system developed which deified the forces of nature. Long afterwards, in the nineteenth century, it was revived under the name of Shinto, meaning 'the way of the Gods'. But it took time to establish Japan in anything resembling its modern form. The country was fragmented as late as the eighth century AD. When it did unite and develop, it did so strongly under the influence of Chinese civilization. China even baptized Japan, whose very name of 'Japan' is derived from the Chinese 'Je-pen', meaning, since the sun always rises in China's east, the land of the rising sun.

By AD 1200 or so Japan was a military feudalism, much disrupted by bloodthirsty struggles between warlords and clans. Bitter rivalries and bloody vengeance came to be glorified in a code of honour which the seventeenth-century warring factious (and the imperial army of the Second World War) were to call the way of the warrior, or *bushido*.[14] For three centuries before 1600 Japan experienced an endless series of civil conflicts. Only at the end of this period did Oda Nobunaga and his lieutenant and successor, Toyotomi Hideyoshi, end the constant warfare. And only then could Tokugawa Ieyasu, following a decisive victory in the battle of Sekigahara, set about reorganizing the entire state.

By that time there had appeared, on the southern fringes of these principalities and civilizations, strange new ships carrying a strange new group of people. They were rough, crude, poorly dressed, fierce and greedy, but equipped with powerful weapons. There were not many of them, and at first they seemed just another barbarian group wanting to trade for local delicacies, luxuries and crafts. For the major empires of the region they were of entirely marginal significance; and for two hundred years they would be confined to small coastal encampments, while the kingdoms of South and East Asia worried about much more important matters. The newcomers were Europeans.

2
Explorers, Soldiers, Priests and Traders

Until the start of the sixteenth century Europeans knew almost nothing about the Asian-Pacific area or its peoples and empires. Contacts were erratic and sparse. Some Europeans, their numbers much diminished during the fourteenth century,[1] were eager to import Eastern spices, Chinese silks and even bureaucratic principles, not to mention technologies including gunpowder and the magnetic compass.[2] But even educated folk were only dimly aware, through news by caravan or occasional travellers like Marco Polo, of the civilizations and riches of the fabulous East.

Late mediaeval Latin Christendom was a turbulent and dynamic region. Its rulers and peoples were enterprising and energetic, filled with religious zeal and accustomed to war, with one another or against the constant threats to Christendom's very existence. From the East came Magyars, not settling but raiding deep into Christian Europe year after year. Until the tenth century there was the scourge of the Northmen. These lethal marine bandits could attack coasts or take their light boats up rivers to strike inland for plunder or the simple fun of rape and killing. They roamed Europe's western coasts and further, to Sicily and Italy. Other Viking groups went east to the land of the Rus (Russia), some bands travelling as far as Constantinople. Different raiders came from the south. Saracens, North African Moors, sailed across the Mediterranean, setting up bases from the French coast to remote alpine mountain fastnesses to prey on trading routes.

Above all, there was the general threat of Islam, whose armies swept with fire and sword through the Middle East, North Africa and Iberia, determined to kill or convert the infidel wherever they could get at him. Back in AD 732 Charles Martel, the grandfather of Charlemagne, had led an army of armoured knights to victory against them. Near Tours he had won a decisive battle, setting a western and northern limit to a Moslem sweep which had begun to seem irresistible.[3] But the Islamic surge continued in other directions. Led by great generals like Saladin, the Moslems expelled the Christian crusaders and their short-lived kingdoms from the Levant. Ships and armies of the Prophet dominated the Mediterranean and occupied much of Iberia. It was one of the great turning points of European and world history when Constantinople fell to the Turks and the Byzantine empire crumbled into dust. For over two centuries after its fall they would surge northwards, carrying the crescent banner to Kiev and the plains of Hungary.

As is so often the case, people learned much from their enemies. Wars and crusades did not prevent Christian princes from making treaties with non-Christian rulers. Nor did they prevent trade from flourishing. In the Levant, as well as in Spain, Arab culture began to civilize the Western military barbarians who had ridden forth carrying the cross and the sword. Europe was taught Arab architecture, mathematics and astronomy as well, occasionally, as civilized manners. The Alhambra in Grenada remains one of Europe's loveliest buildings and modern science would have been impossible had not the Arabs transmitted from India one of the greatest of mathematical discoveries: the figure zero. Until at least 1 100, Moslem science and technology far surpassed that of Europe and was only stopped in its tracks when some of Islam's own religious zealots began to demand spiritual conformity. All truth, they maintained, had already been revealed in the Koran, which was all-encompassing and therefore beyond possibility of challenge.

However, learning from Arabs was one thing, the defence of the Christian West quite another. And in time, defence extended into expansion. That took three directions, and for the princes, priests and merchants of the West all three drives were shaped by a confused mixture of strategic necessity, religious enthusiasm, and a thirst for gold, slaves, adventure and discovery. One thrust, spearheaded by fighting orders like the Teutonic knights, drove eastwards from Germany into non-Christian regions along the Baltic, to Poland and beyond. That produced Germanic settlements in a belt of territory from the Baltic to the northern Balkans and the Black Sea. They would endure for seven centuries, only to be obliterated in 1945. A second direction was towards the eastern Mediterranean: Egypt, Syria, Byzantium. Above all, into the Holy Land of Palestine and, holiest of all, Jerusalem. The first European crusade to liberate Jerusalem set off in 1096, though liberation hardly seems the right word for the way they behaved when they got there, or for the three days of murder, rape and robbery which the Fourth Crusade enjoyed, *en route* in 1204, in still Greek Christian Constantinople. In any case, the whole thing was short-lived. By 1187 Saladin destroyed a force of heavily armed Christian knights and recaptured Jerusalem. Unlike the Christians, he spared his captives.

The most important prong of expansion was therefore the third. It went south and southwest, from Iberia across the seas. It began with Christian reconquests in Sicily and Spain. For the devout, and the church in particular, here too was a war against the pagan, for the strengthening and expansion of Christendom and for the honour of God. It was a struggle in whose conduct all means were legitimate and Christian knights could get remission of their sins. In time, the energies released by the Catholic counter-reformation reinforced such impulses. Ignatius de Loyola founded the Society of Jesus in 1534 and within a couple of decades Jesuits were to be found on the shores of the spice islands, in the observatories of China or debating fine points of philosophy with princes in India.

Religious and strategic motives were inextricably intertwined with economic ones. Although for a thousand years before 1700 per capita income in Europe (and probably everywhere else as well) grew at a mere tenth of a per cent per annum,[4] Venice and Genoa had long grown rich and powerful by dealing with Greece and the Levant in goods which included trans-shipped silks and spices from the East. (In an age which knew nothing of artificial refrigeration, spices were very important in preserving Europe's food or making it edible, as well as for broader medicinal purposes.[5]) Traders had even penetrated into Africa. But the decline of the Mongols meant insecurity on many old trading routes, while the East became even more inaccessible with Turkish conquests and the growing isolation of Ming China. The flow of silks and spices to Europe declined. Not only that, but there was little demand by the East for European goods. That meant paying for purchases in gold; which increased the need for gold from Africa, often brought north from the Niger by trans-Saharan caravan. As the transit routes to the East became more difficult, it also became more urgent to seek alternatives, obviously by going round Islam's flanks.

There was more. Supplementing strategic imperatives, religious enthusiasm and the search for wealth were popular notions of chivalry and adventure, stemming from the romances of Amadis de Gaul or Ariosto. There were fantasies about fountains of youth, cities paved with gold or tribes of dangerously delicious Amazons. There were heated tales of the sexual inventiveness and enthusiasm of the East, of sultans and the exciting habits of their concubines. Further east still lay the fabulous city of Xanadu, which Marco Polo had spoken of and about which Samuel Taylor Coleridge, relaxing in an opium-dazed dream, would write a poem in 1797 which late twentieth-century Chinese archaeology discovered to have been astonishingly close to the truth.[6] In the opposite direction, far to the west, must lie the equally fabulous land of Atlantis, of which the ancients had written.

The story of Europe's irruption into the Asia-Pacific region begins, then, as an early fifteenth-century extension in space and time of these drives. It starts with the religious devotion, the drive for conquest, the avarice and the sheer curiosity, hardihood and brilliant seamanship of the Portuguese, joined, shortly afterwards, by Spain. But at first, it only seemed a minor extension of earlier travels. Even the Romans had vaguely known about the Azores and Canary islands which the Italians and Portuguese found by the fourteenth century. The Portuguese search for African gold was a century old. So was the need for slaves, not only to cope with labour shortages in Portugal itself, but for the tough business of growing sugar cane in hot island climates.[7]

In the early 1400s Portugal was neither large nor rich. Its population was only around one million. The capital, Lisbon, had a mere 40 000. The tiny commercial community was not even Portuguese but Venetian or Genoese. There was a small, war-like aristocratic class, ruling a lot of very poor landless labourers. Yet Portugal lay on the Atlantic. It was a unified country, the Moors having been expelled as early as 1249, leaving it with no more land to reconquer. More importantly, its aristocrats, who were to lead the sea voyages, were adventurous, even reckless folk with a strong crusading impulse. It is therefore a paradox that the single most important figure in promoting exploration was a reclusive, devout person who never sailed distant seas. He was born in 1394, the third son of the King: Prince Henry, of the royal house of Aviz, nicknamed (much later) 'the Navigator'. He promoted a series of voyages. But he did much more. By this time Iberian sailors were equipped with new ships: long, sleek caravels and larger carracks, developed over the previous centuries from mediaeval cogs and galleons. They were faster, better and more seaworthy than the fragile Arab vessels of the Mediterranean. Moreover, being sturdy, they could carry artillery. Their navigators had quadrants, astrolabes and even magnetic compasses. Henry employed Arab and Jewish astronomers and organized enormous advances in cartography and the nautical and navigational sciences. His people produced, for the first time, a reliable table of solar declination for sailors to steer by, meaning that sailors would no longer have to hug the coast to know where they were.

Henry's motives in all this were religious and strategic, personal and, not least, astrological. They had very little to do with commerce. He wanted to smite the heathen, convert pagans, reward his servants and retainers.

Portuguese ambitions were at first vague. Henry and others wanted to find a path to the Indies – meaning all of Asia east of Arabia, including the Indonesian archipelago and Japan. He also thought about contacting the legendary Christian king, Prester John, believed to live somewhere in the depths of Africa, or maybe Asia, who could help in the battle for the cross and against the crescent. Anyway, there were pagans to be brought to Christ. Not until the 1480s, under the forceful King John II, did Portuguese strategies became more firmly linked to the search, in or through or around Africa, for a path to the wealth of the Indies. Even then, it was a search for souls, Saracens, slaves and gold – more or less in that order.

The first step, in 1415, was to capture Ceuta, on the North African coast opposite Gibraltar, and one of the great gold ports. Five years later, other expeditions reached Madeira, which the Portuguese colonized with happy consequences for Europe's wine drinkers. Shortly afterwards they started to sail along West Africa. By the middle of the century, Henry's captains were discovering the Azores. By the time he died in 1460, they had opened up trade in gold, ivory, pepper and slaves as far south as the Gold Coast and Sierra Leone. Three years later they captured Casablanca and by 1471 they had Tangier. By the 1480s they built forts on the Gold Coast, and were sending some 10 000 slaves and 700 kilos of gold a year to Lisbon. Then came one of the greatest sea voyages of history. In 1487–8 Bartolomeo Diaz rounded the southern end of the African continent – which his king named the Cape of Good Hope – leaving a pillar with inscriptions on the eastern side, at Mossel Bay, before returning home. At the same time another expedition, under Pedro de Covilha, was sent to Ethiopia to contact Prester John and look into the patterns of Indian ocean trade. Ten years later an even greater sailor, Vasco da Gama, crossed the ocean beyond the Cape and reached Calicut, in India. His mission was not conquest but to find Christian sovereigns and to establish Portugal in the region's trade. He managed to acquire some pepper and cinnamon and returned to Lisbon. The journey took him two years and he came home with just fifty-four of his original crew of 170 left alive.

By this time Spain, too, was looking overseas. Its reconquest from the Moors had been a long and painful business.[8] Cordoba, once the greatest centre of learning in Europe, had fallen to the Christians in 1236.

But not until 1492 did the armies of Ferdinand and Isabella complete the *reconquista* with the capture of Granada,[9] after which they compelled Moslems and Jews to leave Spain or convert. The court also found the money to send an adventurous character called Christopher Columbus across the western seas. He expected to reach the Indies by sailing westwards from the Canaries to Japan, thereby establishing a link that would compete directly with the eastward thrust of Portuguese journeys around Africa. Such a project seemed quite plausible to the scholars and cartographers of the time. Columbus himself thought, until the day he died, that he had actually accomplished it; and that his journeys had been under divine guidance and his achievements were triumphs for God. The Portuguese were fired by similar religious ardour. They achieved many conversions. Other natives they often killed. When Alfonso d'Albuquerque attacked Malacca in 1511 his first objective, he said, 'is casting the Moors out of the country and quenching the fire of the sect of Mahomet ...'.[10]

Evidently there would have to be some demarcation of responsibilities in new lands – ones not already possessed by a Christian prince – as between Portugal and Spain. The accepted source of mediation in such matters was the Pope, as he had once been the authority for launching crusades. Back in 1452, the Papacy had authorized the king of Portugal 'to subdue Saracens, pagans and other unbelievers inimical to Christ, to reduce their persons to perpetual slavery and then to transfer for ever their territory to the Portuguese Crown'. Now, in 1493, Pope Alexander Borgia issued a bull giving the Spanish monarchs dominion over all the lands they discovered more than 300 miles west of the Cape Verde islands, on condition that they converted its peoples to Christianity. He similarly recognized Portugal's monopoly of the coasts and discoveries of Africa. A year later, Portugal and Spain signed the Treaty of Tordesillas on 7 June 1494, shifting the Atlantic divide a further 700 miles westwards.

For both Iberian powers the search for wealth was soon dominant. It was the huge Portuguese profits from spices that made the Spanish crown insist on access to the Pacific and the Indies. And while Portuguese expeditions were usually led by aristocrats, few of the early Spanish commanders belonged to the gentry. That class had better things to do at home and in Spanish Europe than in dim and distant corners of the earth. Even much later, the usual role of the aristocracy in the colonies was to administer and perhaps lead fleets. Most of the actual *conquistadores* came from a very different social background. Many were simply the riff-raff of Spain. They just wanted to escape poverty, get land and wealth, gold and slaves, achieve status, be noticed by the king and if possible be ennobled. It was all nicely summed up by a companion of Hernan Cortez, the conqueror of Mexico, who said: 'We came here to serve God and the King, and also to get rich.' And indeed, as one disgusted Aztec noted, 'they lusted like pigs' after gold. They were also tough, reckless, arrogant, cruel, extravagant and easily provoked. Many of those who came after Columbus had campaigned in Italy or Africa or, more to the point, against West Indies tribesmen. Yet it was also remarkable, both among Spaniards and Portuguese, how many of these early, often uneducated and cruel sailors, conquerors and administrators also turned out to be men of astonishing ability. Their monuments were not just battles won against fearful odds, or settlements established, or even empires conquered and organized, but in many cases writing of very considerable merit.

Even more remarkable was the speed with which the Portuguese and Spaniards, working with – by modern standards – absurdly primitive transport, weapons and communications established the first global navigation and trading, and therefore also political and strategic, network. Diaz rounded the Cape of Good Hope in 1487. Columbus landed on the island of Hispaniola in 1492. By 1500 the Portuguese were sending every available ship and man to follow da Gama's route to India, starting with the thirteen ships led by Cabral, who accidentally discovered Brazil. (While sailing through the South Atlantic to catch favourable winds to take him east around the Cape of Good Hope to India, he was blown off course and found the Brazilian coast.) By 1501 da Gama had returned and was bombarding Calicut. In 1504 the Portuguese set up the first *feitoria*, or factory – meaning a warehouse for an agent or 'factor' – at Cochin in India. In 1510 they captured Goa, the entry point to southern India for trading goods including Arabian horses. On the landward side they dug protective channels which they stocked with crocodiles. They held Goa for 450 years until it was seized in 1961 by the newly independent India. By 1517 they established another *feitoria* at Colombo. Further east, in 1509, five ships under Diego Lope de Sequeira visited the fabulously rich entrepot of Malacca, on the threshold of the Indonesian archipelago. Two years later, d'Albuquerque arrived with 700 Portuguese and 300 Indians and seized the place.[11] (He went on to capture Ormuz, at the entrance to the Persian Gulf.) In 1514 the first Portuguese ships reached China. By 1516 other Portuguese adventurers were exploring the coast of Indo-China as well, followed by Dominican missionaries in 1527. Thirty years later the Portuguese occupied Macao – with the connivance of Chinese officials – trading from there to Nagasaki in Japan.

The westward route to the Indies was also explored, as was the interior of the Americas. In 1512, Balboa sailed around Cape Horn into the Pacific. In 1519–20, Ferdinand Magellan, arguably the greatest seaman in history, crossed the Pacific in the first circumnavigation of the globe.[12] In the meantime, Hernan Cortez sailed from Cuba with eleven ships, 600 men and sixteen horses to begin the conquest of Mexico. By 1533 Francisco Pizarro had more or less conquered yet another empire, that of the Incas in Peru. Simultaneously the Portuguese were settling Brazil – largely to forestall the French. And in 1542, a bare half-century after Diaz had rounded Africa, a Spanish expedition from Mexico, by this time safely in Spanish hands, also crossed the Pacific, laying claim to the Philippines in 1564[13] and hence to its dealings with the spice islands and silk trade with Canton. A year later one of Spain's soldier-sailors who had become a monk, Father Andrès de Urdaneta, also discovered a way to sail back eastwards from Manila to the Americas. It was the beginning of a Spanish domination which made the Pacific Ocean, for a while, into a 'Spanish Lake'.[14]

On the ground, Spanish and Portuguese policies and institutions were very different. Portugal, with a population never greater than one and a half million, was too small to create an empire of settlement. For all the inflated pride of its court and nobles, it was too weak, and its people too few, to occupy large regions. Instead, the Portuguese built a network of forts-plus-factories reaching, by 1570, from Morocco to Nagasaki. To be sure, they did settle in a few places. Goa became famous for its riches and cheerfully inter-racial hedonism, which the church could never curb. Macao became a reliable, if unofficial, entrepot for trade between China and Japan and a home for rich Chinese and Portuguese merchants surrounding themselves with every luxury, including famously lovely Chinese wives and mistresses. There were Portuguese centres in Timor and remarkable efforts by Portuguese Jesuits in Japan which, by 1600 or thereabouts, had converted some 300 000 people to Christianity. But only in Brazil did many Portuguese colonists settle, and only there did Portuguese language and culture make a lasting impression. Brazil apart, what characterized the Portuguese was not occupation or settlement, but trade.

Even while Diaz sought the ocean route to the East and the kingdom of Prester John, he was also looking for spices. Da Gama sailed under royal orders to stop all Arab shipping between India and Arabia. And d'Albuquerque was told to destroy all Moslem shipping between Malacca and Goa. After he seized Malacca, other expeditions went to Siam (Thailand), China and the Moluccas, again mainly in search of spices. There was pepper from Sumatra and other islands, cinnamon from Ceylon, camphor from Borneo, nutmeg from the Banda islands, cloves from the Moluccas and so on. They were ideal trading goods. Spices weighed little, the volume was small, demand high and the profit enormous. Magellan's *Victoria* was the first ship to bring cloves directly from the Moluccas to Europe; at a profit, it is said, of 2 500 per cent. Even later, one hundredweight of pepper, bought in Calicut for three Spanish ducats, could be sold in Venice for eighty.

However, and for all the importance of spice trading, matters almost immediately became more complex. Holding Goa or Malacca brought political problems. Malacca was the richest commercial entrepot between the Pacific and Indian oceans. One awestruck Portuguese described it as 'the richest place in all the world'. It was therefore important not only for trade but for influence in the entire region. The Portuguese drive for monopoly meant war with Javanese traders, and the destruction of all Indonesian naval power. Policing the sea routes to India and Arabia also hurt the trading cities of Syria and Egypt and therefore the Ottoman Sultan whom the Christians were fighting in Europe and the Mediterranean. In the meantime, d'Albuquerque's capture of Ormuz gave Portugal access to the Persian Gulf, to Persian silks and silver, and Arab horses. The Portuguese also continued to get gold, ivory and slaves from West and East Africa, while controlling a coastal stretch of Brazil.[15] The result was the first virtually global trading network.

It included footholds in China and Japan, though activities there were much more tentative. The first Portuguese ships reached the Ming empire as early as 1513. By the 1550s a ship a year carried European goods from Goa to Macao, which also became the chief export centre for Chinese silks and porcelain. From there, goods could go westwards through Malacca or eastwards, by way of the 'Manila galleons', to the Spanish Americas and thence to Europe. Macao even became a semi-official entrepot for trade between China and the Japanese, whose direct entry China had banned because of Japanese piracy. But Macao traders could sell Chinese silks at Nagasaki, usually in exchange for silver.[16] Indeed, China had a bottomless appetite for silver, whether from Japan or the renowned mines of Potosi in Peru.

However, getting an empire, or a trading monopoly, was one thing: keeping it was quite another. Portugal being small and poor, there were never enough ships or men to control large possessions or even to monopolize the spice trade. Even in a major centre like Malacca, there were seldom more than 600 Portuguese. Matters were made worse by

Portugal's loss of fit young men, so many of whom died or settled overseas. Administration was also inadequate. Soldiers and sailors, getting little or no pay or supplies from home, would sell off royal property, or set up in business, or simply desert. Men were constantly leaving for Spanish settlements, or to enter Persian or Japanese or even Mogul service. That left even fewer men for the armies and ships Portugal needed, let alone to provide enough officials, clergy and settlers for her possessions.

There were not even enough ships. Portugal never had more than around 300, nowhere near enough for trade as well as policing global shipping lanes. There was not even enough timber to build more, yet losses from weather or piracy were always significant. Moreover, losses increased as the quality of ships and crews declined. The upshot was that the Portuguese increasingly depended on others for weapons, food and transport.

Meanwhile, many local officials were making private fortunes. Even the clergy traded in everything from silks in the East to sugar and slaves in the West Indies. St Francis Xavier was scandalized by the immorality, greed and worldliness of officials and clergy. After visiting the Moluccas he remarked that the knowledge of the officials 'is restricted to the conjugation of the verb *rapio* [to steal], in which they show an amazing capacity for inventing new tenses and participles'. Yet everyone left Lisbon to pay for defence and administration, and central revenues were declining. Portugal was even getting less and less African gold. Royal debts increased. By 1560 the treasury was technically bankrupt. Unsurprisingly, piracy and foreign competition increased, and trade began to flag. Indeed, by that time the quantity of spices reaching Europe through the Middle East and Alexandria was no more than it had been sixty years earlier, and quite as much as Portuguese shipments around Africa. Twenty years later, when Philip II of Spain added the Portuguese crown to his own (although Portugal broke away again in 1640), the Portuguese empire was clearly declining, overtaken by stronger European powers. Even the English were plundering Portuguese ships in Asia and the Atlantic. In the East the Portuguese even depended quite largely for transport and supplies on the Dutch. Yet it was these same Dutch who, greatly superior in wealth and ships, were Portugal's strongest competitors in the Indies and the South China Sea after the 1590s.

Strategic weakness, a distant home base and vulnerable communications were not the only reasons for the fragility of the Portuguese trading empire in the Indies. Sophisticated Asians looked after their own interests with ingenuity and guile. European religious intolerance, arrogance and contempt for natives exacerbated local hostilities. The slightly baffled sense of virtue of the Portuguese had special problems with Islam, which spread even faster than Christianity. In Portuguese eyes, all Moslems were infidels and enemies, and all Moslem shipping was fair game. Da Gama, during his second voyage, capped a victory at Calicut by cutting off the ears, noses and hands of some 800 'Moors' and sending them to the local ruler, saying he should make a curry of them. Where Portugal ruled, temples and mosques were apt to be demolished and churches built instead. Non-Christian priests, teachers and holy men were to be expelled, their sacred books destroyed, the name of the Prophet not mentioned. Christians were not to live or lodge with non-Christians. At best, this earned much resentment. The very presence of the Portuguese and their priests created strong Islamic resistance. Yet the Portuguese needed local allies, supporters and auxiliaries to have any hope of controlling such large and varied populations. But in spite of the difficulties, the empire was run with a skill, or at times benign neglect, which allowed parts of it to endure. In Goa and East Timor, and even more so in Africa, it lasted, until the middle of the twentieth century.

Spain shared the Portuguese dedication to religion and conversion of the heathen but concentrated mainly on conquest and colonization. Portugal might be too small and poor to create a lasting territorial empire, but Spain was not. With some 7.5 million people, devout, hardened by climate and by war, accustomed to victory, Spain on the eve of exploration was one of the strongest powers in Europe. Empire was powerfully driven by religion. In the Philippines, for instance, the true colonizers were friars and monks who converted the locals and created a European system of churches and schools. But the profits of empire,[17] especially the gold and silver of the Americas, quickly became essential in maintaining Spain's position in Europe. And beyond lay all the wealth of Asia. It was for this that Columbus, who was expected to meet local princes, was given the title of Viceroy and Admiral of the Indies. He also had a letter of introduction to the 'Grand Khan' plus two blanks to be presented to any other rulers he might come across. His expedition even included a Jewish convert who understood Arabic, then believed to be the mother of all languages. And as added incentive, he was promised 10 per cent, tax free, of all the gold, gems, spices and merchandise that trade with those countries and rulers might bring.

He sailed with three ships. The largest was the *Santa Maria*, possibly as much as 100 tons, carrying forty men.[18] On landing, he found natives who had gold, and convinced himself that here were huge

Asian gold deposits. Within a few years Spaniards had settled on Santo Domingo, Cuba and elsewhere, acquired land and the Indians who lived on it, and started to exploit the locals with bestial and wanton brutality where they did not simply massacre them.[19] As early as 1516 a group of Dominican friars complained to the Spanish court about unspeakable atrocities.[20] But Spain was far away, and instructions could take months, even years, to arrive. So disobedience was rife and the native Caribs were almost wiped out. By 1500 other explorers had followed, including the Italian sailor Amerigo Vespucci, who explored the coast of Venezuela and gave his name to the entire continent.

There followed the conquest of Mexico and Peru, which changed the face not only of the Americas but of world politics. Here were major empires and sophisticated cultures, large populations capably organized, with substantial armies. Yet both succumbed – the Aztecs of Mexico more quickly, while the Peruvian Incas put up a stouter resistance – to forces composed, or at least led, by a few dozen Europeans. Spain did not plan this. It was local commanders who conquered most of the Americas south of the Rio Grande, in a single generation, and entirely without royal authority. Spanish sovereigns were, if anything, worried about these events, their information invariably months out of date. Only in retrospect did Spain approve what had been done, once the situation was irreversible and especially when it became clear how much gold and silver might be had. Also, the Spaniards quickly found they had to rely on local peoples both in war and peace. In time Spanish administration, like the Roman empire before it and the British and French afterwards, developed a great sense of imperial mission, based on classical ideals. It reserved high office for its own citizens and subjects. It employed the best university graduates. It controlled by enquiry and inspection of all departments, and local people and institutions.

Not that empire was an unmixed blessing. The riches it produced, especially the bullion, became increasingly essential to pay for Spain's armies in Europe. But the military and naval burdens quickly became greater still. There were times when Spain's Atlantic shipping had to cope with losses, from weather or enemy action, of up to 30 per cent per annum of the ships that sailed. Other issues were more subtle and more inescapable than those of foreign policy or even money and strategy. For instance, the religious intolerance which made things difficult in the East had even worse consequences at home. In both Spain and Portugal it produced intellectual and scientific decline. By 1500 the Portuguese had forcibly converted some 70 000 Jews and

2000 more were killed in the 1506 Lisbon pogrom. Not surprisingly, given the importance of Jews in scientific and commercial life, a mere half-century after Henry the Navigator's death Portugal faced a shortage of astronomers. Soon afterwards it lost its primacy in navigation and map-making. By 1540 the Inquisition was installed and after 1580 Portugal, and the entire Spanish empire, suffered Philip II's relentless persecution of heretics and the consequent impoverishment in people and resources. Losing the Netherlands, especially, meant losing Spain's richest possession. The church increasingly controlled education and rigorously enforced book-bans. (As late as 1746 the Jesuits banned the works of Copernicus, Galileo and even of Isaac Newton.) It was the end, for the time being, of speculation, science and much philosophy. Indeed, Spain displayed a remarkable combination of religious devotion, political rigidity, military valour and economic incompetence. Partly as a result, even this large empire's resources ultimately proved inadequate.

In spite of such difficulties, the skill, courage and tenacity with which Spain ran its empire was at least equal to that of the Portuguese. In the Americas, the Pacific and in Africa, it endured for 400 years. Spain left an indelible imprint on the cultures, institutions and languages of the Americas and many island groups, even on the peoples' genes. It was left to Commodore Dewey and the US Navy to drive Spain from the Pacific at the start of the twentieth century.

However, whether in Asia or the Americas, Spain and Portugal were challenged, virtually from the start, by European competitors. Iberian claims to a new world monopoly were greeted with scepticism, or simply ignored. King Francis I of France, on hearing of the papal bull apportioning continents to Portugal and Spain, remarked to the Spanish ambassador that he 'would very much like to see Adam's Will, to learn how he divided the world'.[21] The English and Dutch, especially, had important advantages. Their easy access to the naval matériels of the Baltic gave them more, cheaper and often technically better ships. They had more commercial attitudes and much more sophisticated financial practices and institutions, from banks to the new chartered joint stock companies. They had many fewer commitments, and therefore distractions, in continental Europe than did Spain.

Neither English nor French legal conservatives accepted that the Pope could award regions to particular European sovereigns; or that such awards should decide maritime law. They thought that beyond the mid-Atlantic European claims and frontiers were meaningless. Protestant Englishmen asserted other claims against Catholic Spain, based on the 1497 voyage of John Cabot, who had claimed the new lands for King Henry VIII. It was also soon clear that Spain, and especially Portugal, were highly vulnerable at sea and their weaknesses were exploited by English, French and Dutch traders and privateers as well as more official expeditions. Not that it was always easy to distinguish between legal and illegal activities. Twenty-first-century states claim a monopoly of the use of force which, five centuries earlier, rulers were only beginning to establish. Around the 1550s to 1580s there was privateering and semi-official raiding by everybody. There was plain piracy, too, by colourful blackguards whose legends remain fresh. But it was not always clear what activities were illegitimate. How, for instance, should island governors deal with trading ships claiming to have been blown off course? Or with non-Spanish ships on the 'Spanish Main' threatening force, not to rob but to compel trade? Or with foreign ships which found local people, irritated by a Spanish monopoly on trade, actually asking the foreigner to 'compel' them to trade? Local settlers often proved grateful. Not so the Spanish authorities, worried about their monopoly but often unable to supply the needed goods. Commerce therefore overlapped strongly with more doubtful activities.

Anyway, adventurous Englishmen wanted to profit from Spanish America's need for West African slaves. The Spaniards attacked them. The English returned, led by men like Sir John Hawkins, his cousin, Francis Drake,[22] Walter Raleigh and others, to prey on Spanish shipping. By 1576 John Oxenham had slipped into Panama, brought his guns across the isthmus, built a small ship on the Pacific coast and captured a Spanish coastal vessel carrying 38 000 pesos. A year later, Drake left England in the *Golden Hinde* to sail round the world. Over three years he raided the western coasts of Spanish America, crossed the Pacific and returned to Portsmouth with treasure worth around 600 000.[23] By 1600 the English had made deals with Javan and Moluccan princes, visited Goa, brought home goods from China and established consuls at Tripoli (in North Africa), Basra and Babylon.

The threat to Spanish interests was obvious. But it was all horribly confusing for European politics, where Spain was England's traditional ally against France. Maybe, now, England should switch alliance to France. The passions of the counter-reformation and Spanish repression of Protestants in the Low Countries suggested no less. Patriotism, a strategic contest for power, greed for gold and profit, and profound religious faith were deeply involved on all sides. English evangelicals especially, seeing themselves as the elect, creating God's kingdom on earth, supported both the Dutch and the French Huguenots. West country sailors like Drake came from such groups; so did the Pilgrim Fathers who sailed to North America. The upshot was a long drawn-out struggle on sea and land. Spain had to convoy its trade and bullion shipments from the Americas and station naval squadrons in the western approaches of Spain and in the Caribbean. Even so the 1620s and 1630s saw a Dutch offensive against Spanish shipping in the Caribbean – like Piet Heyn's capture of the Spanish silver fleet off Cuba in 1628 which seriously interrupted the entire silver flow from the New World. In these contests the English greatly expanded their naval and ship-building capabilities.[24] They developed ship-board artillery much superior to Spain's, demonstrated in the climactic battles against the Spanish armada, sent to invade England in 1588.[25]

But the Americas contained more than Spanish colonies, ships and plunder. There were fertile and uninhabited islands, highly suitable for growing tobacco and sugar. The French seized Guadeloupe and Martinique in 1635, the Dutch took Curaçao and established Surinam. The English took Barbados in 1635 and Jamaica in 1655; and it was Barbados, particularly, whose sugar helped to transform the entire Caribbean economy. It also created a huge demand for black slaves to work the fields, in a climate often fatal for Europeans; and Bristol became immensely wealthy from its near monopoly of that slave trade. By the second half of the seventeenth century many people in England thought the whole value of overseas possessions lay in the sugar islands. Meanwhile, on the North American mainland occupation also produced settlements, like Virginia whose early wealth also came from tobacco. The French went still further north. In the 1530s they founded Montreal. In 1603 Samuel Champlain moved further into the future Canada. Other Frenchmen built Quebec and discovered the Great Lakes.

What about the East, destined to become the heart of the British empire following American independence? The English East India Company, founded in 1600 by Royal Charter, was formed by London merchants who wanted direct access to the Indies. When they arrived, they found the Dutch well entrenched and determined to keep new-comers out by diplomacy and guns. And the London government left traders and colonists to their own devices. There was little government money to spare and anyway, these explorers and adventurers were just trying to become rich, so they could look after themselves. The English therefore tended to settle where there was little local resistance.

A foothold in India was at first quite incidental to the company's interest in the spice islands. In 1608 a Turkish-speaking Levant trader named Hawkins sailed into Surat and arrived in Agra, the capital of the Mogul empire, with an escort of tough, bearded Pathans. He presented a letter from King James I to the Emperor, who equipped Hawkins with an Armenian Christian wife, though nothing much else came of the mission. Seven years later, a formal embassy under Sir Thomas Roe was received at Agra, and the Emperor granted the company the right to trade. Within two decades the Portuguese had accepted the company's right to set up trading posts and warehouses ('factories') on the coast. Other English sailors and merchants went to Masulipatam, commanding the Coromandel coast, and to the Ganges estuary, which dominated the rich hinterland of Bengal. By 1639 they also possessed a strip of coast which would become the sovereign enclave of Madras. Then the Cromwellian republic became more assertive overseas. It emphasized military power and by 1659 the East India Company's monopoly had been confirmed with a new charter. Possession of the island of Bombay followed in 1665,[26] complementing a naval power with which no Indian ruler could compete. The foundations of the three chief English 'Residencies' of Bombay, Madras and Bengal had been laid.

By this time the Mogul Emperor Aurangzeb had conquered southern India and was promoting a intolerant Islamism. It was the heyday of his empire and England took care to be well informed about it. Charles II's poet laureate, John Dryden, even wrote a play about the succession struggles in Delhi. In India itself, though the death rate among English merchants could be one out of three, the others lived very well. They even hired soldiers to guard themselves and their convoys, and to enhance their status. By 1690 the company was setting up a trading station on the river Hoogli, destined to grow into Calcutta; while Bengal textiles would become a vital part of the company's exports to England.

For the French, overseas expansion was hampered by the distractions of war in Europe. Also, French overseas efforts were largely instruments of state power. France, with its enormous natural wealth, had maybe twice the population of Spain and eight times that of the Dutch.[27] And for men like Cardinal Richelieu in the early seventeenth century, all overseas expansion was part of the larger struggle against Spain. So French colonies became part of the royal domain of an absolutist monarchy. Government was by royal agents, taxes imposed by royal command. It was in this context that private companies were set up and had to maintain troops. Even then, for Louis XIV's great finance minister Jean-Baptiste Colbert, and his successors, trading operations were a protected environment, with colonies trading exclusively with the mother country.

Still, there were early commercial relations with North Africa. Further afield, De Gonneville had reached the coast of Brazil in 1504 and other expeditions reached Madagascar and Sumatra shortly afterwards. To the East the French came rather later than the English. Though there was some French trading from 1604, the *Compagnie des Indes* was only founded in 1664, six decades after its English and Dutch rivals. It was created on the initiative of Colbert, one of the founders of the modern, centralized French state. It had a royal charter, and royal patronage remained critical to its operations. Trading was largely based in Bengal and on the Coromandel coast but was only moderately successful, in part because the French court had ulterior motives. Louis XIV supported the company largely to provide a base for Jesuit missionary operations; and the connection between commerce and conversion remained close. In any case, European wars drained French resources.

Nevertheless, India looked politically and strategically promising as the Moguls, around 1700, began to lose control of the religions and tribes they had held together with a strong hand. Local quarrels erupted and rulers began to enlist European help. At first, the French seemed to have the edge as Hyderabad, Mysore and the Mahrattas bought equipment and hired instructors from them. In contrast, the English company appeared content merely to trade from its three main factories, virtually unconcerned with India's volatile politics. This situation remained true until around 1740.

In spite of these activities, it was not the English or the French who posed the greatest challenge to the Portuguese and Spanish trading empires. It was the Dutch. For while the Iberians were expanding overseas, the Low Countries were the main beneficiaries of some fundamental changes in the political economy of Europe. States were showing the first signs of national as well as administrative cohesion. That meant novel obligations and loyalties, growing trade and some specialization of production. In these conditions new kinds of commercial entities and banking operations, needed for distant and costly trade, emerged among the cosmopolitan and tolerant Protestants of Antwerp. The city became the centre of the spice trade. It was in Antwerp that great German banking houses like the Welsers and Fuggers opened branches soon after 1500. Simultaneously, the flow of gold and silver from the Americas made Antwerp into Europe's chief financial centre. As the Spanish government spent its revenues, merchants and bankers dispersed the money throughout Europe, much of it to finance trade deficits with the Levant and the East. The money market flourished. For a time, Bills on Antwerp became the commonest international currency (a kind of early Euro). Europe's commercial and maritime supremacy shifted from the Mediterranean trading cities to the Protestant northwest.

Indeed, Antwerp became the capital of a whole new commercial civilization, and the commercial and financial capital of the Spanish empire itself. Although Spanish soldiery sacked the city in 1576, furious because the King couldn't pay them, its entrepreneurs and capitalists fled to Amsterdam, whose ruling merchant oligarchy welcomed profitable business. The Dutch of Amsterdam therefore quickly replaced Antwerp as the unchallenged metropole for Europe's marketing and finance. The Bank of Amsterdam was founded in 1609 and the city soon developed the world's most sophisticated capital markets.[28] Others followed – in 1694 the Bank of England – but it was Holland which remained the chief financial and trading centre of Europe. It offered low interest rates, secure international payments, free capital movement and an adequate flow of savings to provide finance. The excellent Dutch credit rating allowed them to borrow cheaply. As late as 1660 the Dutch States General could decline a loan offered at 2.5 per cent, in a period when England had to pay over 6 per cent. Both London and Amsterdam were eclectic in personnel and techniques. They borrowed economic ideas and techniques from Italy; and the bankers were not just German or Dutch but also Italian: like the 'acclimatized Italians' of the Vernatti family in Holland, or the Cavalcanti and Pallavicini in London.

Furthermore, by the middle 1600s the Dutch controlled much the largest merchant fleet: half a million tons. Indeed, Spain's entire Atlantic shipments were only a tiny fraction of Holland's huge trade with the Baltic. The economic and shipping development of the maritime provinces of Holland and Zeeland was perhaps the greatest single reason for the evolution of the Dutch nation and its success in the long struggle against Spain, which only ended in 1648.[29] In that process, the Dutch also created a military – and therefore also administrative – revolution in Europe. In a mere half-century or so, they went from political insignificance to world power. By the end of the sixteenth century they posed a major threat not just to the Iberian empires but to the prosperity, even the economic survival, of England.

Yet dominance in commerce and finance, in industry and shipping, did not automatically translate into imperial possessions. Portugal and Spain might come to depend on Holland for munitions, even food. Their commerce might rely on Dutch ships. But the impact on the political or strategic balance outside Europe took time to develop, especially since, in the East, the Dutch were late arrivals. For a long time the main focus of Dutch trading was on the Baltic and on Lisbon. They happily relied on Eastern goods brought through Alexandria or Constantinople and across the Mediterranean. Even after the Turks controlled Eastern Mediterranean ports, the Dutch continued their profitable exchange – often through Lisbon – of wood and fish from the Baltic for Mediterranean oil, wine and fruit. However, King Philip II's wars with Protestantism made life more difficult for Dutch heretics, especially after he annexed Portugal in 1580. Spanish customs officials had to close their eyes to the Dutch grain ships which Spain badly needed, but other vessels might be confiscated. For the Dutch, trading directly with distant regions looked more and more attractive. By 1621, they had between half and two thirds of the entire trade between Brazil and Europe.

The Dutch also tried to get to the Indies, at first via the Arctic Ocean. When that proved impossible they followed the Portuguese and the English, mostly by going round Cape Horn. Things became more organized in 1594, after they built a new type of ship for transoceanic voyages, and once nine Amsterdam merchants had founded the *Compagnie van Verre* (Company of the Far Regions). The first voyage, in 1595 under Cornelis Houtman, was with four ships and 240 men. Only three ships and eighty-nine men returned two years later, but they brought some pepper from Bantam. So twenty-two ships set out in 1598 and though only fourteen returned, they came laden with spices which may have given the investors a return of around 400 per cent. Such ratios, between lives lost and profits gained, continued. It was not unusual for an expedition to set out with 250 or 400 people, of whom maybe forty-five or sixty would come back alive. For instance the first commander to follow Magellan's westward course set out in 1598 with four ships carrying, among other things, around 130 guns, thirty English musicians and 8000 gallons of wine. Only one of the ships managed to reach Japan in April 1600, with a quarter of the original crew of 110 still alive and only five really fit to stand on their feet.

By that time the States General was suggesting that merchants might do better to cooperate rather than compete. So, in 1602 the Company of the Far Regions became part of the United Netherlands Chartered East India Company, which was awarded a monopoly of trade east of the Cape of Good Hope and west of the Straits of Magellan. By 1615 the Dutch, in a markedly national as well as commercial effort, were sending still more highly organized expeditions, trying to dominate the distribution of East Indies produce. But trade again brought politics. It meant safe anchorages in the East for ship repair. It meant protecting goods and stores in a secure entrepot. Since trading posts had to be protected against rivals or local rulers they required some kind of fort. Communications needed security; and a monopoly, like that of spices from the Moluccas, required still more naval and military protection. Accordingly, the company was empowered to build strongholds, to conclude treaties and alliances, and to wage defensive war. Moreover, the Dutch authorities supported the company not only because of the wealth it brought but because it was a useful instrument in the wars against Spain and Portugal. The company therefore became a general instrument for war and conquest in the East and something of a state within a state.

Defensive efforts inevitably sowed the seeds of territorial acquisition. Even if the area of direct Dutch rule was limited, local dynastic or factional rivals sought Dutch support, so that in time many native states ceased to be fully sovereign. The Dutch might support a native prince, but in effect became his overlords. Moreover, as Dutch economic power penetrated the life of the islands native trade declined, local society became more authoritarian and standards of living eventually became more precarious.

In Europe, the company became the strongest trading corporation of the seventeenth century and in the East it had, by the 1620s, seized a number of Portuguese colonies. The Dutch captured Amboina in 1605 and went on to take other Portuguese possessions in Ceylon, the Moluccas, India and Malaya. Notably Malacca, whose conquest in 1641 sealed Dutch dominance in Malay waters. Dutch factories also appeared in India as far north as Bengal. Although the Dutch were generally not keen on territorial governance, they made more and more agreements with local rulers, giving them more and more reasons for political intervention. In 1667 they conquered Macassar, in the Celebes, a major spice port. They also came to control regions of Java. By the 1670s its sultans were depending on Dutch help in their succession struggles; and it was local Dutch initiatives, not decisions at home, that were leading to conquests in the remainder of Java. During the second half of the century Dutch authority extended still further over the various Indonesian principalities, including Aceh in Sumatra. By the 1670s the Dutch had made Mataram into a protectorate: a decade or so later, they also controlled the Sultanate of Bantam which commanded the pepper trade.

The pursuit of trade and profit therefore took them way beyond Java or the realm of spices; though even as late as 1730 they were bringing as many spices to London as the English East India Company was gathering from the entire archipelago. The Dutch traded in Coromandel, bought Indian textiles for sale in Indonesia and conquered Ceylon, which incidentally stimulated Indian overseas trade and shipping. Further East lay access to Chinese arts, crafts and inventions, including silks and ceramics. Also gunpowder, which Europe may have started to acquire from China as early as 1400. By 1614 the Dutch potteries at Delft were imitating Ming blue-and-white ceramics. Chinese linen turned out to be much better than the equivalent Dutch product. From 1660 *chinoiserie* materials and decorations became prized in Europe. Indeed, by 1700 European demand for Indian textiles, and silks from China or Persia, was more important than demand for spices. Soon afterwards the demand for tea and coffee also soared. In the meantime, the role of Japanese silver, and later copper, in Eastern commerce became highly important as well. Of particular value, and a favourite in the Bengal trade in particular, was opium. A century and a half before the disputes which led Britain and China into the so-called 'opium war', Dutchmen were delighted to be able to buy it for 70–75 rupees in Calcutta and sell it in Batavia for 220–25. Nor was it by any means simply a matter of economics or trade. Chinese culture, especially, had a profound impact on the educated classes of Europe not least because of its undogmatic beliefs and its civil service system, open to merit and assessed by examination – all of which resonated with Europe's philosophical bent as ideas moved towards the Enlightenment.

In the meantime, in 1618 the Dutch Indies acquired a new governor general, a ruthless, God-fearing, energetic and cruel fellow named Jan Pieterszoon Coen.[30] A year later, in defiance not only of the Sultan of Bantam but of the company's directors back home, he occupied the town and port of Jacatra. It was a hub for the traffic of the Indies, and Coen built a fort there. After rebuffing the English, he built Jacatra into the fortress of 'Batavia'. Its Dutch garrison was said to spend its days in prayer and its nights in orgies with drink and women. This city of Batavia – much later the modern Jakarta – became the capital of the Dutch East Indies for three centuries. Shortly afterwards, Coen claimed surrounding territory as well, and drove the English from the Moluccas, Amboina and Banda. His methods were not gentle. He almost exterminated the Banda islanders. On Contor, he tortured and killed the islanders' leaders, destroyed villages and took the inhabitants as slaves to Java. In other places, including the island of Run, he simply had all the men killed. On Ambon, the Dutch killed the ten Englishmen, eleven Japanese and one Portuguese who occupied a fort there, on charges of somehow conspiring to overthrow Dutch rule.

Coen's plans went further. He tried but failed to seize Macao from the Portuguese. The Dutch sent ships to Japan. They moved to Formosa (Taiwan), with its fine harbours and strategically important location and built a settlement for the flourishing trade with China's Fujian province. Formosa, lying halfway between Manila and Nagasaki, controls the coast of much of southeast and eastern China and became one of the most profitable of all Dutch holdings. The Spaniards, who had been there first, objected to the Dutch presence and built two competing forts. But in 1640 came a Chinese revolt which the Dutch suspected Spain of inciting; a year later, both Spanish forts were taken. The Dutch in their turn were expelled by Coxinga, a Chinese pirate king who, chased out of China, fled to Formosa with 25 000 men. He ruled until his death in 1662.

Coen was convinced that the region's commerce was essential to the prosperity of the Netherlands, which had a legal right to a commercial monopoly. He wanted to limit territorial holdings, but those he had should be settled by Dutch colonists. They would cut out both European competitors and native merchants. More colonists could be brought from Burma, Madagascar, China, by force if necessary; preferably Chinese, who were industrious and not war-like. He also planned to use thousands of Japanese soldiers who 'are just as good as ours'. He needed a strong fleet and built extremely efficient Dutch-style shipyards. He would create a vast, monopolistic commercial empire from Aden to Nagasaki. Most of its profits would come from intra-Asian trade, for the profits from Asian and European trade would be proportionate to the wealth and populations of the two regions. The system would bring all the commodities of Asia to Batavia – silks from Persia and China, cinnamon from Ceylon, Chinese porcelain, copper from Japan – there to be exchanged for spices which the Dutch East India Company alone would carry to Europe, in ships each of which would be worth a king's ransom.

The trouble was that so vast a colonizing scheme, quite apart from being hugely expensive, was simply not feasible. While Dutch officials tried to impose a command economy in the East Indies, most of the soldiers and officials were trading privately on their own account. Anyway, too few Dutchmen, and fewer Dutch women, came out, the Dutch being less keen than some other Europeans on becoming colonists, since life was easy and profitable at home. Those who did go out tried to carry their dress and way of life with them. They lived like princes, though their houses and canals were stinking with filth. Very many died, whether of disease or, even more frequently, of drink. Coen himself said: 'our nation must drink or die', but often they did both. Not surprisingly, the Dutch service came to include a lot of Frenchmen, Germans and Englishmen. Marriage with locals could not solve Dutch problems either: Asian women of good social standing, or high caste, would not marry Europeans, least of all ordinary soldiers or clerks. Most Asian women who married outside their race, caste and religion abandoned not only all ties to family but all claims to respect. Much the same applied to European women marrying locals. There were other problems, many of which were to be replicated in British, Portuguese and French colonies, especially in the tropics. Europeans often had little to do and it takes character to withstand the rigours of indolence. They, and not least the women who acquired much higher social standing in the colonies than they could claim at home, began to insist on the finest and most absurd social distinctions or issues of precedence.

This also led to an insistence, even stronger among the Dutch and British than among Spaniards and Portuguese, on white folk living 'alone and apart' from the locals. That often involved little more than a few hundred Dutchmen trying to recreate a bit of Holland while maintaining the prestige of distance from the natives; but it could also mean imposing Dutch standards in social and legal matters. For over two hundred years Indonesian contracts were usually drawn up in Dutch, and local rulers had to sign papers, dealing with trade or garrisoning, whether they understood them or not. Meanwhile the Dutch, like the British and French later in Vietnam, China and India, retained their own harsh jurisdiction over their compatriots, even in criminal matters. But where Dutch interests were not affected, native rulers and local laws were usually left in place. The system had no room for assimilation, let alone acquisition by the locals of Netherlands citizenship.

Nor did the Dutch have much of a missionary purpose. Not that religion was irrelevant. Devout Protestants fervently believed in the guidance of heaven and their own role as God's elect; and were convinced that commercial success was indissolubly linked to divine favour. But neither the Dutch nor the English were particularly keen to carry the cross into new lands and convert the heathen. Missionary activity proper was a very subordinate business. In two hundred years of operation, the Dutch East India Company sent less than 1 000 preachers from the United Provinces out to the East; and the Dutch Reformed Church in Asia was, and remained, very much subordinate to the civil power. Roman Catholicism proved much more attractive to natives partly, no doubt, because of the higher quality of the Catholic clergy. But it was also because of Dutch Reformed intolerance of local beliefs, especially Islam.

In the meantime, Dutch expansion created conflict not only with the English, but with the Spaniards, for whom Dutch irruptions threatened not only the 'Spanish Lake', but Spanish territories in Peru and Mexico. At issue were enormously important economic interests, including the 'Manila galleons'; vital trade between Manila and Mexico, exchanging American silver for Chinese silks, that began in 1564 and went on for 300 years. To make matters worse for the Spanish authorities, in the Philippines they were not just fighting the Dutch – who briefly seized Manila around 1570 – but dealing with local turmoil like Chinese revolts or Moro[31] uprisings (which would continue, off and on, into the twenty-first century).

As for the English, in the early days they had only about 10 per cent of the capital of the Dutch company. Where the English East India Company sent twelve ships to the East between 1600 and about 1610, the Dutch sent fifty-five. For the next century and a half, Anglo-Dutch relations varied from cooperation to bickering, both in the Indies and in Europe, where the two were initially allied against Spain. Both companies were, theoretically, in favour of freedom of the seas and of international trade.[32] But in practice there were complex negotiations about respective interests. The Dutch wanted to keep their monopoly of the East Indies spice trade and to seize property, while avoiding major conflict. Indeed, around 1600, the Dutch government wanted good relations with the English (and French) in opposing Spain. Yet King James I of England spent from 1613 to 1621 seeking a Spanish royal marriage for his son and wanted no Spanish quarrel. Not that any of this decided Anglo-Dutch relations far away in the Indies. There, the Dutch relied mostly on their ships, local fortifications and strong garrisons. In time, they largely succeeded in frightening British traders away.

Altogether, therefore, the final years of the sixteenth century and the first half of the seventeenth saw much confusion, with Dutch, Portuguese, Spaniards and English manoeuvring, trading, cooperating, competing, sometimes fighting. But not everywhere. Burma, Siam, Annam and Cambodia had no interest in trading with the Europeans. There was some local xenophobia and resistance to Portuguese freebooters and to the Dutch in Siam. Indeed, the Siamese appealed for French aid and Louis XIV briefly put a French garrison into Bangkok.

But in general, some of the rivalries could be fierce. There were bitter, if small-scale, battles between the Dutch and the Spaniards off Corregidor. Some conflicts, virtually guerrilla wars at sea, involved not just the Dutch, the Portuguese and the Spaniards but all sorts of other folk: slaves, local inhabitants, Japanese mercenaries and cut-throats of every description. The English and especially the Dutch search for monopolies and profits meant not only getting trading privileges from local rulers but cutting out Arabs, Chinese and Javanese as well as European rivals. A good deal of what went on was not much better than privateering, even piracy. Nor did the early English or Dutch administrators and captains – unlike the Portuguese and Spaniards – have much by way of strategic motives. What drove them all was the hunger for profit. As West African blacks told the Dutch, much as the Aztecs had once said to the Spaniards: 'Gold is your God.'

But Dutch curiosity also took them further. One result was the discovery and mapping of Australia by Abel Tasman and Frans Visscher. (Or maybe rediscovery. There is uncertain evidence that some Portuguese had found the coast earlier.) Like finding Brazil, discovering Australia was an accident. The Dutch had found that the best way to get to the Indies was to sail directly eastwards from the Cape of Good Hope, using the strong winds in the latitude of the 'forties, instead of sailing north along the African coast and turning eastwards only later. The new course kept well south until the ship reached a latitude where turning north would bring it quickly to Java. This was sure to mean that, sooner or later, someone would overrun the eastward leg and, turning north, bump into Australia. In October 1601 someone did, finding land on the western tip of the Australian continent. Other ships followed in 1605, and in 1623 another expedition went to the Gulf of Carpenteria. One of its ships, the *Arnhem*, gave its name to the northeastern shores of the Gulf: 'Arnhem Land.' By 1640 the Dutch had an outline knowledge of the Australian coast from the northwest Cape to parts of the south, as well as of the whole Arnhem Land coast. Two years later still they sent two ships, with 110 men commanded by Abel Tasman, to find out more. In a very considerable feat of seamanship Tasman sailed right around Australia, making a landfall on the island named after him – Tasmania – and also discovering New Zealand.[33] The ocean thereabouts is mapped as the Tasman Sea. A century and a half later still, the explorer Matthew Flinders named two Tasmanian mountains after Abel Tasman's ships.[34]

There was much more to these travels than spices or gold. The Portuguese, English and Dutch explored and described these new worlds of men, of nature, of land and weather. They produced volumes of maps, description and comment. Much of the early literature described the Mogul empire in India. But the Dutch, in particular, produced charts and maps from their expeditions throughout the region. The Netherlands were already well known for printing, book production and mapping.[35] Printing had been invented around the ninth century by the Chinese, who even developed movable type. But Europe's interest in writing grew well before Gutenberg used such type to print the first Bible in 1452–5. The new techniques were in great demand, especially as towns grew and governments and bureaucracies demanded more records.

It was, altogether, an age of scientific and navigational innovation. Telescopes and microscopes were invented in the Low Countries around 1600. In 1675 King Charles II set up the Greenwich observatory, with its new meridian which suited astronomers, who could construct accurate tables of the movements of the moon. Greenwich went on to become the primary base for plotting global location. Though mechanical clocks had appeared in England and Italy by 1300 it was left to John Harrison, also in England, to revolutionize timing for navigation. In the early eighteenth century he built a chronometer without a pendulum (which could be disturbed by a ship's roll or pitch): it would therefore be accurate over a voyage of many months. It became possible, for the first time, to calculate longitude accurately out of sight of land.

Meanwhile, amid all the manoeuvres, explorations and squabbles of the Europeans from Nagasaki to the coast of Malabar, two major polities paid virtually no attention. China and Japan had largely passive roles in the critical opening phases of European expansion. Each became inward-looking, albeit for different reasons. China concentrated on Central Asia. Japan simply closed its doors. It is surely one of the oddities of this era that the largest and most accomplished societies in Asia played almost no part in its broader commercial and political developments.

For Chinese statesmen, real threats seemed bound to come from the north. And for a long time, defences there were inadequate. The empire was neither able to make the Central Asian tribes pay tribute nor to make them reliable allies, though it had usually been possible to absorb invaders into China's civilization. Although the Great Wall of China is said to date from around 200 BC, it seems more likely that only after yet another defeat by the Mongols in 1550 did the empire begin the colossal, and colossally expensive, enterprise of building this 1 550-mile protective wall.[36] But walls are not everything. Before 1600 the Ming emperors had become ineffective and it was court eunuchs who controlled armies and the secret police. In the wars and famines of the later Ming period China's population actually fell. Then a new and even more formidable tribal confederation appeared, based in Manchuria, beyond China proper, hence known as the Manchus. By 1616 they had their own Khan, or emperor. In 1644 they replaced the Ming on the peacock throne of China. They concentrated on providing firm authority at home and protecting the northern frontiers. They sent armies into Xinjiang to subjugate its Turkic tribes, made Outer Mongolia into a tributary, occupied Inner Mongolia and strongly garrisoned Manchuria. But they also, as early as 1668, banned Han migration into Manchuria, lest it become swamped by ethnic Chinese. The result, Manchurian underpopulation, was to have far-reaching political consequences. These Manchus, or Qing, became the last dynasty, occupying the throne until the empire's collapse in 1911.

In the meantime, a new kind of threat was emerging far away in the northwest. The duchy of Muscovy (Moscow) had managed to survive repeated assaults from Central Asia. As late as 1571 Moscow itself had been burned by Tartar raiders. Yet those immense Central Asian plains equally tempted rulers to seek defensible frontiers further east. Peasants, too, sought free land there, very much as American, Australian and Afrikaner settlers were to move into their own hinterlands in later centuries. Above all, there were furs in extraordinary abundance: squirrel, otter, marten, beaver, ermine, mink and sable. By 1584 Muscovy's rule extended as far as the Urals. But as fur supplies west of the mountains became exhausted, hunters moved beyond. Within half a century the Russians had moved into Siberia. Fortified stockades were built at Tyumen in 1584, Tomsk in 1604 and Krasnoyarsk in 1628. By 1647 the Russians had reached Okhotsk and the Pacific Ocean. Spearheading the movement were Cossacks, foreign mercenaries, Ukrainians, Swedes, Germans, adventurers and blackguards of all denominations.

Moscow tried to impose some order in Siberia, whose furs may, by 1660, have yielded fully one third of Russian treasury receipts. But controls were fragile. Russians treated native Yakuts with unparalleled brutality and Moscow failed to stop a slave trade in local women. In Kamchatka the natives were in such despair that when the Russians were not slaughtering them, they killed themselves. By the middle of the seventeenth century the Russians had moved to the Amur river, which continued to mark the Sino-Russian border three and a half centuries later. Here was a warmer, more fertile region. Unlike the snow-clad north, it could produce food.

For the Chinese, this was a very different group from the wild horse warriors who had threatened China from time immemorial. These newcomers could not be defeated or accommodated or absorbed. Chinese officials reported to the emperor that 'man-devouring demons' had come to infest the region. The first response was to offer trade in return for a Russian withdrawal. But the Chinese wrongly assumed that Moscow, rather than Russian freebooters, was in actual control. When Moscow did not respond, the Chinese tried force. To no avail as more Russian peasants, rebels and vagabonds made their way east. Muscovite and Manchu delegations finally met at Nerchinsk in 1689. The Russians wanted the Amur river to be the agreed frontier. The Chinese suggested Lake Baikal, some 600 miles further west. Eventually the Russians gave up the Amur valley but got an agreement to trade.[37] For the next century, Russia looked, not south towards China, but eastwards, to the Okhotsk seaboard, Kamchatka, the Kurile Islands and eventually North America. By 1740 they had founded the port of Petropavlovsk, getting half a century's start over Britain and France in the North Pacific.

For China and its rulers, these northern concerns remained incomparably more important than external relations in the south, where no serious threats could be expected. Although Japanese pirates could endanger the coast and even sail up the Yangzijiang, it was cheaper to buy them off. Foreign trade was not important to Chinese society, even if it might sometimes be for Chinese individuals or families. The abrupt end, from 1430, of China's seaborne expeditions therefore seemed logical. In any case, a new emperor listened to Confucian mandarins who despised commerce and hated the eunuch-admirals who commanded China's naval expeditions. Profit from the expeditions had been meagre, fleets and maritime power expensive, and neither trading nor even collecting tribute seemed worth an effort that diverted substantial resources from the north. Expanding contacts southwards could only bring other barbarian influences into the properly ordered Chinese realm. Unsurprisingly, by 1500 Chinese public and private fleets had shrunk and ships were going no farther than the Philippines or Malacca. In that year, the Emperor forbade his subjects on pain of death to build a ship with more than two masts. In 1525 the empire even destroyed all ocean-going ships and arrested their owners. It became a capital offence to put to sea at all. Similarly, the empire was wholly indifferent to the fate of overseas Chinese, even when there were massacres in Manila or in Batavia in the mid-1700s. Altogether, the Manchus wanted to throttle contact between the people and the outside world. Chinese were not allowed to emigrate. They were forbidden to travel on foreign ships. They were not allowed to become Christians. To teach the Chinese language to foreigners became punishable by death.

This kind of thing made the simplest trade extremely difficult. Foreign traders were confined to a few ports administered by the central bureaucracy. They lived in separate residential districts, with what later ages would call some 'extra-territoriality' and with their own head man. It had been so with Arab traders in the China of Marco Polo's time, as with Javanese traders in Malacca earlier still. Such foreigners always depended on the local potentate and were subject to arbitrary exactions by officials. Even so, the Portuguese lived in Macao a good century before the Ming empire ended, and before the Qing had been thought of. Similarly, the English East India Company started trading at Guangzhou Canton in 1637, and established a factory there in the 1680s. For the politics of the empire, however, these foreigners were entirely insignificant. The official view was very much that expressed by another emperor, a century later, to a stunned British envoy: 'We possess all things. I set no value on objects strange or ingenious, and have no use for your country's manufactures'.[38]

It was nevertheless the British who were to make the greatest Western impact on China. For two centuries after their arrival, mutual frustration and misunderstanding were almost complete. The British tried to expand their commerce. The Chinese resisted by obstruction, delay and, locally, extortion. Foreign trade was increasingly focused on Guangzhou and then confined there by another imperial decree. The foreigners could live in Guangzhou only during the trading season; then they had to leave for Macao. They were forbidden to bring their wives to China or to learn Chinese. They could not row on the river or ride in a sedan chair. They were effectively confined to their factories. Even so, by the end of the seventeenth century their presence became permanent and sixteen years later British agents could stay all year round.

In Japan, the decisive switch to isolation came around 1600, after Tokugawa Ieyasu crushed the feudal lords and became the master of Japan's destiny. He revived the old title of shogun. Japan was given a military regime, with the shogun virtual commander in chief, responsible for Japan's defence. Real power was henceforth in his hands, though he remained nominally responsible to the emperor. Moreover, the shogunate became hereditary in the Tokugawa family; and lasted until the middle of the nineteenth century, lending its name to an entire historical era.[39]

Ieyasu was anxious to promote foreign trade, so for three decades shipping and trade flourished. Still, there was a note of caution: trade gave access to foreign religion and therefore possible subversion. Trading was mostly with China but also with the Indies and Manila. At first Ieyasu distributed favours to rival foreign missions, depending on their efficiency in bringing trade. But in 1600 an English sailor and ship-builder named Will Adams came to Japan, built an eighty-ton ship for Ieyasu and persuaded him that the English, unlike the Spaniards and Portuguese, did not want to proselytize. They and the Dutch only wanted to trade. By 1612 he was Ieyasu's interpreter and trusted adviser; while the Dutch, whom their head office wisely instructed to be 'modest, humble, polite and friendly', were installed as traders.

But foreigners brought problems as well as opportunities. The greatest foreign influences were Christianity and weapons. Cannon were first used there by 1560 and the firepower of a musketeer corps quickly became decisive on Japanese battlefields. That made it vital to control the ports through which guns could be imported. As for Christianity, Japan quickly became much the most promising Asian field for Jesuit and other missionaries. In 1600 there may have been 300 000 converts and by 1615 perhaps half a million. But the links between Japanese Christians and their distant, alien Pope suggested that Christianity might be subversive. Ieyasu's last years therefore saw careful manoeuvring between the Japanese and three or four foreign trading powers. There was an anti-Christian backlash and some Christians were burned. In 1610, for instance, a Macao ship, the *Madre de Deus*, came to Nagasaki, was attacked and had nearly fought her way back out of harbour when a chance shot set her on fire. The Captain, Pessoa, threw down his sword and shield, took a crucifix in one hand and a torch in the other, and threw the torch into the ship's magazine. He became a hero of local Japanese folklore.

Not that Ieyasu wanted to dispose of the foreigners. But he did want to ban missionary efforts while milking European knowledge and activities. He manipulated the various Europeans for the best deal. There was even, in 1614, a Japanese mission to Europe, received with considerable splendour in Rome, Venice, Madrid and Seville; although Europe was, for obvious reasons, reluctant to give away the secrets of modern navigation and ship-building – much as the United States in the 1990s tried to deny strategic technologies to China or Iraq. In spite of such exchanges, Japanese controls on foreigners were tightened. Priests and foreigners might live close to their ships but in 1614 a new edict ordered the deportation of all missionaries and some of their followers.

After Ieyasu's death controls were tightened further. All foreign shipping except Chinese was confined to Nagasaki or Hirado. In 1622 over fifty Christians were put to the sword or burned at the stake in Nagasaki. Public sympathy for the victims only deepened official xenophobia. The following year a new Shogun celebrated his investiture by burning another fifty. Spanish envoys were told that talk of trade was merely a cover for subversion. Englishmen, Mexicans and Spaniards from Manila were banned altogether, and life even for the compliant Dutch became more difficult.

By 1636 there were new decrees. No Japanese ships were to leave for foreign lands. Any Japanese returning from abroad would be executed. Rewards were offered for the denunciation of Christians. Children of foreigners by Japanese mothers would be expelled. The artificial island of Deshima was built in Nagasaki harbour, to which the Portuguese were confined. The last straw was a peasant rebellion in Kyushu. Whatever its origins, its war cries were Jesus, Maria and Santiago; and its banners carried Catholic symbols. The rising began in December 1637 and the rebels quickly entrenched themselves at Hara castle, near Nagasaki. There were 37 000 of them, including 15 000 fighting men. The first government attacks were repulsed with heavy losses. Help was then demanded from the Dutch: guns were sent, and a ship, which bombarded Hara for a couple of weeks. In April 1638 Hara fell, and every soul in it, man, woman or child, was slaughtered.

Naturally the persecution of Christianity became more intense. The Portuguese were told that if any more monks or priests arrived, the regular Macao vessels would be burned with everyone on board. Shortly afterwards all Portuguese were banned from Japan on pain of death. Then local xenophobia reached new heights. An inspector found, above the doorway of some factory, the date of construction: AD 1637. It was enough: within the hour all buildings dated by the Christian era had to be destroyed. The Dutch were allowed to stay. But their commander had to be replaced each year. All of them were moved to Deshima island which became, for two centuries, Japan's only window on the outside world. On its 1.25 hectares lived some twenty Dutchmen. Except for concubines and whores, no Japanese was allowed to stay overnight. Boats were forbidden to approach. There was a single footbridge into the town, and the compound was contained by some 250 guards and officials.

The question which this complex story raises, and on which historians cannot agree, is how the Europeans accomplished so much on so slender a resource and population base, and with such primitive means. The explanation is not European technology. Indeed, the Europeans did not have major technological or even military advantages in most of Asia before 1750 or 1800. They were handicapped by small numbers and their distance from home. It is true that the Portuguese, English and Dutch established a decisive Western superiority in fighting at sea, relying on stout and weatherly ships, on daring and expert seamanship and, most importantly, on the invention of heavy ship-board artillery, which made it possible to sink rather than board enemy vessels. In 1512, for example, the Portuguese destroyed an armada of 300 Javanese ships sent to attack Malacca. Yet they quickly began to use Indian-built ships, as Indian carpenters learned to use local hardwoods to European specifications. Indeed, by the mid-1500s many Portuguese ships, and later English and Dutch ones, were distinctly inferior to Indian-built ships. The Europeans used native crews, too. Sometimes the entire crew was native, except for one or two dozen officers, gunners and soldiers.

Asian folk were also quite familiar with metals, metal-working and weaponry. Europeans themselves frequently employed local people and weapons, and local rulers quickly acquired guns and European military skills. Some employed Europeans to teach locals how to make and use the weapons. Other guns were bought or simply recovered from European wrecks. As early as 1508 the ruler of Diu may have had a hundred Portuguese guns recovered in this way. And in 1565, a Moslem army defeated the Hindu kingdom of Vijayanagar, in south India, using an artillery corps of 600 guns, as well as superior cavalry. Nor can it be said that the Europeans, for all their occasionally desperate courage and ferocity in battle, were more courageous than the fighting men of Java or India or, for that matter, Mexico.

Other factors mattered more. One, maybe even more important in the Americas than in the Indies, was disease. Although the Europeans were not immune to Asian or New World parasites, they brought with them diseases of which local peoples had no experience and to which they had no resistance. They died in their thousands, even millions, of typhus, smallpox, measles and influenza. Equally important were moral factors. That went far beyond the matchless determination, ferocity and battle-discipline of the Europeans. There was also the towering European self-confidence, for the Iberians particularly underpinned by religion, but in any case so total that it was often simply accepted by the local population, which created few problems in places like the Indonesian archipelago, whose peoples were in any case accustomed to strict obedience to God-like rulers.

Most important of all were surely three other factors: the political and social condition of the local societies, the cultural superficiality of the European impact, and the fact that only towards the end of the seventeenth century did Europe itself begin the socio-economic revolutions which would allow massively increased power to be deployed overseas.

One is struck by the political, social and religious fragmentation of the societies which the Europeans encountered in Asia.[40] The sole exception is Japan and it is precisely there that, given a centralized and effective shogunate, foreign influence could be effectively contained. Elsewhere, no society had the organization or unity against outside power that one would expect of a modern nation-state. Nor was there any coherent inter-state system, still less any mutual assistance among local principalities. There were certainly empires in northern and southern India, in Mexico, Peru and in China. None of them was capable of united and effective action against the Europeans. They could not even deny the outsider substantial local support from dissident, hostile or merely ambitious groups. And there were endemic local hostilities: between Shia and Sunni Moslems, Moslems and Hindus, rival princelings, between Amerindian tribes. The Aztecs were hated by their subject peoples. In Java, the kingdom of Mataram was riven by dynastic wars and the island principalities had constant feuds. The seventeenth-century populations of Indonesia may have despised Christians, and been hostile to the Dutch, but there was nothing like united resistance. On the contrary, the Dutch were constantly involved in native wars. Even in China, central edicts were apt to be as honoured in the local breach as in the general observance.

Except in Japan and possibly China, the Europeans rarely encountered large-scale or sustained opposition. Instead, individuals, rulers and groups made their own local arrangements. Indeed, the European achievements would have been impossible without active support from local allies, auxiliaries and mercenaries. Cortez campaigned in Mexico with thousands of non-Aztec auxiliaries who provided transport and intelligence, while the high-born Aztec lady who was his companion provided excellent political and strategic advice. In Peru, the Spaniards were helped by the Incas' enemies, some of whom were experienced local engineers. When Diego de Almagro marched from Peru down into Chile, he had 12 000 Indians with him. It was much the same in the East. D'Albuquerque at Goa had forty Hindu captains and their troops serving under him, and the Portuguese variously employed Goan and Malabar troops, a Japanese detachment in Malacca and even used infantry composed of black slaves from Guinea. In time, not only did the English and French ally themselves with one prince against another, but each prince recruited, trained and used substantial local forces of his own. By the time the English defeated a well-equipped Indian army of some 50 000 cavalry and infantry at Plassey in 1757, they did so with a force of only 1 000 European and 2 000 Indian troops.

Moreover, as the eighteenth century began, the political and especially the cultural impact of Europe remained insignificant. The Europeans were established traders. They commanded a number of ports and entrepots and demonstrated their military and naval prowess. But they quarrelled busily with each other. In places like Goa or Malacca they were only one part of a complex religious, ethnic and cultural jigsaw. Even anti-Moslem campaigns, like those of the Portuguese in Goa, were brief, ineffective or both. In most places, where they ruled they did so through local princes and institutions. Even missionary efforts usually allowed for local traditions. The very fact that in Java Europeans held themselves aloof or, as in China, were kept at arms length, limited their cultural and religious influence even further. Everywhere, their presence was too slight to change the pace or direction of deeper local currents.

Not only that, but European efforts themselves were not based on organized state activity. French colonial enterprise was indeed part of the state's domain. Dutch activities also seemed in many ways state based. And the English East India Company, although a private commercial entity, run by a board of directors and funded by private capital, had implications which almost immediately attracted the attention of, and soon supervision by, the government in London. Yet the forms of organization – of loyalty, of administration, of finance; the capacity for mobilizing socio-economic effort – were still, by later nation-state standards, quite slender. It was an age, still, when Germans became Russian generals or English kings, when Scots served in the armies of the king of France, when Dutch sailors went over to Islam or became pirates and Frenchmen could serve Indian rajahs. And no one spoke of 'traitors'.

In other words, while Europe's efforts attracted commercial and political attention at home, none of them were yet 'national' in a modern sense and none rested on the organizational powers of a modern state. Yet within barely half a century multiple transformations in Europe itself, of philosophies, of social and political organization, of administrative and military practice, would wholly alter the position of these powers in the East. It was only then that their role would begin to change from that of mere trader to imperial rule. It was the national revolutions of the eighteenth century in Europe which largely made the colonization efforts of the nineteenth possible.

3
Nationalism and Revolution in Europe

These European transformations began with radically new ideas not only about Europe's place in the world but about humanity's place in the universe. One reason was knowledge of the earth and its peoples brought back by explorers. Scholars and cartographers had known since the 1300s that the earth was round, which Plato, Aristotle and Eratosthenes had understood one and a half millennia earlier and Saints Augustine and Thomas Aquinas since. The Catalan atlas of 1375 marked an 'Asia' that might be reached by sea. Ptolemy's 'Geography' became known around 1410. However, even a century after Columbus, European geographers entirely underestimated the size of the globe, or the ratio of water to land, and seriously misunderstood the shapes and relationships of the continents. The discoverers changed all that. Soon after 1600, not only Africa but India, China, Japan and Brazil, and much of the Atlantic, the Indian Ocean and the Pacific had been charted and mapped with reasonable accuracy, their characteristics and peoples described and analyzed, often in a markedly detailed and sympathetic way. Scholarly writings dealt with the Congo, Japan and China. Closer knowledge of these civilizations inevitably changed assumptions about Western Europe's uniqueness.

Other discoveries proliferated in this dawn of modern Western science. In 1546, only a year after the Spaniards started to work the silver mines of Peru, the astronomer Tycho Brahe was born, eighteen years later Galileo and Johannes Kepler in 1571. Their discoveries changed forever Europe's view of the place of the earth, and of mankind, in the universe. They did more. They may not have touched the deep layers of ignorance and superstition of ordinary folk; but for the educated classes, they entirely altered the relationship between scriptural authority and human reason, observation and experiment.

They implied a fundamental challenge to accepted theories of knowledge, the nature of learning, to intellectual authority. This had profound consequences even for the idea of God.

Together with that came radical shifts in reigning social and political philosophies, and the beginnings of modern nationalist forms. Ethnicity was taken for granted as the primordial building block of society, since ancient times prior to, and often a condition of, statehood.[1] Men, following their biological disposition, were everywhere ethnocentrist. However, mediaeval Europe was not composed of clearly defined states. It had a kaleidoscope of political patterns and competing sovereignties, their relations depending almost as much on litigation as on personal relations or force. Rights and privileges were constantly granted, changed or withdrawn. Hence the rule of law took hold as a practical cement of society. The territorial state, a monarchy within more or less clearly defined borders, only appeared in Italy around the fifteenth century and was strengthened by the revival of classical ideas about legitimacy, secular sovereignty and non-interference in the internal affairs of independent states.[2] The Renaissance and Reformation brought further challenges to the unity of Christendom and the authority of the papacy. The doctrinal and structural changes sought by men like Martin Luther and Calvin went far beyond internal church reforms.[3] They destroyed the political unity of Christianity and, in time, removed religious sanction from sovereigns. That affected relations between kings and subjects everywhere. Scientific criticism of Christian tenets was also encouraged; so was a Christian humanism foreshadowing the eighteenth-century Enlightenment. Thinking about state and nation also came to a head. One of Luther's most famous statements, in 1520, was addressed *'An den christlichen Adel deutscher Nation'* (To the Christian nobility of the German nation). Similar thoughts surfaced, more or less simultaneously, in Britain, France and Holland.

Developments naturally differed from place to place. For the French, national pride was natural. Already in mediaeval times they had seen themselves as the cultural heirs of Greece and Rome. French political and economic consolidation took the king as symbol of the state. By the fifteenth century this polity claimed to be unique and superior, with king and *parlement* working together, under law, for the glory of God and the common good. From the beginning, too, centralization made the state, requiring a professional bureaucracy, in the form of the king's council, (later the *Conseil d'État*). In time, the ties of king and kingdom to the larger Christian commonwealth loosened.

There were fierce social cross-currents. Calvin began work in Geneva in 1541; twenty years later there were several hundred Calvinist churches in France, which became the foci of discontent. Religious turmoil led to civil strife, including the Saint Bartholomew's massacre of Huguenots (Protestants) in Paris in August 1572. Many Huguenots fled to the Low Countries, England and north into Germany. There were Jansenists,[4] whose rejection of mysticism also undermined the old faith. There were even 'new' Jesuits who believed in freedom and science, their intellectual curiosity tending towards faith in nature and progress, producing a humanism and worldliness leading to their suppression in 1773. By the later 1600s the French court itself was full of scoffers. Louis XIV, the 'Sun King', applauded performances in which Molière, the greatest playwright of the age, ridiculed the entire programme of the Catholic counter-reformation. Yet Louis' court preacher, Bishop Bossuet, who was also the great theorist of the divine right of kings, urged Louis to wipe out heresy in France. Louis therefore continued the persecution of Huguenots, Jansenists and others. Tens of thousands more took their skills north, to the safety of Prussia or Holland. The Prussian court, in particular, warmly welcomed them: to this day Berlin has a French cathedral and a Huguenot museum.

But the divine right of kings implied the 'deification of the French polity'.[5] And by the later 1600s the king personified society. The phrase for which History has remembered Louis XIV, who came to the throne in 1661 and reigned until 1715, is *'L'État c'est moi'* (I am the state). The country, *la patrie*, became one with the king's person and worthy of any individual's sacrifice. The test of an obedient subject was to be a patriotic Frenchman. Furthermore, since the authority of the king was that of God – in the eighteenth century, kings still appointed bishops, as in Britain they still do – the state became an end in itself and a source of moral as well as political authority. It was the power and welfare of the state which mattered, not that of individuals or of the people.

As the power and scope of government grew, so did resistance. An alternative vision of social order saw the people as the victim of monarchical oppression. Louis' persecution of the Huguenots removed some of the most dynamic elements in French society. This, together with tough administrative controls and taxation, led to the alienation of large segments of a middle class, which was growing in size and prosperity. Such political frustrations were to contribute greatly to the outbreak of the French Revolution a century later. Even the elite saw its liberties and privileges infringed and its political influence diminished. But such resentments also contributed to the emergence of a modernized national consciousness. As the King stripped the nobility of power, many of them joined the Parisian bourgeoisie in scoffing at sacerdotal kingship and opposing excessive centralization. Many disappointed aristocrats became sympathetic to ideas of the people as the bearer of sovereignty, and of the state rather than the king as the focus of loyalty. While the state continued to be monarchical, the view gained ground that the king was supposed to serve the state, not the other way round. Gradually, an individual identity as the king's subject gave way to one based on membership of a civil society of citizens. The state, *la patrie*, became an object of loyalty for all members of 'the people', thus implying political liberty through participation. These sixteenth- and seventeenth-century tensions therefore put greater emphasis on Frenchness. So did constitutional ideas which invested the community with sovereign power and gave it the right to oppose an unjust ruler. Constitutional rule and respect for the rights of the people became more and more a condition of royal authority.[6]

In the Low Countries, too, the Reformation period stimulated political change, even revolution, and a national separatism. Calvinism may have rejected Rome, but it had a clearly defined concept of society and the state, and insisted on organization and discipline. It began its conquest of men's minds in the 1550s and 1560s, at first in the French-speaking regions of the south, infected by the winds of religious change from the French Huguenots. The newly established Dutch Reformed Church provided dissidents with coherence and discipline. At its first synod in 1568, that defiant and democratic church directly challenged Rome. Discontent was fed by Spain's taxes and heavy-handed administration. By 1566–7 William of Orange led an armed revolt in defence of traditional liberties; though allegiance to Spain was only denounced in 1581. The Dutch argued that princes were appointed to be the shepherds of their people. God did not create subjects for the benefit of the prince. If the prince was tyrannical the subjects, being duty bound to preserve their freedoms, had a right to depose him. Some Dutchmen even started to say that true sovereignty resided in the people, drawing a fiery response from Philip II of Spain. But William, with the help of Dutch scholars, waged a press campaign at the bar of European opinion. He could also count on help from England, which had no wish to see Spain regain full control of the Channel coast.

In these struggles the northern Netherlands developed a claim to sovereignty based on separate Dutch identity. Moreover, the Dutch rebelled against Philip II not only on religious grounds but to oppose Spanish centralization. The new Dutch state therefore became an umbrella for local and provincial selfishness. Loyalty was chiefly to the city or province, not to the United Provinces. The state was loosely federated and the States General at The Hague was for a long time the sole administrative body of the Dutch Republic. Unlike England and France, this state was not designed for efficient external action. No political grouping in Europe, it was said, had less sense of sovereignty and fewer ambitions for conventional forms of power. The provinces would concede power solely to ensure the Republic's survival and protect its trade. National taxation and policy were a kind of last resort, a residual after provincial and commercial interests had been catered for. Much effective power remained with the benevolent dictatorship of town merchants, who set their faces against any notions of sovereignty which might conflict with their commercial interests. What the canvases of Rembrandt and Frans Hals record are just such sober, cautious men, complacent even, not given to flamboyance or show. 'By and large the wealth of the Dutch was the result of a multiplicity of individual commercial transactions. State intervention was minimal.'[7] Not that this, or the small Dutch population – as late as 1600 it was only around one million – prevented them from fighting in Europe's eighteenth-century wars, or from action overseas. But the Dutch state and nation were very different from France and England.

It was in England that a recognizably modern nationalism first took root. National consolidation and a stronger state were critical in solving King Henry VIII's dynastic and foreign problems. They provoked his quarrel with the church and the claim to absolute governance of the English state, to which the church became subordinate. That denied the unity and indivisibility of Christendom. It also encouraged the despoliation of church property for the benefit of the royal finances.

This process consolidated national consciousness. The King's struggle against Rome became part of maintaining England against foreigners; the popular sense of English difference becoming tinged with Calvinism. Protestant English resistance to Rome was also strengthened by the new literacy, and reading the new vernacular bible which appeared in the 1520s and 1530s. The papal bull deposing Elizabeth I caused vast resentment and reinforced her struggles against Spain. By the end of the century England had a new national identity, conceived as an autonomous community. Also, it was a period when both the gentry and the professional and commercial middle classes grew in numbers and influence, a community whose members were equally secure in their civic liberties. The state needed the gentry, as well as the nobility, to enforce its laws as unpaid justices of the peace. And the new professional groups, especially lawyers, tended to value achievement rather than family status alone.

These classes began to assert themselves partly to support an embattled national consciousness and partly in response to Henry's financial and political needs in his struggle with the church. Henry had to rely increasingly on support from the House of Commons. Where equivalent institutions elsewhere, the *Cortes* in Spain and the *États-Généraux* in France, became inconsequential, the Commons of England grew in importance. By 1600 Englishmen thought it their right and duty to take part in politics. Patriotism had to do with the rights of members of the nation, equated with the country. The next three or four decades were a time of religious turmoil and of incompetent rule by a government without a standing army and therefore incapable of repression. The terms of the struggle for power implied that sovereignty attached to England, not the king. England, particularly in its Puritans, was nationalist. Popular sovereignty and nationalism were identical twins. Shortly after the accession of James I parliament already claimed an equal share in government. In 1604 the Commons used unprecedented language, asserting that '... the voice of the people, in the things of their knowledge, is said to be as the voice of God'.[8] At the same time King James, in urging the union of England and Scotland, referred to them as two nations. His son was even more insistent on England's character as a national entity. And the philosopher Thomas Hobbes thought that civil war and revolution were really about 'that liberty which the lower sort of citizens under the pretense of religion, do challenge to themselves'.[9]

The early and middle 1600s saw continental devastation in the Thirty Years' War,[10] revolts in various places including Catalonia and Bohemia, and civil war in England. England's turmoil centred on the twin issues of faith and political authority. Contemporary writings stress the ideas of the nation and of England, opposition to the crown being framed in national as well as religious terms. The King's opponents accused him of trying to destroy the established rights 'of freeborn Englishmen'. When put on trial in 1649 he was charged with having been 'trusted with a limited power to govern by and according to the laws of the land and not otherwise'. John Bradshaw, sentencing Charles, pointed out that monarchy was a contract, a bargain between king and people.[11] The House of Lords was abolished because it was 'useless and dangerous to the people of England'.[12] Even the brilliant flourishing of science which accompanied and followed the foundation of the Royal Society was due, the public thought, to the peculiar genius of the English nation; and scientific effort was welcomed as promoting the nation's prosperity.

Although the monarchy was restored in 1660, by 1688 James II was driven from the English throne. Once again, revolution was a move to restore the ancient rights of Englishmen. James was accused of promoting Catholicism, of reasserting royal powers and tampering with property rights. The political class declared the throne vacant and offered it to William of Orange (whose wife Mary was James II's daughter). William and Mary accepted 'on the conditions laid down by a Convention of past and present leaders of the English people'.[13] So William had been chosen not by God, or the church, or normal rights of succession, but by the people of England. He accepted conditions implying profound constitutional change. Parliament, which had not met for several years, was immediately summoned. It passed a Bill of Rights prohibiting taxes not levied by parliament or keeping a standing army in peacetime. The first removed the financial power of monarchs and the second forbade any repetition of the Cromwellian military regime.[14] The Bill also extended civil rights and called for free elections to frequent parliaments, whose members would enjoy free speech. The king remained head of the executive, but could only govern with the regular consent of parliament. In sum, England acquired a limited monarchy and took a long step towards a constitutional one.

It was the first of the three great eighteenth-century revolutions – 1688 in England, 1776 in America and 1789 in France – and the overture to reshaping the principles of European politics, dovetailing with the whole intellectual upheaval of the Enlightenment, destined to reformulate ideas of state legitimacy, largely in national terms. Not that the growth of national passions in Europe was anything like linear. Ideas overlapped, were often confused, unclear, even contradictory. Still, ideas are dynamite in human affairs, and never more so than in eighteenth-century Europe.

Enlightenment attitudes derived from Galileo, Kepler, Newton and a series of discoveries, from that of the circulation of blood, by William Harvey, to the invention of probability theory by Blaise Pascal and Pierre de Fermat in the 1650s. Men began to conclude that all real questions were in principle capable of being answered, by someone, somewhere, sometime. Reality was a body of facts to which all men must submit; and all answers about the physical but also the social worlds were inherently knowable. They were discoverable, but only through the unfettered reason accessible to any man, not through faith or priests. Society's problems could be analyzed like those of the physical universe, and even designed as mechanisms. They could yield to what later centuries would call social engineering. The science of the seventeenth century therefore bred the faith in reason and progress of the eighteenth. It produced a temper that rejected authority and asserted the Rights of Man. It made government a science, and led to the bureaucratization and centralization of the state, as in the monarchies of Frederick the Great of Prussia and Joseph II of Austria.

A seminal figure in these philosophical shifts was probably the Frenchman, René Descartes. If Calvin paved the way for secularizing society, it was Descartes who developed, from self-evident first principles, a science which would explain with mathematical certainty not only biology and physics, but metaphysics, psychology and therefore social reality, too. God himself was turned into a mathematician, or the clockmaker of this mechanical universe. In contrast, Blaise Pascal reaffirmed the vital need for personal communication with God; and a series of new movements sought religious certainty. There were Jansenists in France, Quakers and Methodists in England, Pietists in Germany and Catholic lands, and millenarian splinter groups in many places. Still, after Descartes many reasonable men thought there were indeed universal laws of human behaviour, as there were for nature; and if only they could be understood, harmony might be established among men as there was harmony in nature. Crime and folly would be abolished by reason.

France naturally played a key role in developing these and other social and political ideas. For the entire seventeenth and eighteenth centuries she was the intellectual, artistic and spiritual leader of Europe, the brilliance of her civilization impressing itself on the European mind in spite of her civil and religious strife, corruption or frequent mismanagement of public affairs. It was no jest when Frederick the Great, the soldier-King of Prussia, remarked to the encyclopaedist d'Alembert that he would rather have made the French poet Racine's masterpiece, *Athalie*, than won the Seven Years' War. In the earlier eighteenth century the – largely French – founders of the Encyclopaedia, like Diderot and d'Alembert, sought to spread reason and benevolence to the masses. They wanted to fight obscurantism with science and knowledge. The great Voltaire, whose wit and wisdom made him the leader of the European Enlightenment, insisted on reason, compassion and freedom. He admired the liberties and democracy of England and emphasized the political role of reason, liberalism and consent. He insisted on the innate similarity of men, their capacity for reason and the importance of a cosmopolitanism which two centuries later would be called multi-culturalism. He believed in material prosperity and social planning, and thought peace among individuals and nations was truly possible.

The tumult of Enlightenment ideas moved across frontiers as religion had done in earlier times. One strand stressed science and scientific materialism as the gospel of freedom from superstition. Some went even further, like La Mettrie who remarked that 'man is a machine, but also a plant' (an idea still, or again, much in vogue at the beginning of the twenty-first century). Another gave birth to Romanticism and the celebration of individualism and will. Yet other strands went in for scientism or technology or occultism and magic. After 1770 or so, a host of sects flourished in France, Prussia and southeast Germany, devoted to Eastern theosophy, mysticism, séances. Some were linked, not incidentally, to a pan-European revolutionary optimism.

When philosophers like Diderot, Voltaire or John Locke argued against superstition, they also spoke about injustice and inequality. They tended to argue that, as government derives its powers from society, for whose sake government exists, so society can change, limit or revoke those powers. John Locke's apologia for the 1688 revolution had already argued[15] that morals exist before politics. The Stuart kings had violated their implied contract with the people, who were therefore justified in making another contract elsewhere.

However, the central figure in changing accepted philosophies of politics was Jean-Jacques Rousseau. A thorough-going neurotic, he came from Geneva, that refuge of heretics, and tried his hand, unsuccessfully, at trades like engraver and watchmaker. He was moody, unreliable, sentimental, arrogant, ultra-sensitive and aggressive. He could be dishonest and cruel. A man opulent in his contradictions, he preached the gospel of the family but abandoned his children to a public asylum. A philanthropist who loved mankind, he could not live with anyone for long. He scoffed at the religious and sexual promiscuity of the woman who loved and kept him for years, poor Mme de Warens. He quarrelled with his friends. Yet he was also the herald of popular democracy and came to be revered, even in his own day, as a prophet if not a saint. Even Immanuel Kant, the greatest philosopher of the age, for whom God remained the final guarantor of all human and physical systems, saw him as the voice of conscience.

His two key works were the *Contrat Social* and *Émile*. In the first, he argued that the association of individuals in a community creates a collective moral body to which the individual surrenders himself and his rights. That body, consisting of all the voters, receives from this assembly and its votes its life, will and common identity. 'Those who are associated in it take collectively the name of people, and severally are called citizens, as sharing in sovereign power, and subjects, as being under the laws of the state.' Citizenship has to do with active participation and freedom with self-determination.

Passing into this civil state is the meaning of morality, for society is a law unto itself and all values derive from it. Hence 'whoever refuses to obey the general will shall be compelled to do so by the whole body, this,' Rousseau famously maintains, 'means nothing else than that he will be forced to be free.' And since sovereignty cannot be alienated, nor divided, it cannot be represented by any mere part of the whole. Law itself is only the 'declaration of the general will'. Government is merely an intermediary between the individual and the sovereign community, its task being to execute laws and preserve liberty. The people's community, the nation, is therefore supreme. Indeed the citizen's mind must constantly be concerned with *la patrie*, defended at need by the nation in arms.

Not that Rousseau was a twenty-first-century Western liberal democrat. Indeed, he is arguably one of the intellectual ancestors of twentieth-century totalitarianism.[16] He thought democracy demanded altogether too much perfection. 'Where there is a people of gods, their government would be democratic. So perfect a government is not for men.' Consequently, the best practicable government is an elective aristocracy, rule by an enlightened elite. Equality means 'uniformity of the populace [at large], which was a condition for the unity of the nation [and] facilitated the expression of the general will, and therefore ensured its freedom'.[17] Following Rousseau, Hegel went even further and saw the state as an ethical idea made actual, a quasi-divine entity representing the unfolding of the universal spirit on earth. So, while Montesquieu had thought the diversity of races and nations merely a set of variations on a theme, for Rousseau and Hegel, it was part of the great drama of a historically inevitable evolution of mankind from childhood to maturity. It was only in the service of the state that the individual could fulfil himself and become truly free.[18]

In some respects, these changes returned to ideas about the will of the people prefigured in fifth-century Athens and later in Roman Law, and foreshadowed by the Henrician Reformation and subsequent civil war in England. But the stress on nationalist assertion, and the supremacy of the nation, was new. Before 1750 'nation' had been a fairly harmless concept. In France especially, *patrie* often had to do with city or clan rather than France. But the revival of the classics focused attention on the Greek *polis*, the city state whose rights were superior to those of the citizen. Repeated wars with England also encouraged national feeling. In 1755 the Abbé Coyer was writing that mothers should understand that they were bearing children for *la patrie*; that soldiers should learn to die for it and their parents to be glad of that; and that priests belonged first and foremost to the nation.[19] By 1781 Joseph Servan was coupling the ideas of citizen and soldier in his *Soldat Citoyen* and seven years later the Abbé Sieyès[20] could write that 'the nation exists before all, it is the origin of all. Its will is always lawful; it is the law itself.'[21] In Germany Herder, too, was celebrating the uniqueness of national identity.

Rousseau also became an important source of nineteenth-century Romanticism, whose ideas paved the way for romantic nationalism. *Émile*, published in 1762, was a treatise on education. It launched a cornucopia of ideas on nature, and man's responses to it. Rousseau criticized the established church and unrestricted rationalism, both of which trampled underfoot the sense of reverence and the natural in man. Perhaps fortunately for the book's broader reputation, the *Parlement* in Paris objected to its anti-Catholic sentiments, had it publicly burnt and a warrant issued for Rousseau's arrest. While the *Contrat Social* proposed a reign of reason and justice, *Émile*'s reverence for the natural proved no less important. Romanticism became a celebration of individual genius and will[22] and a passionate protest against universalism. It celebrated spontaneity, the uniqueness of individuals and, by extension, of nations. Nor were these new ideas and nationalist stirrings confined to France. In England, war also promoted national feelings while passions were strengthened, everywhere, by religion or domestic unrest.

England saw other kinds of unrest also, especially about political and parliamentary reform. There was much inchoate radicalism in places like London. For most of the eighteenth century government was 'the King's Government', with ministers appointed or dismissed individually, at the monarch's pleasure, so reform smacked of Jacobinism. By the 1760s, radicalism was personified in the unlikely figure of John Wilkes. He was the second son of a pious distiller, sent to school to study Greek and Latin at the age of nine. After studying further at Leiden he acquired a rich wife and went in for drinking, debauchery and a spot of devil-worship. He became a Member of Parliament, a brilliant journalist and a thorn in the side of king and government. Not that he had a coherent programme; he was a stormy petrel rather than a revolutionary. But his theme, that a tyrannical executive was violating the liberties of Englishmen, echoed the issues of 1688–9, and resonated particularly in the City of London. That was important, since London remained the centre for insurance, banking, trade and ancient crafts. It was also a city of grinding poverty, crime, entertainments like bear-baiting and cock-fighting, not to mention women prize fighters. Highwaymen operated in the middle of town and as late as the 1770s the Lord Mayor was held up at pistol point just west of London. A decade later the Prince of Wales himself was robbed in Berkeley Square. (Presumably the nightingales forbore to sing.) There was endemic rioting: against Catholics or Jews or Dissenters or Scots or just to promote the cause of some populist hero. John Wilkes managed to harness the political energies of thousands outside the political class. Here, for the first time, was a mass radical movement in Britain.

The same principles of popular representation became accepted in Britain's North American empire, which brought wealth, but also heavy defence costs. Here was a dumping ground for convicts. Between 1715 and 1775 some 30 000 convicts – like Moll Flanders – were transported across the Atlantic. But Puritanism, and the puritan libertarian populism, went too. As early as 1638 a Connecticut preacher told his flock: 'The choice of public magistrates belongs with the people by God's own allowance. They who have the power to appoint officers and magistrates, it is in their power, also, to set the bounds and limitations of the power and place unto which they call them.'[23] Difficulties of communication and control also produced, in practice, much political and economic independence in the American colonies. London's attempts to limit this independence led to friction,[24] disputes and riots. The immediate issues centred on taxation.[25] But for London, the underlying problems were strategic and constitutional: the danger of letting the important American colonies slip into the orbit of France; and colonial defiance of British parliamentary sovereignty. For the colonists, however, the basic grievances were about representation and rights. Most settlers, in the Americas and elsewhere, thought they were citizens and subjects overseas, with the same rights as in Britain. Indeed, George Washington and his colleagues, like the English revolutionaries of 1641 and 1689, claimed that they only wanted to preserve their traditional English rights, appealing to John Locke's natural rights principles: no taxation without representation. The English government insisted that colonies owed loyalty to the crown and were instruments of overall British policy. Yet by May 1775 the colonials would no longer accept the authority of parliament in London, let alone that they should contribute to the general expenses of the empire. They were in open rebellion.

As Plumb has pointed out:

> ... America began to announce that it was the victim of tyranny at the same time that many Englishmen were beginning to develop exactly the same attitude to their own government ... Americans and Englishmen felt themselves to be the victim of the same wanton prejudice, the same blind insistence on the letter of constitutional rights, the same ignorance of the broader principles of justice and humanity ...[26]

It was no coincidence that the Founding Fathers of the American Republic were deeply learned in the ideas of the French *philosophes* and the European Enlightenment. Their resentment of London's high-handedness became explicit in the American Declaration of Independence:

> We hold these truths to be self-evident, that all men are created equal, that they are endowed by their Creator with certain inalienable Rights, that among these are Life, Liberty and the pursuit of Happiness – that, to secure these rights, governments are instituted among Men, deriving their just powers from the consent of the governed ...

with the obvious implication that 'consent of the governed' meant majority voting and rule. Here was the original doctrine of self-determination, which was to cast a very long shadow indeed.

The rebels' principles found strong support in London, which undermined the government's war effort. Charles James Fox and many Whigs had long maintained there was a fundamental right of resistance, even rebellion. Edmund Burke protested bitterly against royal policies. Britain should keep her colonies by bonds of affection and let them become independent if they wanted to. Byron wrote a panegyric to George Washington: 'The Cincinnatus of the West/ Whom envy dared not hate/ Bequeathed the name of Washington/ To make man blush there was but one.' Chatham (William Pitt the elder) was sympathetic. Even some of the generals due to command in America, like Lord Cornwallis, thought the colonies should not be taxed by coercion. Some economists argued that the colonies were no benefit to

Britain anyway, and certainly not worth a war. Adam Smith said much the same in his *Wealth of Nations*, published in 1776, with its promotion of free trade. 'Great Britain', he said, 'derives nothing but loss from the dominion which she assumes over her colonies.'[27] Britain should only trade where that made economic sense, whether the partners were colonies or not. Some of the opposition formed itself into groupings like the Supporters of the Bill of Rights Society. John Wilkes naturally went much further and wrote: 'The king is only the first magistrate of this country ... responsible to his people for the due exercise of the royal function in the choice of ministers.'[28] He went to prison for his pains, though still a Member of Parliament. He seemed, to Americans as to Englishmen, almost to personify Liberty; the sense, as Rudyard Kipling would so elegantly put it a hundred years later, that men wanted 'Leave to live by no man's leave/ Underneath the law'. Burke pontificated that Wilkes was only being pursued 'for his unconquerable firmness, for his resolute, indefatigable, strenuous resistance against oppression'.[29] There was intense public excitement about his imprisonment, mobs demonstrated in the streets and the imprisoned Wilkes was deluged with presents.

The war stretched Britain's governmental wisdom, as well as resources, to breaking point. The French Foreign Minister, the Comte de Vergennes, saw immediately that London could not win. 'It will be in vain,' he said, 'for the English to multiply their forces there, no longer can they bring that vast continent back to dependence by force of arms.'[30] Britain's increasing diplomatic and strategic isolation underlined the point. While the Americans, confronted by poorly led British land forces, held their own, it was probably the intervention of the French which turned the tide. In March 1778 they declared war on England, followed by Spain and Holland. The French Navy played a decisive role: its blockade of the American coast compelled the 1781 surrender by Cornwallis at Yorktown, which was critical in persuading Britain to abandon the war. By 1782 ministers in London, overburdened with domestic dissent and war costs as well as worries in the West Indies, in India, with Spain and France, almost welcomed American independence and sensibly tried to make the break as amicable as possible.

The opposition in London also reflected further movement towards notions of representation and accountability. The loss of North America naturally weakened the crown's dominant political influence. In 1780 Dunning's resolution in the Commons declared, echoing parliament's resistance to King Charles I, that 'the influence of the crown has increased, is increasing and ought to be diminished'. Defeat in the American war strengthened, as defeat so often does, a mood for change. Many of the reforms sought in the following decade by senior parliamentary figures like Fox and Burke meant reducing the crown's political influence. Parliament already controlled the power of the purse, but the 1780s saw moves to change the entire ministerial system, making government dependent upon parliamentary rather than court support.

The Dutch also supported the Americans, were enthusiastic about the Declaration of Independence and became the second country to recognize the rebels. Although the states of Holland had banned Rousseau's *Contrat Social* and his *Émile* – which naturally made the books more popular – the Americans' resistance to dictates from London roused Dutch folk memories of their own resistance to Spain. It promoted the 'Patriot' movement within Holland. There were other motives also for sympathy with America. One was the hope for trade once North America became independent. And while Amsterdam remained Europe's chief money market, and the creditor of virtually every European monarchy, the Dutch were no less pleased to lend money to the Americans.

Then came the French Revolution. The impact of the English ones of 1649 and 1688 had been relatively localized. The American one of 1776 had, in the short term, only limited and temporary consequences for the larger balance of power. By contrast, the events of 1789 in France were a political and strategic earthquake which shook European society to its foundations. Like all great upheavals it had complex causes. They included increasing confusion and self-doubt among the ruling elites. Major segments of the aristocracy and the *haute bourgeoisie* rebelled against the reforming initiatives of an irresolute absolutism. Unrest was stimulated by the American example. Dissent was legitimized by an appeal to libertarian principles alleged to have been violated. But it was not immediately obvious that this upheaval would lead to a quarter of a century of large-scale war in Europe. Even in England, the revolution had many early friends. The young Wordsworth was full of fervour.[31] Edmund Burke, later a fierce opponent, at first looked kindly on moves to free the French people, to establish checks and balances against tyranny. William Pitt himself at first sympathized with the revolutionaries' devotion to liberty (as well as their fiscal policies). Indeed, by 1792 both Pitt and Tom Paine were predicting fifteen years of peace. But by 1793 matters had changed, as more and more people were fed to the guillotine, as Paris spoke of exporting revolutionary principles and as the prospect of French fleets in the Scheldt raised fears about an invasion of England.

In Paris the principles of Rousseau, of French nationalism and of the early English populist radicals, were taken much further by deeply earnest revolutionary and post-revolutionary nationalists. In the words of Article 3 of the 1789 Declaration of the Rights of Man and Citizen: 'All sovereignty resides essentially in the Nation. No body, no individual, can exercise authority which does not explicitly emanate from it.'[32] The Declaration of Rights of 1795 repeated: 'Each people is independent and sovereign, whatever the number of individuals who compose it and the extent of the territory it occupies. This sovereignty is inalienable.' Here was the insistence on each nation's right to self-determination, completing the transformation of the idea of 'nation' from a prepolitical community with a shared historical identity to a coherent political actor, a democratic polity of active and committed citizens.[33] Even ethnic or cultural commonalty became subordinate to, albeit an essential factor in, republican participation.

The struggle for power extended from the domestic into the international realm. French nationalism, republicanism and statism, surrounded by enemies of the revolution, became fiercely militant. From 1792 France was at war with Austria and Prussia. Early defeats produced panic measures, including the execution of the King. Revolutionary sentiments and principles were most fearfully on display during the Jacobin 'reign of virtue' when, in the terrible words of Saint-Just: 'The Republic consists in the extermination of everything that opposes it.' Like other revolutionaries before and since, Robespierre and the other Jacobins could claim hecatombs of victims in the name of abstract nouns.[34] In the name of purification and reason they called for the head of the King in 1792, of the Girondins in 1793, of the aristocrats in 1794 and after that started on one another.

What developed in this maelstrom of ideas and passions was a new basis for national identification, unity and loyalty, new ideas about the structure and unity of society, and new ways of symbolising its continuity and mobilizing its resources. The locus of legitimate political authority was no longer the country or the king or the church or even Christendom, but an entity called 'the people'. It was a concept of the most far-reaching importance. It implied a need to distinguish, not only emotionally or politically but administratively as well, between members of 'the people' and others. It established clear distinctions between citizens and non-citizens and implied equality of fellowship among citizens. It followed, too, that decisions could only be legitimate if taken by a majority of this fellowship's members. The centre of gravity of the political system shifted, organized society became dominant and the forms of political action foreshadowed those of the modern world. Wider political participation also made room for various forms of radicalism; while the need to rally majority support promoted the organization of political parties. Not surprisingly, within fifty years France had achieved universal manhood suffrage.

Problems remained. What, precisely, made for membership of this national fellowship was not easy to define. The French Revolutionary Constitution of 1793, in Article 4 defining 'The Status of Citizen', granted every adult foreigner who lived in France for one year the rights of residence and of active citizenship. In time, that turned out to be too generous. Furthermore, the idea of 'the people' clearly assumed the territorial state. Beyond that, things were less clear. Montesquieu had written half a century earlier[35] that environmental influences like climate and terrain were decisive in developing politics and institutions: different circumstances called for different systems. Dominant German views, following Herder, Fichte and the Romantics, held that there was something organic and special about any national group. The nation was not only an active and participatory social grouping but a prepolitical community and culture with a shared historical destiny. To be French or English or Chinese, as Isaiah Berlin has put it,

> ... is to belong to a unique society ... and ... what it is to 'belong' cannot be analyzed in terms of something which these persons have in common with other societies ... but only in terms of what each of them has in common with other [members], each group having its own ways of talking, eating, concluding treaties, engaging in commerce, dancing, gesturing, building ships, tying shoelaces, explaining the past, worshipping God ...[36]

These French views made nationalism more rigorous but also more political and democratic. Nor was the march of liberty and human betterment to be confined to France. The revolutionaries called on other oppressed peoples to rise against rulers and landlords. They, too, should throw off privilege and dictatorship. So nationalism attached itself to the universalistic principles of the Enlightenment and the defence of liberty against the oppression of church or nobility or king. The state was to become the instrument of the 'nation' and of 'liberty', in whose service, as the Anglican prayer-book says in a rather different connection, 'is perfect freedom'. It was that concept for which revolutionary armies were willing to fight, it being the revolution's historic task to bring enlightenment and freedom to all nations. Liberty, Equality and Fraternity – the new trinity – would produce a league of like-minded nations, and extend the struggle against Liberty's enemies. It was on such grounds that Dutch republicans joined with France; that Italian and German intellectuals and bourgeois expected revolutionary France to sponsor their own nationhood; or that Beethoven wanted to dedicate a symphony to Napoleon the great Liberator.[37] As late as the mid-nineteenth century Mazzini, the father of Italian unification, saw national statehood as the only proper end of revolutionary activity, and the condition from which rights and liberty would flow.

Even once that conjunction of nationalism and international libertarianism faded, nationalism remained as a, perhaps *the*, principal means of identification, self-determination and political assertion. Not that its progress was smooth. After 1815 the victor powers were hostile to nationalism and its twin, revolution. Metternich understood its disruptive potential and how fatal nationalism would be to Austria. At the same time, though there were middle-class protests against foreign rule in Italy, Ireland, Greece, the peasant masses were barely affected. Until the later nineteenth century, and in most places, people were more attached to locality or province than to the nation. Only gradually did nation-state identification gain ground outside Western Europe and become the principal framework for participation in the affairs of society.

One of the most powerful drives in this growth of nationalism was the desire for assertion by the despised, oppressed or defeated. So was exile which, Lord Acton once remarked, is 'the nursery of nationality'. Napoleon's campaigns produced national reactions in Spain, Russia, Germany and elsewhere. Indeed, romantic German nationalism itself was largely a reaction to feelings of inferiority among Germans confronted by the military and political ascendancy, and the matchless cultural brilliance, of eighteenth-century France. It all underlined the 'highly competitive character of European nation building'.[38] A more modern example is the fierce nationalism (Zionism) of first-generation Jewish immigrants to Palestine, before and after the Second World War, leading to the creation of Israel.[39] Nationalism had similar roots in Europe's colonial world. As Soetan Sjahrir, first prime minister of the Republic of Indonesia, said: 'The source and lifeblood of all nationalist extremism is the socially and intellectually inferior station in which the Indonesians are forced to live. Extremism springs from the resentment that they … feel at being looked down upon as an inferior race.'[40]

But these developments did much more than change dominant political philosophies. They changed the nature and structure of the state which became the institutional embodiment of the nation, just as the sovereign nation became the sole legitimate basis of the state. In creating new kinds of coherence between state, government, territory and popular loyalties it created a variety of novel socio-political structures and the conditions for stronger and centralized state administration, new forms of finance and even the industrial revolution. All this created unprecedented capacities for social mobilization and mass enthusiasm in the pursuit of a common 'national' end. Employed by the new administrative state, it promoted a fearsome degree of social efficiency, demonstrated in dramatic fashion by the administrative and military efforts of revolutionary France and the Napoleonic state.

As the state was nationalized, so the nation became statist and its administrative machinery more complex and powerful. With the transition to popular political principles and more modern social organization, accompanied by scientific and industrial advances, revolution made the state even stronger. 'Without planning to do so, the revolutionaries [i.e. in France in 1792] rebuilt the edifice of absolutism into a bureaucratic structure a great deal larger and more solid than ever before ... the state apparatus became society's instrument for accomplishing the general will. This depersonalized the exercise of state power ...'.[41] Economic and social modernization may have isolated the individual, but national consciousness could also mobilize individuals in the shared general interest. The nation embodied a higher good than any citizen or group. It, and its state, therefore acquired moral connotations. Patriotism became progressive and constructive, competing loyalties regressive, the former acquiring a corporate, as well as emotional and popular, quality which became the hallmark of the effective nation-state.

It was war, more than almost anything else, that consolidated the new principles of national identity, democratized governance and centralized state power. Furthermore, it promoted new kinds of military organization and compelled the growth of new economic activities, new kinds of administration and finance, and the development of new social structures.[42]

The creation of modern military organizations goes back to Maurice of Nassau, Prince of Orange, commander in chief of the army of the United Provinces at the start of the 1600s. Taking command of mercenaries and soldiers of fortune, he drilled them into a model army. He provided regular pay, regular food, equipment and even housing, partly to avoid raids on the citizenry. He imposed iron discipline. When his men were not upon campaign, he gave them constant, endless drill. He divided the army into battalions, companies, platoons and squads, with a clear chain of command from every squad up to Maurice himself. The result was that he could move troops around a battlefield like chess pieces, and his formations could fire concerted volleys.

But foot drill is also hugely important in bonding men to their fellows. As any drill sergeant knows, soldiers who have drilled together form a special bond. Where, before Maurice, foot soldiers – coming mostly from the poorer or vagabond classes – had been a disruptive element in society, once drilled these peasants or cut-throats became reliable and obedient. Soldiers, as William McNeill has pointed out, '... became replaceable parts in a sort of human machine, and so did their officers'.[43] Other European powers quickly imitated Maurice.

The first to follow suit were the Swedes, followed by the English and then the French. By 1700 the French had created a centralized military machine capable of putting several hundred thousand men into the field. Once again, envy and imitation went hand in hand. Other major powers, notably Prussia and Austria, acquired standing armies of a type the twenty-first century would have understood: disciplined, with regular, often standardized weapons and equipment, regularly housed, fed and paid, capable of fighting other states as well as compelling tax-payers to maintain both them and the general state machinery. Only in Britain did the memories of Cromwell and James II, as well as the primary expenses of naval power, severely limit the crown's ability to keep an army. These developments and their effects were not confined to major states. It was Mars who presided over the consolidation of the Dutch Republic. And the effects were felt around the world. The Seven Years' War of 1756–63 was fought in India, the Americas, and the East Indies as well as Europe. It has been called the first world war.[44] Other global conflicts followed. Napoleon's 1797 invasion of Egypt gave severe headaches to a London government worried not only about Europe but about attacks, via the Middle East, on India.

Not that European opinion was united in such matters. On the contrary, the more professional the military became, the less did the growing and increasingly comfortable urban commercial classes sympathize with policies likely to lead to war. The men of the eighteenth-century Enlightenment were no more willing than Western liberals two centuries later to accept war as necessary or inevitable. And however profitable war might have been in earlier times, economists followed Adam Smith in believing that wealth would come by peaceful commerce. Indeed, in an illusion which has persisted ever since, they thought trade would produce peace. Wars stemmed from vested interests and false perceptions, from which enlightened modern man should free himself.

All of which was far removed from the needs of the embattled French revolutionary state, which produced innovations that would change the organization not only of war but of society. Military necessity strengthened the new principles of national unity and the capacity for mobilization. National manpower and resources were harnessed by a ruthless populist authority. As the law of 23 August 1793 succinctly put it: 'From this day until that when our enemies have been chased off the territories of the Republic, all Frenchmen are on permanent requisition for military service.' This produced a capacity to raise, organize, supply and deploy larger and much more effective armies than those of the revolution's combined enemies. By the end of 1794 France had over a million men under arms.[45] Four years later the revolutionary authorities adopted conscription as a permanent national policy: every able-bodied young Frenchman would serve in the military for five years. It was, for the first time, a 'nation in arms'.

As national principles and patriotic enthusiasm promoted wars, so wars promoted national principles still further. For the first time peasants from obscure provincial villages, who had never before been away from home, were dressed in national uniforms, in a national army, in some foreign place where the locals regarded them as *Frenchmen*. Furthermore, these revolutionary armies were forcibly democratized. They were led by officers advanced on merit. Though core personnel tended to be former royalist professionals, Napoleon's generals and marshals came from all social classes, like Murat, the innkeeper's son who became Europe's premier cavalry commander. National flags, previously unknown, were introduced in 1791 by the national convention, which ordered the use of the tricolor. Moreover, the new mass army – one uncommonly ready to spend men – was suffused by the ideology of revolution, moved by the display of brilliant uniforms, by symbols and abstract ideas. Instead of being drilled automatons, its soldiers were full of initiative and flexibility. Inevitably, this egalitarian mass army also had profound effects on France's social structure.

These armies carried their principles with them. French soldiers found that in Italy and Germany they were heralds of liberalism, national self-government and the end of autocracy. It did not last, of course. Provincial Germans welcomed them at first, but by the mid-

1790s, under the mounting pressures of war, the armies were bleeding food and fodder from occupied areas. The 'sister republics' found themselves mere pawns of French diplomacy. In 1796 the Directory informed General Jourdan that the great art of war was to live at the expense of the enemy; but friends were not much better off. Europe became less conscious of liberation than of hardships imposed, for instance by Napoleon's attempts to block trade with England. French invasions therefore also served, especially after Napoleon's retreat from Moscow, to stimulate a German – as distinct from merely Prussian or Saxon or Bavarian – national enthusiasm.

The organization of European wars also hugely increased the demand for money and strong administration. Civil administration in Europe had its roots in mediaeval royal households. From these developed a threefold division between treasury affairs, a high court and the royal council, all of them served by expert functionaries. By the fifteenth century, courts had become more costly, and rulers tried to reclaim power from the unruly mediaeval aristocracy, which meant expensive guns to breach the castle walls of rebellious barons. Longer and more expensive wars at home and abroad further increased the need for money, which meant more sophisticated administration to mobilize resources. That strengthened the King's council (later the *Conseil d'État*) and its bureaucracy, increasing the domestic power of the new territorial monarchies in France, Spain and England. It also increased demands for representation as a basis for taxation.

In both France and Britain the scope of royal administration increased greatly in the sixteenth century.[46] In England the administrative genius of Henry VIII's officials, like Wolsey and Thomas Cromwell, strengthened the grasp of central government. This was enhanced by the novelty of printing, which greatly increased central resources, allowed laws and instructions to be circulated widely, accurately and quickly, and made government influence more uniform. But the growth of government also underlined the weakness of any systems where the king became the chief clerk of the realm, working without adequate delegation. The result was to enhance the role of an educated and often secular class of officials. The new aristocracy of Tudor England was largely composed of such functionaries, replacing both the clergy and the old nobility of the Wars of the Roses. A century later, administrative centralization had evolved even in further in the Cromwellian republic, in which '... a new kind of public service, in some ways a new administrative system, was coming into existence ...', supported by an annual public revenue of some £1.5–1.7 million.[47]

The power of the state also grew hugely in the France of Louis XIV. The Sun King relied on a group of middle-class ministers, of whom Colbert is only the best known. Colbert's Code imposed 'the largest politically unified area of the contemporary world',[48] with corresponding wealth and power. He regularized taxation, organized local and army administration, saw to education, commerce and industry. In time, French administration even acquired some *de facto* autonomy.[49] In finance, for instance, in the thirty-five years before 1789, France had nineteen ministers. Effective power naturally devolved to long-serving officials.

Within a short time other European governments, notably that of Prussia, had followed suit. Indeed, modern European public administration is probably traceable not only to France but to seventeenth-century Prussia and late eighteenth-century Britain.[50] In Britain, administrative reform had various causes: the desire to limit the political influence of the crown, the pressures of global conflict, government inefficiencies over America, impatience with administration as a tool of personal politics. Moreover, the growing scope of government and administration made the customary overlap of administration and political functions simply less feasible. Few individuals could combine the two roles. A sharper separation of the two was needed.

In France, the revolutionary period produced great changes in administration, as in other areas of French life. In improving social efficiency it vastly increased bureaucratic power.[51] The totalitarian revolutionary state not only conscripted all Frenchmen, but produced a planned economy: with 'national bread' and ration cards, a requisitioning of all crops not needed for local consumption and the regulation of foreign trade by a central commission. Rules were enforced by the guillotine. Naturally total rigour proved unsustainable and corruption and a black market emerged. Still, it was an unprecedentedly 'national' effort.

The civil service, like the military, became a career open to talent. Officials were no longer responsible to a king but to the state. They were instruments of public power and of burgeoning administrative law. Their role was depersonalized. Even Edmund Burke could not refuse reluctant admiration to these new energies and efficiencies:

What now stands as government in France is struck out at a heat. The design is wicked, immoral, impious, oppressive; but it is spirited and daring; it is systematic; it is simple in its principle; it has unity and consistency in perfection ... It is military in its principle, in its maxims, in its spirit, and in all of its movements ... We have not considered as we ought the dreadful energy of [this] state ...[52]

All this was further strengthened by Napoleon. Administration became more complex, and more like a military organization. It was organized on Enlightenment principles of universality and rationality. Authority attached to the office, not the man. The service was given a clear, hierarchical chain of command. France had new territorial divisions: *départements, arondissements* and so on, all linked to a national Ministry of the Interior. Nor did the emperor overlook the need to train expert staff; he founded the *École Polytechnique* to train specialists and administrators. The *Conseil d'état* acquired intellectual as well as judicial authority. These practices, too, were quickly copied by other countries.

War vastly increased the need for money. So did new technology. That meant new methods of public finance. In the eighteenth century several states started to widen their tax base. Since military expenditure rose even faster, wars were mainly financed by loans. In the Netherlands the war of independence from Spain had already highlighted the tension between provincial autonomy and the federalized decision-making needed for a common war effort. Coherent administration and economic management, however unwelcome to city oligarchies, had been essential for success. However, no centralized fiscal mechanism was developed; the seven provinces remained financially autonomous, and until the Napoleonic period even defence spending was only by joint action through the States General. Though financial unity did eventually lay the foundations for the modern Dutch state, 'The creation of a protected colonial outlet for Dutch textiles in the first half of the nineteenth century and the expansion of the national railway system in the 1860s were probably more decisive preconditions for internal economic integration and economic development than fiscal unification'.[53]

In Britain, too, administration required more revenues. The centralized national fiscal system which evolved relied a good deal on indirect taxes.[54] Adam Smith regarded this as one of the main causes of Britain's prosperity. Barely recovered from the civil strife of the 1640s, the English found themselves fighting a war against France, from 1688 to 1697, in which military expenditure was almost 75 per cent of government spending. Fifty years later the Seven Years' War seems to have cost a grand total of some £160 million (£13.1 billion),[55] or about twice the 1760 gross national product. The Napoleonic wars may have cost Britain, each year, £60 million (£1.9 billion) or 25 per cent of the national income. Throughout this period the fiscal burden per head was much heavier in Britain than in France, with British taxation being maybe twice to three times as high.[56] But growing percentages of British military spending were funded not by taxes but by government borrowing. During the American revolution loans funded some 40 per cent of defence costs. The pattern continued. 'The treasury raised money by issuing government securities, usually in the form of long-term bonds with a guaranteed annual premium. The service costs … were financed by the nation's increasingly effective tax system.'[57] It is not too much to say that this system of loan financing created by the Treasury and the Bank of England was quite as responsible for the string of victories over France as Wolfe or Wellington were on land or Nelson at sea. And in war or peace, government financial operations went on growing. Between 1750 and 1850 public revenue (in current pounds) multiplied by nine: from £7.5 million (£613.2 million) in 1750 to £57.1 million (£2.8 billion); while the interest payments on the national debt grew from £3.2 million (£261.6 million) to £28.5 million (£1.4 billion).[58]

The consolidation of these nation-states, and their wars, also forced general economic, industrial and trading growth. At first, this came through policies of economic nationalism known as mercantilism. Mediaeval Christianity (like Islam) had the utmost suspicion of 'usury': lending money at interest or making undue profits. That changed with the appearance of Protestantism. Calvinism, especially, made commercial enterprise respectable, even Godly. Hard work was righteous. Success was a reward of virtue. Here was the origin of the 'Protestant ethic' which, three centuries later, Max Weber was to see as a chief motive of the Western capitalist economies. Not that interest rate management was abandoned. In England, for instance, it was forbidden from 1700 to 1714 to charge interest rates higher than 6 per cent; and from 1714 to 1832 the limit was lowered to 5 per cent (though the limits did not apply to government borrowing).

Other developments were already in train by the time Martin Luther triggered the Protestant revolution. Mediaeval Europe's economy was fragmented and localized. Then came a more interconnected network, increasingly dependent upon the involvement of sovereign power. Nationalism therefore became an economic force well before becoming a political fact. Moreover, once state power came to depend not only on control of territory but on effective use of resources, trade became a matter of state competition and the 'balance of trade' a way of measuring national advantage.

The dominant economic assumptions of the seventeenth and eigh-teenth centuries were therefore clear-cut. Wealth was finite; gain for one implied loss for someone else. A state became rich by conquest or by getting a larger share of a static pie. The result was a kind of partnership of merchants and officials, pursuing both private profit and state power. The state encouraged private enterprise so as to increase its own wealth. Strong government was thought an economic necessity and a defence against dislocation, including unemployment which, given no effective policing, could easily lead to violence and unrest. The establishment of mercantilism is '... not, in fact, intelligible except as an organic part of the whole process of state-making ...'.[59] The process also justified dis-crimination against outsiders. After all, law-making is always political and instrumental, and here external and domestic needs came together. These mercantilist concepts, including the use of state power to facili-tate commerce, first appeared in England. Indeed, 'For much of the sev-enteenth century and most of the eighteenth, British statesmen tried to divert the economy toward geopolitical ends ...'.[60] In France, mercan-tilist and quasi-mercantilist policies took on even more statist and authoritarian forms, including regulations to impose social discipline and ensure product quality. The machinery established by Colbert and his successors clearly implied that public administration was incompa-rably wiser and more important than mere trade and industry.

By the 1720s the classical apparatus of mercantilism was complete. In parallel, there was protection for domestic industries and, abroad, increased nationalism and belligerence. Government was the protector of markets and shipping. Self-sufficiency in strategic and exotic goods also meant having a large merchant navy, just as commanding trade meant assured work for home manufactures. In consequence, everyone combined the search for wealth with a drive for strategic power through stronger shipping resources and colonial monopolies. The English Navigation Acts of 1651–63, for instance, were meant to protect England's trade with the colonies and the English shipping to carry it. The Anglo-Dutch wars that followed stemmed largely from Dutch insistence on unrestricted freedom of the seas and of trade, versus England's insistence on absolute sovereignty over home waters.

Given mercantilist orthodoxies and national competition, colonial issues were mere tools of home policy. Having colonies opened up new fields for economic enterprise. Owning them, and especially their trade, became significant factors in the Europe-centred competition for power. London's strategic plan was therefore to make Britain and its colonies self-sufficient in strategic materials, especially naval stores, including the tall trees needed for main masts. Similarly, one reason to protect merchant shipping was to control, as against the Dutch or French, the transport of colonial staples like sugar and pepper to Europe. Another was to train enough sailors to man the navy in wartime. All this lessened the importance of territory in Europe compared to trading and finance, where Britain was strong. Similarly, the system favoured trade surpluses and hoarding bullion, whether for reserves, or to give purchasing power to armies and navies overseas, or as a lubricant for trade. Indeed, without bullion, trade with the Levant or the East Indies might have died.

The French and English wars with the Dutch in the late seventeenth century had clear mercantilist motives. In 1664 Colbert wrote to his king that the Dutch were trying to capture world trade to increase their strategic power. The assumption was that trade was finite and monopoly possible. Similarly, after de Ruyter reorganized the Dutch fleet and humiliated the English in 1667, England's navigation acts were amended and certain commercial advantages conceded. These wars were about economic dominance, command of trade with the colonies and reserving raw materials for one's own domestic industries. Anglo-Dutch rivalry only faded in the following century, overshadowed by the political and strategic implications of growing French hegemony. By then, the British empire was regarded as the world's largest area of unrestricted trade.

Before Adam Smith there was no real champion of *laissez faire*. Only then did the mercantilist orthodoxy start to give way to his argument that it was pointless to manufacture at home what one could buy more cheaply abroad. In Italy and Spain mercantilism was unsuccessful anyway, its ideas being largely derived from English, French and Dutch models. It was northwest Europe that had effective merchant communities and corporate organizations, while Spain and Italy were dominated by lawyers and clergy. Not surprisingly, it was in northwest Europe, where the political economy approach dominated, that the word 'capital', in its modern sense, appeared around 1630,[61] while the modern usage of 'economic' and 'economist' dates only from the nineteenth century.

In the eighteenth century, at any rate, England still fought mainly for trade. In France, Louis XIV was much concerned with royal revenue, but took no interest in commerce. Colonial issues were more marginal than for England and settlers and adventurers were often left to their own devices. Industry and commerce were the servants of state policy rather than policy serving commerce. William Pitt, by contrast, thought that England's prosperity and greatness depended strongly on commanding world trade. Trade meant wealth and power and England's only real rival was France: or, as Pitt put it in 1763: 'France is chiefly, if not solely, to be dreaded by us in the light of a maritime and commercial power ...'[62] England's aim in the Seven Years' War must be to capture French trading posts, command the produce of the West Indies and keep supremacy at sea. Canada should be captured with its fur and fish trades and naval stores, and fresh markets gained for home manufactures. Pitt was therefore concerned to seize France's trade rather than destroy her empire. Only then could England gain enough wealth to subsidize her continental allies in Europe's wars. His, and England's, success was measurable. In 1700 almost 80 per cent of Britain's exports were going to Europe. During the next century, Britain's export industries grew almost four times faster than those directed at home markets;[63] yet by 1800 only 45 per cent went to Europe. In 1770, the East India Company's trade alone was worth some £1.7 million (£100.7 million).

Not only, therefore, did the sixty years of almost continual warfare from the 1750s prove hugely successful, but war turned out to promote all forms of economic and industrial growth: it was good business. The napoleonic wars especially stimulated British trade, with exports growing some 3.8 per cent per annum faster than either before or afterwards; French trade, by comparison, was thoroughly disrupted.

The consolidation of the nation-state, and its wars, had even broader implications for general economic and industrial growth than for trade. In confirming borders, they unified national markets and provided a basis for the industrial revolution. They created the boundary conditions for a modern capitalist economic system and the domestic pressures for its growth. Demography reinforced change. Populations grew at rates unprecedented in Western Europe. So did towns. By 1700 London and Paris each had populations of over half a million people. Growth had many causes, including earlier marriages, better health and declining infant mortality.

Table 3.1   Increasing population figures (in millions)[64] 1700–1900

	1700	1800	1850	1900
England and Wales	5.2	9.6	22.3 (UK)	38.2 (UK)
France	21.0	26.0	36.5	40.7
Netherlands	–	2–2.5	3.1	5.1

That growth helped to liberate the popular and social energies that went into the 'industrial revolution'. And the new industrialism of the seventeenth and eighteenth centuries, the gathering of people into towns and the relative decline of the countryside, the discipline of factory life, improved education and wider communication helped still further both to increase social wealth and to make an even more national society and consciousness possible. Indeed, modern nationalism as well as industrialism seem to have been essentially urban phenomena.

Moreover, strong central government had always involved much more than protection against outsiders. Protection remained significant, for instance for England's woollen industry. But government also provided the infrastructure for a domestic administration disciplined by the rule of law. Even in Britain, let alone in more highly controlled France, it meant legal restrictions on prices and wages, a ban on the export of textile machinery and some other technologies, as well as on the emigration of skilled workers. For a long time, it also meant a ban on incorporation, since there was a general horror of 'speculation', no doubt reinforced by the South Sea Bubble of 1720.[65]

The British state may have offered strong government, but it did not promote the growth of particular industries. William Pitt had read Adam Smith and believed, like Margaret Thatcher two centuries later, in smaller government and fewer taxes. There was a clear, even guaranteed, sphere of individual enterprise and action free from state interference. That turned out to be of special importance and highly productive. Innovation and enterprise have always blossomed in informal settings rather than under tight conservative rules. Yet the general connection between private wealth and public power has always been a primary concern of governments. And with tighter regulation, heavier taxation and increased government borrowing, official financial policy became the biggest single influence on economic activity. As Marx pointed out later, while capitalism did not liberate anyone or promote democracy, it did require a political system which operated in the interests of capitalists; once older social links and customs had begun to give way to the market, political power gravitated towards the holders of money.

National wars also stimulated industrial development. The military market for mass-produced goods was probably a critical stimulus to the entire industrial revolution. Armed forces needed uniform cloth, guns and other paraphernalia; and for much of the sixty-year period before Waterloo Britain had, often at short notice, to make some 100 000 of its poorest men into fully clothed and armed sailors and soldiers. It is no accident that the industries most critical to the war effort, including the metal industries and textiles, were also those in which innovation and industrialism was at first concentrated. Their production spread, for example to iron works in Scotland. At the same time, entrepreneurs sought to even out the erratic flows of government orders by seeking complementary or alternative markets, including ones overseas.

In France the story was very different. Down to the late eighteenth century it led the world in the sheer volume of industrial production, as well as in domestic and foreign trade. But trouble gradually built up. The expulsion of the Huguenots had deprived France not only of important skills but of much entrepreneurial dynamism. The Colbertian regulatory system became in time both tyrannical and corrupt, stifling innovation, or, more precisely, its exploitation. Eighteenth-century France was full of innovations, only to find them developed and applied in Scotland and England. It was rather like twentieth-century English inventions being taken up by American business. In both cases, France in the late eighteenth and Britain in the twentieth, the most important social groups were not industrialists and merchants but lawyers and financiers. Before 1800, by contrast, England gave priority to production and official decisions were carefully based on furious lobbying by interested economic groups. In France, regulations were apt merely to be handed down from on high by a bureaucracy somewhat contemptuous of mere trade and industry. There were other differences. In Britain, even as the agricultural sector underwent relative decline, its productivity increased. France also became richer, but kept a large and low-productivity agricultural sector. In Britain, some 18 per cent of the labour force worked in industry in 1688; by 1840–41 the figure was over 47 per cent. The comparable number in Western Europe seems to have been around 25 per cent.

In any event, as Plumb has observed, the English '... changes in industry, agriculture and social life of the second half of the eighteenth century were both violent and revolutionary'.[66] It is not surprising. As Schumpeter famously pointed out in the 1930s, 'creative destruction' is of the essence of capitalism and the idea of a stable capitalist system is a contradiction in terms.[67] In the first three or four decades of the eighteenth century, population expansion was prefaced by a rapid expansion of British trade and markets, at home as well as abroad. That particularly affected the lower middle classes with enough education and technical competence to use the new possibilities. It also fuelled the industrial revolution, a term first used by French commentators in the 1820s for an economic transformation which they thought as overwhelming as the French revolution of 1789. Its structural economic changes were made possible by innovations across the board: in technology and machinery, transport, industrial organization and finance. They produced a substitution of machines for human effort, the use of new and abundant raw materials, and a switch from animate to inanimate sources of power, especially steam. There was also a fundamental redeployment of resources away from agriculture and towards the industrializing sector.

By 1700 England (and Holland) were already the greatest textile producers of Europe, had the greatest merchant fleets and were the biggest traders. In 1760, nine years before James Watt's steam engine inaugurated the age of steam, Britain imported some 2.5 million pounds of raw cotton for its textile mills, then the most important sector of industry. Seventy-five years later, that figure had grown to 366 million pounds.[68] Again, between 1688 and 1901, the share of national income provided by mining, manufacturing and construction virtually doubled, to 40 per cent, and between 1700 and 1850 Britain's exports of iron and steel increased from 1600 tons to 1.2 million tons per annum. These shifts involved unprecedented productivity increases and a steady rise in income per head. They were accompanied by infrastructure developments of turnpikes, canals, ports and coastal shipping. In the process, industrial development also tended to unify the country. Coal and metal-working, especially iron, needed not only large amounts of capital but nation-wide transport and supplies. By 1800 '... the gap between Britain and the most advanced other economies in this field was quite unprecedented, and unrepeatable'.[69]

Naturally, the balance of domestic political power was also transformed. Local isolation broke down as England's economic interests became more closely linked. The notion of 'society' expanded beyond the local. So did values, as the new industrial and middle classes concluded that a principal, if not sole, measure of virtue was immediate social value. The new industrialists were equally interested in law, order and efficient administration: especially in the towns, populated by more energetic citizens, local government and administration were tightened. The result was a greater common interest between the industrialists and the new administrative classes. It was all strengthened by religion, especially a Wesleyanism which also complemented the new faith in economic *laissez faire* with an unprecedentedly close-knit social organization.

The new national state, then, consolidated domestic markets. Borders and border controls became clearer, transport and communications more secure and the writ of the central government ran more quickly and securely throughout the national territory. Conditions became more secure for the growth of new kinds of banking, insurance[70] and financial arrangements, not to mention the exploitation of new inventions. The new nation-state therefore also helped to make possible the financial and banking revolutions of the nineteenth century.

But matters did not stand still. In the first industrial revolution, unambiguously led by Britain, agricultural productivity increased, steam power was developed, the factory system spread and corporate forms of business organization grew. In the second, from the middle 1800s, Britain's lead was increasingly challenged, especially by the US and Germany. Communications and transport were revolutionized by steamships and railways, electric motors, internal combustion engines and oil fuel became common. Big business and professional management made their appearance. For Britain, the upshot was that, as far as one can tell, the rate of economic growth was 0.7 per cent per annum in 1700–80 and 1.8 per cent in 1780–1801 but shot up to 2.7 per cent in 1801–31,[71] in spite, if not because, of the Napoleonic wars. Substantial growth continued. In the 170 years from 1820 to 1990 Britain's per capita income multiplied by a factor of ten.[72]

The Dutch journey to the industrial world and the centralized state was different. By 1600 the United Provinces were full of folk who had fled north from the Spanish Netherlands and France. These Huguenots, Calvinists, Jews, merchants and artisans of all kinds quickly developed thriving industries and crafts in the northern Dutch provinces. They produced fine linen, cut diamonds, made renowned Dutch pottery, built sugar refineries and produced fine textiles, like brocades. They also tended to dominate Northern European fisheries and much of the seaborne carrying trade. Together with that went an absence of servility, a sense of equality, and good education.

Furthermore, from the sixteenth century the Dutch enjoyed a high savings ratio as well as substantial profits from trade. In the two centuries which followed, there was much outward foreign investment, especially through the East and West India Companies. But by the later seventeenth century Dutch economic expansion came to a halt and the eighteenth was a period of economic and social decay. The reasons are clear enough. The country relapsed into commercial, industrial and technical conservatism. Reform was stifled and taxes were heavy. Though taxes were low everywhere by twenty-first-century standards, for most of the seventeenth and eighteenth centuries the tax burden in

Holland was higher than in other countries. Around 1800 it seems to have been some 12 per cent compared with 5–10 per cent elsewhere. It has been estimated that in 1510 a worker in Holland would have had to work some seven working days to pay his taxes. By 1790 the figure was over thirty-three days.

Some of the chief industries declined, including fisheries, the timber trade and the formerly flourishing textiles industries, which now suffered from foreign competition. Even ship-building, where the Dutch had long been leaders, declined. In 1697 Czar Peter the Great of Russia came to Holland to learn ship-building. Thirty years later, the Dutch were themselves hiring English shipwrights. Even their navigation and ship-handling declined. As the industrial revolution began, Holland suffered further from lack of iron or coal as well as its small population. Instead of industrial development, there was a flood of low-priced manufactured goods from Britain and, later, from Germany and France as well. What industrial development there was went, like the inflow of British investment and technology, to the Catholic south, the future Belgium. Dutch public debt increased, too. Together with that came a shift from trade or production into reliance on income from foreign government bonds, investments which were largely liquidated during the Napoleonic wars. And until almost 1800 the state remained riven by provincial separatism and jealousies, stifled by administrative bureaucracy, and hampered by the emigration of skilled workers.

Even more important than size and lack of industry may have been some other factors. One was the huge drain of many of the youngest and fittest men who went to the colonies. Emmer has estimated that during the eighteenth century 4000–5000 unmarried men went out each year to the Dutch East India Company's possessions in Asia, where two thirds of them died. Even if half the total were foreigners in Dutch service, that represented one tenth of every cohort of young men born in Holland.[73] The total Dutch population in 1800, as we know, was not much over two million. A crude calculation would suggest the following. Assume that one quarter of the total population, or 500 000, were able-bodied men, the rest being older men, women and children. In that case 4000–5000 going East would represent around 1 per cent of the country's able-bodied men. If two-thirds of them died in the Indies, that would be around 0.66 per cent of the total. Even if one assumes that Emmer's numbers are too high, because as many as half the men going East were foreigners entering Dutch service, the *annual* losses would be of the order of 0.33 per cent of all able-bodied men in the Netherlands. An equivalent order of magnitude of losses in the United States or Britain in the 1990s might be around 225 000 and 48 000, respectively. These are figures that might be expected in the case of modern world war. If the Netherlands did indeed suffer an annual loss of young men, presumably including some of the fittest and most enterprising, on anything like this scale, that must have had hugely debilitating moral and social effects in the country.

Together with that came the consequences of European wars. The late seventeenth century wars against France and, even more, those of the later eighteenth century against England, badly overstrained Dutch strength. Between 1688 and 1713 the republic's national debt multiplied by five and while the English Treasury could raise loans at 6 per cent, the Dutch had to pay 9 per cent. By 1780 the Dutch Navy had declined so far that Dutch sailors preferred service in foreign merchant navies. Some 20 000 of them served in English ships.[74] Support for the Americans in 1780 proved especially ruinous, with the British blockading Dutch ports and interrupting traffic with the Indies. The Dutch merchant fleet was swept from the seas and the peace treaty of 1784 broke its shipping monopoly with the East. The East India Company was ruined and in 1796 both its empire and its debts were taken over by the state.

Only then did reform come. By the 1780s came a rebellion – quickly stifled – against the House of Orange. The dissidents called themselves 'patriots', following the American example, but were crushed within a couple of years. Then, in 1794–5, came occupation by French revolutionary armies, with government replaced by a revolutionary committee. In May 1795 the United Provinces became the 'Batavian Republic'. It was compelled to house and pay 25 000 French soldiers and to form an alliance with France in its war against Britain. That republic lasted from 1795–1805. Propped up by French bayonets, it was despised by everyone as a creature of French policy; while both before and after that, the French assumed the Dutch were mere tools of the British. Napoleon wrote the Dutch off as a legitimate national entity. But it was not quite true. In the Netherlands, the French armies confronted a dour republicanism expecting self-determination and willing to be difficult. In effect, between the arrival of King Louis Bonaparte in 1806 and the return of the House of Orange in 1813, the seven Dutch provinces became a united nation. This kingship and French occupation saw not just the end of the Dutch Republic but the development, under French influence, of a centralized state apparatus. Much was lost, including most of the 15 000 Dutchmen who marched with Napoleon's *Grande*

Armée to Moscow. But by the time a new Dutch state under King William I emerged, following the downfall of the Napoleonic empire, it owed much more to that centralized apparatus than to the heritage of the former United Provinces. An evangelical Dutch egalitarianism added representative government by 1818.[75] It was therefore these two decades of French rule, and the subsequent period to 1848, which saw the gradual and intermittent construction of the institutional structure of a centralized nation-state.

As national consciousness and nation-states consolidated, as bureaucratic government expanded and as great armies marched across Europe, relations between all these national entities also became more formal. Clearly a state based on a nation had an obligation to protect not only the security and material well-being of the citizens, but also their identity. There might be arguments about the cultural aspects of nationalism, but national identity clearly had to be distinguishable from the identities of surrounding states and societies. These considerations, and the whole turmoil of the seventeenth and eighteenth centuries, encouraged the elaboration of laws of conduct between nations. Such laws had begun to emerge much earlier, with the disintegration of the universal political organization of the *respublica Christiana*. Where Hobbes and Machiavelli had regarded states as confronting one another in a moral and social vacuum, later writers developed notions, often based on the revival of classical ideas, of the legitimacy of the secular state, of non-interference, and of their common interest based on natural law. The Dutch, in particular, developed, not just in practice but in theory, influential ideas about non-hegemonial principles and the development of a law of nations.

It was Hugo de Groot (Grotius), the former child prodigy driven from Holland by religious differences, who sat in Paris in the middle of the seventeenth century and wrote the first standard treatise of international law, *De jure belli ac pacis* (The law of war and peace). Here was the idea that states were free, equal and independent; and that international society could only escape anarchy by developing mechanisms of human society through international law. That notion of the fraternity of nations was to reappear in many forms. In the short term, it produced a common culture of inter-state behaviour, regulated by the establishment of resident missions and embassies, and of a balance of power and clear rules for dealing with issues of war and peace. For it was the national state which claimed, as the legitimate agent of the community, the monopoly of the use of armed force. Any erosion of that monopoly was usually assumed, on excellent historical evidence, to be likely to lead to social chaos and barbarism. But more was to follow. In the nineteenth century Mazzini used the elegant analogy of nations being like members of an orchestra in which individual musicians, each with a separate instrument, play the same music. The same thought was to lead to the formation of the League of Nations and the United Nations of the twentieth century.

At least three conclusions can be drawn from this story. First, the new European form of the nation-state had by 1800 developed a degree of economic, social and military efficiency which was not only unprecedented in Europe's own history but without parallel in the rest of the world. Secondly, this new social and political organism rested on complex and interrelated developments in such fields as moral impulse and political thought, as well as industrial and financial power, administrative organization and military might. Thirdly, as the military and economic capacity of the European powers increased, and the European balance of power tended towards equilibrium, the importance of strengthening one's position by making territorial and economic gains outside Europe increased yet further; while events overseas were increasingly determined by metropolitan domestic politics. Up to the end of the Napoleonic wars (and again later) the expansion of Britain and France, in particular, was driven by Anglo-French contention in Europe rather more than by developments in Asia.

4
From Trade to Empire

These changes in the nature of the European state were the basis for developing colonial power. They made themselves felt overseas only slowly and in erratic fashion. But as overseas trade and conquest became increasingly important factors in the European power struggle, peoples in the Americas or Asia became pawns in the game of European politics. Conquests could become negotiating chips. English gains from France in the colonies, for instance, could be exchanged for parts of the Low Countries vital to the security of the British isles. It was all summed up in the famous comment by Macaulay on the importance of a war, around 1740, between the King of Prussia and the Empress of Austria, about possession of the central European province of Silesia:

> The whole world sprang to arms ... The evils produced by his wickedness [i.e. that of the King of Prussia in seizing Silesia] were felt in lands where the name of Prussia was unknown; and in order that he might rob a neighbour whom he had promised to defend, black men fought on the coast of Coromandel, and red men scalped each other by the Great Lakes of North America.[1]

By the later eighteenth century the Franco-British contest in the East focused strongly on India. The British East India Company monopolized British-Indian trade from 1698 and within half a century its trade seems to have turned over some £1–2 million per annum (£82–164 millions). Being content, until around 1740, merely to import and export goods, and virtually unconcerned with the local politics, such clout as it had was parasitic on the Mogul empire. Yet within a mere seventy-five years, with no deliberate plan, the company found itself governing Bengal, much of central, eastern and southern India, and maintaining the most powerful army in sight. Indeed, the company, whose support the local princes found increasingly useful, began to behave like an important Asian power, conducting armed operations not just in India but in Java, Malacca and even Arabia.

The process began with the death of the Mogul emperor Aurangzeb in 1707. The successors of Akbar had expanded the empire, for instance to include Assam. Yet by 1700 Mahratta horsemen from the south were ravaging the Deccan and confronting the Moguls. After Aurangzeb the empire began to disintegrate. In 1717, the East India Company was granted a measure of territorial autonomy. Twenty years later the empire was too weak to maintain its territory, let alone to impose peace on the Europeans. Imperial authority shrivelled. Security declined, and provinces became independent states. The Persians captured and plundered Delhi in 1739 – when Nadir Shah carried off the jewelled magnificence of the peacock throne – and the Afghans did it again eighteen years later. The kettle-drums of the Mahratta cavalry could be heard probing further and further into imperial domains.

In 1742, there appeared on this disintegrating Indian scene the most dangerous of the East India Company's opponents. He was Joseph-Francois, Marquis Dupleix, who took up office as governor of the French *Compagnie des Indes*. His arrival heralded two decades of struggle between the English and French in India. Within four years Dupleix captured, and briefly held, Madras. Then he decided to extend French influence throughout the surrounding region of the Carnatic. Control would mean, among other things, collecting land tax – almost £550 000 (£45 million) in 1753 alone, it is said[2] – together, naturally, with something for French officials, including himself. The upshot was that the English and French found themselves sponsoring rival rulers in the Carnatic, backed by armed force. Dupleix' masters in Paris did not want to fight the British or to gain larger territories. They wanted to be neutral in intra-Indian politics. Indeed, in the 1750s and early 1760s, France itself was consumed by the European campaigns of the Seven Years' War, and the struggles against Prussia. Nevertheless, by 1750 the two sides were at war in India. In the end, the French company was ruined, though as late as 1768–9 it still sent fifteen ships to India and made a profit of some £700 000 (almost £41.5 million).

The British, too, had more vital interests than India. They owed their dramatic victories there to a most unlikely figure. He was an unprepossessing twenty-five-year-old company clerk named Robert Clive. Headstrong, daring and unmanageable as a boy, he turned out to be ambitious, enterprising, a born soldier and a daring and inspiring military commander. He was also a talented political intriguer, who could play in the snake-pit of Indian politics even more effectively than his competitors. He led European troops, together with Indian soldiers trained, disciplined and operated in the European manner, to crushing victories over native levies, even ones equipped with similar weapons. Furthermore, within three years the British and French governments had reinforced their respective sides with professional European regiments, transforming what had begun as a mere quarrel between rival commercial interests.

The major test for British power came not in the Carnatic but in Bengal. Its ruler, the Nawab, worried about company influence and the effect on his revenues, attacked and occupied Calcutta. His treatment of British captives appalled English opinion. The damage to the company's prestige and income, indeed to its entire position in India, was very great. Clive sailed North, recaptured Calcutta and in 1757, by a combination of politicking, bribery and skill, won a stunning victory at the battle of Plassey, crushing the Bengal army at the cost of a mere seventy-three of his men killed and wounded. The land taxes of Bengal and other provinces passed to the company, which won the war in the Carnatic as well. Local rulers scrambled to secure the company's friendship and protection, and to equip and train their armies in the European fashion. By 1763 France accepted that it had lost the Seven Years' War. French competition in India came to an end. Britain also acquired Canada and territories in West Africa. Within a year or so, the Mogul emperor was effectively in British hands. A British commercial enterprise had become a major military power in India.

The transformation was achieved by a very small number of soldiers and officials, who wanted to combine the interests of the company and their country and in the process get rich. Company officers discovered that war could be much more profitable than trade. Soldiers of all ranks learned that going on campaign brought not only cash allowances and opportunities for promotion, but loot. Which meant, at the very least, comfort and status for them and their families if and when they returned home. Moreover, victors were expected to enjoy the spoils of war. And political influence by gifts, bribery and double-cross was entirely customary in India, even more than in eighteenth-century England. It was normal for Eastern rulers to be generous to those who helped them and once the company had become a power, its officials naturally followed custom. In the decade after Plassey a number of company officials received large sums. Some tax-collectors even diverted taxes into their own pockets. Clive himself got almost a quarter of a million pounds (£17.9 million) in cash from the new Nawab alone.

Rapid expansion of the company's power fuelled the desire for yet more. But the high-handedness and venality of the company's officers also did alarming things to its balance sheets. In 1744 the company lent £1 million (£81.7 million) to the British government, but by 1815 it had a 150 000-man army yet was £40 million in debt (£1.3 billion). Early on, directors in London became concerned about the misuse of company resources which were already thinly spread; about the company's debts; about the readiness of senior company officials to use war as an instrument of policy; about the political difficulties stemming from crushing independent states. In 1765 Clive, who had meanwhile gone back to England, returned to Bengal to clean up government. He increased official salaries and promotion by seniority and introduced guidelines banning private trading by company officers, or accepting gifts from native traders. But he had only indifferent success. Later, in London, and having acquired country estates, an Irish peerage and bought a flock of Members of Parliament, he was attacked for corruption. Clive's defence was vigorous. He explained the realities of Indian political life: at one point, he sketched the fabulous riches he had left untouched and exclaimed: 'By God, Sir, I stand astonished at my own moderation.'[3]

However, as the company in India became a state in its own right, it also became too important to remain insulated from British politics. After Plassey, the Prime Minister had rejected Clive's proposal that the government take over the Indian territories, but in 1773 Lord North's Regulating Act brought Indian affairs under the London government's control. Seen from there, some of the company's political and military efforts seemed particularly unnecessary once Britain had to find resources to fight the American rebellion as well as France, Spain and Holland.

Moreover, much that was happening in India looked to London horribly like corruption and bad faith. Mismanagement was rife and the need to restore reasonable standards of probity seemed clear and urgent. It was therefore not just Clive who came under attack. By the 1780s another former Governor-General, Warren Hastings, was charged with corruption and dragged through seven years of an agonizing and highly politicized trial in London. Even if it was true that his activities in India had the best of motives and accorded with local customs, that merely underlined the urgency of replacing Indian customs with British ones. Though Hastings was eventually acquitted, the general trend was clear. In 1784–5 came the India Act placing India under the control of the English parliament, and giving the new official Board of Control the power to dictate to the company.[4] It also separated trade from governance. Shortly afterwards Lord Cornwallis – who had surrendered to the Americans and French at Yorktown in 1781 – went out as Governor-General, to impose London's views and reform company administration. By the time he left in 1793, he had set up a British bureaucracy, professional, well-paid, uncorrupt, which increasingly saw service in India as a calling, and its task as the improvement of the country. Clear distinctions were drawn between government and commerce. Not surprisingly, this system of professional service, its corporate and bureaucratic organization and deliberation by committee, proved to be a much more powerful tool of government than the old Mogul system of a single, supreme ruler.

By 1798 the tenor of Indian administration changed in other ways. Earlier worries about the damage that territorial expansion did to trade and profits fell away. An England once more at war with France became more bellicose and a new Governor-General, Richard Wellesley, changed priorities. Safeguarding the routes to China, for example, meant acquiring Penang, on the Malay Straits, as well as Mauritius, with the best harbour in the southern Indian Ocean. The safety of India itself now meant taking Ceylon from the Dutch, in 1801, and securing the magnificent port of Trincomalee. In southern India, Wellesley crushed Tipu Sahib in 1799 and the Mahrattas in 1803. Simultaneously, the British occupied Delhi, gaining final control over the Mogul emperor. They reduced the princely states of Mysore and Hyderabad to dependencies, removed the ruler of the Carnatic, and by 1818 finally defeated the Mahratta confederacy, making India, effectively, into a single security system. This was not everywhere deplored: by 1809 one of the harbingers of modern India, Raja Ram Mohun Roy, saw British rule as a move to a 'milder, more enlightened and more liberal' government.[5]

Political dominance involved other and more subtle issues, including the divergence of values and cultures. The Americas had been colonies of settlement. India was not. British migrants to the Americas had brought with them Christianity, British values and ideas of government. India was different: no attempt was ever made – the company lacked the means and the attempt would anyway have been futile – to change the beliefs or lives of the Indian masses, to make India into a larger Britain. After 1793 land rights, reshaped, could be bought and sold. But in general, the company administered Indian law and ruled through, not against, Indian political processes, including the established political order of princely states.[6] Hence local social and religious customs were preserved. The forms and even the language of the Mogul empire were retained. Consequently, British rule was, for a long time, irrelevant to local customs and religions, to the India which Pandit Nehru was to describe, two centuries later, as 'an ancient palimpsest on which layer upon layer of thought and reverie had been inscribed'.

The British, like the Moguls before them, were just another set of foreign rulers. Before 1800 or so they did not even proselytize much for Christianity, as the Moguls had so intensively done for Islam. English Governors-General ruled as Indian rulers had always done, making exactions, exercising powers of life and death; with one critically important exception. Under the British it was law that became supreme, not the ruler's whim. The separation of judicial and administrative power began in the 1790s, after which Indians could appeal to law against administrative decisions – Indian law. Even Cornwallis did not impose British law on the mass of the population; though Englishmen remained subject to British law. That rule of law may well have been Britain's finest gift to India.

But political and administrative reform was not enough for the religious and humanitarian zeal of late eighteenth-century Britain. At home, slavery ended in 1774, before the American revolution;[7] and by 1807 English merchants were prohibited from trading in slaves anywhere. In the 1790s Anglicans, Baptists and Congregationalists formed missionary societies, shortly followed by the British and Foreign Bible Society. That did not immediately involve tampering with Indian law or custom, yet it began a much more profound effort to influence Indian cultural patterns. It was done with high moral purpose. But it would strongly contribute, a century later, to the undermining of British rule in India. One should not try to do more good than people will bear.

In the meantime, the period of revolutions in Europe and America proved a turning point for colonizing activities. It confirmed the dominance of European military and naval power wherever it was tested, not least that of the British, for whom the changes altered both the geographic focus of empire, and imperial psychology. Until 1763 theirs had been largely an American empire. By 1815 America had been lost but other territories added, some of unprecedented size and complexity. Now the British concentrated on South and East Asia and Oceania, and later on Africa as well. Like all imperial rulers, they transferred their own ideas and institutions to these colonies. Furthermore, the loss of the American colonies taught important lessons. It had been due to indifference and a failure to understand that colonies, like young people, grow up. Even in the eighteenth century, with trade strongly controlled in Britain's own interests, and in spite of the constitutional pot-pourri of British affairs and the distances involved, the colonists had very considerable autonomy in practice.[8] Now it was even clearer that colonies should, and would, have their own destinies; and that colonies of British settlement, in particular, would demand the same rights and institutions as people at home. Growing colonies of settlement would need a large measure of self-government. By 1850 most of them had it.

There was another lesson. With independence, America could trade with anyone, thus destroying all possibilities of a trading monopoly and therefore most of the theory and practice of mercantilism. The East India Company's Indian trading monopoly ended in 1813 and ports were opened to foreigners. In the 1820s the remaining colonies followed suit. By 1833 the company's monopoly of the Indian market itself was also ended. Within two decades India, whose textile exports had been the mainstay of its foreign trade, was importing textiles from England. Adam Smith had won the intellectual argument about free trade and a new network of international treaties did away with trading obstacles. By the mid-nineteenth century trade was largely free, which undermined the eighteenth-century economic rationale for empire. But not entirely, since new economic needs did suggest managed trade. By 1815 many of Britain's advanced industries, for instance in textiles and metal-working, had grown to meet wartime needs. They were now too large for the reduced demands of peacetime, so additional outlets were badly needed and a properly managed system of willing colonies would, even without mercantilism, be just the thing. Furthermore, the wars had made London into the world's dominant financial centre and Europe's financial hub. After 1815 London handled much overseas financing, especially the issuing of British colonial and other government bonds. As early as the 1820s governments in the Americas were raising loans in London and some Indian long-term debt moved there, too.

Population growth continued to encourage colonial expansion. Britain's population, 14 million in 1780, had grown forty years later to 21 million. In the hundred years after Waterloo some 20 million emigrated. In 1820–40 alone, both Australia and Canada doubled their populations, even though most British emigrants went to the United States. There were new colonies, too, for instance on the tip of southern Africa, acquired from the Dutch in 1798. Migration there was encouraged: in 1820 alone, some 5 000 settlers went out and English became the language of government.

Closer links and swifter communications, such as new roads, and early steam-ships, strengthened the strategic and economic rationale of empire and the impact of its moral purpose. The East India Company governed with a few hundred British officials, often 'Residents' guiding semi-independent princes. Recruitment was concentrated in London where cadets had to study Indian history, laws and languages before sailing. After 1833, four candidates had to compete for each vacancy. Pressure from Thomas Macaulay, who served in Bengal and became Secretary of the Board of Control, encouraged entry by examination. This modernized Indian Civil Service (ICS) tried to avoid needless interference with Indian life. It tried to avoid trouble by keeping missionaries out, as well as maintaining Mogul laws for Indians. These officials often had great sympathy for Indian ways of life, saw themselves as the friends and protectors of the common people, and knew that imposing change would cause conflict and expense. Yet nonintervention in local beliefs proved difficult to sustain. Buddhist and Hindu perspectives on life were difficult to square with European ideas, let alone with modernization, with capitalism, or the Western sense of material achievement. It was also easier to use English as *lingua franca* than to rely on the multiplicity of local languages. In 1828 English supplanted Persian in formal diplomacy. Infanticide was forbidden, *thuggee* stamped out[9] and *suttee*[10] prohibited, albeit with only partial success. The British were convinced that they were the bearers of civilization. Yet distinguishing between European values, rights or institutions and those of others turned out to deepen racial and cultural dividing lines. Frictions grew as this produced a previously quite absent sense of identity on the non-European side and an embryonic desire for representation in government.

After the Napoleonic wars the empires grew, everywhere, by a slow and uneven process which began to look both cheap and irresistible. In 1800, in the whole of Asia, only some Indonesian islands and the Philippines, in Spanish hands, had been entirely under European rule. The key regional powers had still been China, Tokugawa Japan, Burma, Siam, the kingdoms of Korea and Vietnam. By 1850 there were dramatic changes which faced Britain with strategic problems that ultimately proved insoluble. They began with expanded control within India. Like all rulers with insecure frontiers, the British wanted to secure neighbouring areas. That meant expansion across the sub-continent in a process facilitated, as it had been for a century, by the sheer coherence of British loyalties to the nation and allegiance to the crown. By 1820 all of India up to the Punjab was under British control. In 1843 they conquered Sind.[11] Six years later the Sikhs followed. By mid-century the entire Punjab was under the control of the British. They had become the suzerains of India.

This process encountered difficulties on religious as much as political grounds,[12] which culminated in the 1857 Indian Mutiny. By the 1850s the Indian army had a quarter of a million men. As religious movements flourished in England, some officers began to preach to Indian soldiers who feared their own religion might be subverted. The final straw was the introduction of a new rifle. To use its ammunition, the soldier had to bite the paper off his cartridge. The rumour spread that cartridges were waxed with cow and pig fat, alarming both Hindus and Moslems. In May 1857 some soldiers mutinied and occupied nearby Delhi. The mutiny spread, but was defeated, with a cruelty almost equal to its own, by British and loyal Indian troops. India became a territory wholly under London's control: the governor-general became a viceroy and by 1876 Queen Victoria was named Empress of India.

Ruling India, however, also meant defending it. Britain, the greatest naval power in the world, had no significant army: only some 250 000 men for world-wide garrison duties. Though there was an Indian army as well, paid from Indian funds, that was not always enough. The French threat to India might have disappeared by the 1760s, but the protection of India was to bedevil London's global military planning for the next two hundred years. Napoleon's 1798 invasion of Egypt raised the spectre of another French attack on India, this time with help from Persia and Afghanistan as well as Indian allies. That danger, though ended when Nelson destroyed the French fleet at Aboukir Bay, strengthened pressures to secure India through control of the Mediterranean and the Middle East. Hence London worried when Egypt let de Lesseps' French company build the Suez canal, which opened in 1869.[13] Swifter communications also brought as many dangers as opportunities. As early as the 1820s steamships had reduced travel time between London and India – via Alexandria and the Red Sea – from six months to six or eight weeks. The canal reduced travelling time between Europe and India still further.

As the nineteenth century went on, the Eastern empire became central to Britain's entire foreign policy. Russian expansion into Central Asia might pose continuing dangers to India's northern borders and a British expedition into Afghanistan ended in 1840 in a disastrous retreat from Kabul. Moreover, by the middle of the century the security of northeastern India also required the securing of Burma. Burmese civilization centres on the Irrawaddy river valley and is part of an Indo-Chinese cultural area which includes Thailand and Cambodia. Stronger links with China and Tibet produced a cultural separation from India reinforced by geography. As the British 14th Army found to its bitter cost in the Second World War, Burma is divided from India by the forests and mountains of the Arakan. Until the eighteenth century, Burma was virtually impervious to Western influence. Though its people were cheerful and their religion peaceable, their rulers were as hysterical and capricious as any in Asia. It is said that one king, around 1800, not only massacred most of his relations but ordered the queens of his predecessor, and a number of lesser ladies, burnt alive holding their babies in their arms. In one area suspected of conspiracy, he had every living thing, man or beast, destroyed. He carried his frontiers to the Arakan and the borders of India, and invaded Siam. He even invaded Assam where he killed or deported half the population. Under his successor, a Burmese general advanced into Bengal, carrying golden fetters for the British Governor-General, Lord Amherst.

By this time the British were fed up and in 1824 declared war. An amphibious expedition seized Rangoon. As so often in colonial campaigns, the British grossly mismanaged their supply and medical services: of the 40 000 troops sent, 15 000 died, mostly from malaria and dysentery. When the campaign ended, the Burmese paid a heavy indemnity, while Assam and the Arakan were incorporated into British India. The next king denounced this 1826 Treaty but went insane. His successor again killed off much of the royal family, as well as 6 000 lesser mortals.

In spite of all this British merchants, prodded by Europe's new industries demanding raw materials, began to exploit Burma's minerals and teak forests. Unsurprisingly, they also thought that Burma should be annexed. So, in 1852, came a second Burmese war. Some 8000 British and 22 000 Indian troops captured Rangoon and the Irrawaddy valley rice region. A new king, this time a sane and calm Buddhist, came to the throne and established normal diplomatic relations. The province of British Burma was created in 1862 to include the annexed portions of the country.

In the meantime, further south, there was Malaya. In 1780 the British set up a base for the China trade at Penang. During the Napoleonic wars they added Malacca, acquired from the Dutch. In 1811 they took Java and installed the thirty-year-old Stamford Raffles as Lieutenant-Governor and four years later they focused on the Malay peninsula itself. In 1819 the brilliant Raffles, with superb strategic insight, founded the modern Singapore. Indeed, one can still go to the Raffles Hotel in Singapore and have a gin sling at its famous (and refurbished) long bar. In 1826 Penang, Malacca and Singapore were administratively grouped together as the Straits Settlements, under the East India Company. Six years later Singapore had become the Straits Settlements capital, though the peninsula to its north remained dominated by autocratic Islamic sultans. Resource development began late. Some Chinese started to work open-cast tin mines by the mid-1800s, but not until the early twentieth century, with more investment and modern technology, did Malaya start to produce half the world's supply of tin and rubber.

Beyond the archipelago lay the new continent of Australia. There the first British landing, under Captain Phillip, came in 1788 at Botany Bay, now in Sydney. Another fleet followed two years later. In part, this colony of New South Wales was meant as a penal settlement, to replace North America. But convicts were, from the start, in the minority and most of them were released after a few years, and became settlers. From Botany Bay, explorers and settlers went south, to Van Diemens Land – later Tasmania. From there, others sailed north and founded Melbourne, in yet another colony, named after the new young Queen, Victoria. Other colonies and free settlements on the Australian continent – Western Australia, Queensland and South Australia – followed. All of them quickly acquired economic significance. Sydney became the centre for South Pacific whaling; and parts of inland Australia turned out to be good for sheep. By the 1830s Australians were supplying half of Britain's wool imports. Immigrant numbers grew and colonial governments offered bounties to attract yet more.

By comparison, eighteenth-century Dutch colonial efforts suffered from economic weaknesses and repeated foreign policy errors. Not only was Dutch power overextended in the struggles against France after 1700; weakened by the wars of the 1750s – which cost the Dutch some overseas possessions; and weakened yet further with the virtual elimination of Dutch sea power in the 1780s. In addition, Dutch dominance of Indonesian and Malay waters was heavily undermined by local smuggling and piracy, all of which continue in lively fashion to this day.

All the same the Dutch, like the British in India, had by 1800 ceased to be a merely commercial enterprise and become a territorial power in the archipelago. Their trade had turned down rather earlier, but control strengthened. As early as 1677 the Dutch were protectors of the Sultan of Mataram. A century later they had extended their sway over two thirds of Java; all of the island's sultans were Dutch clients; and they controlled the rest of Indonesia by strategic bases or treaties with native states. On the Malabar coast, where the French had first obtained pepper, the Dutch dominated a number of small polities until 1729. This expansion of Dutch rule, especially in Java, was made possible largely by the animosities within and between local states. For instance, the largest Javanese state, Mataram, was repeatedly rent by civil wars.

In this period the Indonesian economy was still largely native. Coffee, introduced by the Dutch, became hugely profitable. Consumption of opium, imported from Bengal, increased – especially among Chinese – despite objections from native rulers. There was much smuggling. But most communities were self-sufficient and had little use for money or trade. The Javanese economy had three main sectors. One was complex cultivation, including that of rice, on Bali and in Eastern Java. But most Indonesians lived in a second, shifting agriculture, with jungle-regeneration. Arabs, Chinese, Europeans and some locals occupied a small third sector, a coastal trading economy.

Consequently, and for all their territorial power, the Dutch remained an alien body on the fringes of Asian societies. (Even more so in China, where they had only trading agencies.) Rule was based, as with the British in India, on governing through local structures. The Indies had, after all, seen several cultural waves: Hindu, Moslem and European. All of them a mere 'thin, easily flaking glaze on the massive body of indigenous civilization'.[14] Not that Javanese society remained entirely unaffected. Dutch rule through local elites, backed by Dutch military force, tended to strengthen aristocratic power. The Dutch had other assistance, especially from local Chinese. As Coen had observed: 'There is no people in the world which serves us better than the Chinese ...'[15] At the same time, however, the company suffered much the same kinds of corruption, abuse of office, and resource diversion to personal trading that afflicted the British company in Bengal. Which contributed to growing company debt at home. In 1700 that company debt was 12 million guilders. In 1791, about when Warren Hastings was being wrung dry in London, it was 96 million and the company maintained its dividends by borrowing. In 1799, when the company collapsed, it was 134 million.

The Napoleonic period changed everything. The new state which emerged after 1815 had representative institutions which began major organizational and financial reforms. These created a modernized state structure with a sharpened sense of national and religious identity. Financial revolution, too, overtook some defence of local traditions. But the public debt had already been amalgamated in 1789, and a national system of taxation created in 1806. The tax burden now started to decline, from around 12 per cent to, eventually, some 7 per cent of the national income. By 1840 further constitutional, fiscal and monetary reforms made possible the creation of a full national financial system.

All this was quickly reflected overseas. Having been taken over by Britain during the war, Java and the other islands were returned to the new kingdom of the Netherlands to help strengthen it as a barrier to French expansion in Europe. By then, Stamford Raffles had abolished hereditary possessions and destroyed much of the feudal system oppressing the common people. He ended slavery and reorganized the government of Java, including the judiciary, relations with the princes and the tax system. Rulers in effect became salaried officials. When the Dutch returned, their relations with the locals also changed. Even Dutch-Indonesian social intercourse, formerly incidental, became more normal.[16]

But the returning Dutch quickly found themselves at war. Local princes took up arms against efforts to stop them selling land to Chinese, Arabs and Europeans, thereby impoverishing the peasants. The war lasted from 1825 to 1830. Victory cost the Dutch some 25 million guilders and the need for money produced the so-called 'cultivation system'. Under this, peasants could either set aside land for crops needed by a new Netherlands trading organization, or else give sixty-six days' labour per annum to the system. The Dutch also introduced new crops like tea, tobacco and palm oil. The system was highly profitable for the Dutch. In 1830 the colonial government could not make ends meet. By 1851 it was sending 15 million guilders per annum to Holland.[17] Over the period 1840–75 it was 780 million; so that, within a couple of decades of returning to the Indies, the Dutch reorganized the economy on more commercial lines. Even the mid-century Liberal revolution in Holland did not protest about economic exploitation, it only wanted private enterprise, equal chances for both races, and that Dutch profits should not be at the cost of Indonesian welfare.

France's colonial operations remained, as always, much more fully under the control of the home government. And Paris also continued to focus on European rather than Asian problems. Few ministries showed much interest in colonies. Primary responsibility for them lay with the Ministry of Marine and, from 1710, a minor sub-department, the colonial bureau. So colonial expansion was slow and consolidation even slower. For much of the eighteenth century, colonies remained marginal for government. Not only that but France, so much richer and more self-sufficient than Britain, was simply less interested in trade. Neither government nor public, raised on Colbertian principles, had much interest in colonies unless they directly supplied France's own needs. Moreover, it was not only India, where the French company's position, and the political role which Dupleix had tried to create, were lost in the Seven Years' War. Canada and other possessions were also lost. Other overseas efforts were less important anyway. When the *Compagnie des Indes* was suspended in 1769, its bases were simply transferred to the crown, but government still had grave doubts whether colonies had any value. After 1776, for instance, Turgot argued in Cabinet that the whole colonial system was doomed by the example of the American rebellion, and French colonies were not worth defending.[18] The implication was that France should simply trade within the new economic system destined to emerge from formerly closed colonial trade.

Not that France was short of explorers and traders venturing into far places. But many voyages were inspired more by scientific curiosity than by commerce or strategy, and organized by government, not private enterprise. In 1682 explorers travelled down the Mississippi to the sea and claimed for France most of the immense interior of the future United States. They named it Louisiana, after King Louis. In 1719 Bienville followed up by founding New Orleans. The French expanded in the Caribbean too. In the 1760s to 1790s, Bougainville and La Pérouse sailed to the South Pacific, including Tahiti and the New Hebrides. They brought back charts, geographic information and descriptions of plants of great interest, but no great economic or political results flowed from their enterprise.

What the journeys did illustrate was another kind of conflict in European expansion, one not confined to the French. Bougainville's sailors, like James Cook's Englishmen, or the Portuguese two centuries earlier, were enchanted by the new customs and races they encountered. One traveller was quite overcome:

> ... If happiness consists in the abundance of all things necessary to life, in living in a superb land with the finest climate, in enjoying the best of health, in breathing the purest and most salubrious air, in leading the simple, soft and quiet life, free from all passions, even from jealousy, although surrounded by women, if these women can themselves even dispense happiness, then I say that there is not in the world a happier nation than the Tahitian one.[19]

But where sailors discovered sun, food, ease and bevies of welcoming girls, the missionaries only saw benighted heathen and promiscuous naked savages. Here were the makings, in much of the tropics, of the confrontation between administrators and churchmen on the one hand, and traders, soldiers, scientists and writers on the other.

Nor did France's decisive role in the American War of Independence bring colonial gains, however important French successes might have been in bolstering national pride or general dislike of the British. In any case, the revolutionary and Napoleonic wars ended interest in Asia and North America for the time being. In 1803 Napoleon sold Louisiana to the new United States for $15 million. After 1805, when Nelson destroyed the French fleet at Trafalgar, Britain seized other French colonies. Remaining colonies were forced into greater self-reliance, further weakening the French state, and by 1815 France had lost almost all her former possessions. In the post-war settlement only Martinique and some trading posts in India were recovered, none with strategic significance. In any case, defeat and exhaustion removed France for a generation from contention for empire in the East, and to an extent even in Africa. In addition, Napoleon's occupation of Spain had greatly weakened the Spanish empire, which also began to disintegrate.

Yet the Revolution decisively changed France's view of colonies. Its principles of equality, and the essential unity of humanity, influenced all later colonial dealings. Most French overseas colonists had shown even before 1789 that they wanted equality within the French state, not independence from it. Now, they got their wish; and equality was not confined to Frenchmen. The 1794 Constitution of the Revolution's Year III changed the status of colonies to that of Departements of France, integral parts of the Republic. The legislation of this revolutionary period became the basis of France's approach to empire for the next century.

Meanwhile, in Asia, most of the now rather faint French interests related to Indo-China. Larger than France, it is a loose amalgam of three areas: Vietnam, Cambodia and Laos. Within Vietnam the Tonkin region always saw itself as intellectually and culturally primary, but had been dominated for nine centuries up to AD 939 by the Chinese. Repeated civil strife followed, including wars between Tonkin and the Cochin-China region in the sixteenth and eighteenth centuries. In the meantime the Chinese, having lost control, nevertheless claimed suzerainty. The first Portuguese ship seems to have reached the central coast in 1535. By the early seventeenth century several countries had trading posts and the first Catholic mission arrived. Vietnam expanded southwards from the Red River delta until around 1757 but threats of internal strife continued, only ended when the Nguyen dynasty united the country in 1802. By this time the French were trying to enter the region as missionaries and traders. With little success, partly because of French weaknesses in India and distractions in Europe, but especially because of Vietnam's sense of cultural and national cohesion, so different from the conditions facing the French and British in India.

India was a patchwork of cultural, ethnic and language groups. In Vietnam, the French had to deal with a people who had identified themselves as a separate cultural and social entity long before the Western idea of a nation-state was conceived. That identity had been cemented during two thousand years of struggle with Chinese power and influence, and would yield to the French as little as it had done to China. None of that stopped unofficial French efforts. For example, Bishop Pigneau de Béhaine privately recruited French officers, technicians, soldiers and sailors to help a Nguyen dynasty prince to conquer all of Vietnam between 1788 and 1802. The prince became the Emperor Gia Long, establishing the last Vietnamese dynasty. Yet it was soon clear that establishing any longer-term French influence, whether for commercial advantage or spreading the gospel, would be hard. The dynasty may have come to power with French help, but the Vietnamese gradually grew more hostile to European influence. They continued to reject all French proposals for diplomatic and trade relations. Most Vietnamese were quite unprepared to accept Western ideas and religions. It was Confucianism that was the backbone of their bureaucracies, as of their Chinese and Korean equivalents. Indeed, some missionaries were executed, together with an unknown number of Vietnamese Catholics, after an uprising for which they incurred some blame. Back in France, some missionaries and merchants began to talk about military intervention, while naval folk looked for Asian bases. But not until 1857 was Napoleon's nephew, the Emperor Napoleon III, willing to organize an expedition into Vietnam.

Beyond India, Vietnam or the spice islands lay the huge bulk of China, governed from 1644 by the Manchu dynasty. In the early eighteenth century China enjoyed a golden age of stability and prosperity under its firm rule. Population, agriculture and trade grew. Scholarship and the arts flourished. The empire made sweeping conquests in inner Asia. Chinese administration was extended into Chinese Turkestan, Mongolia and Tibet. The northwest frontier with Central Asia was sealed. Relations with Korea and Southeast Asia, areas of less strategic significance, were classified, like other trading or diplomatic relationships, as 'tributary', with the customary implication of ceremonial dependence.

This complex empire had long been regarded in Europe with general and ill-informed admiration. Impressions of China were heavily influenced by reports from early Jesuit missionaries, and later by writers like Voltaire or Leibnitz. It was regarded as a land of great culture, flowing with milk and honey. In 1686 Robert Hooke told the Royal Society in London that a better understanding of China would 'lay open to us an Empire of learning, hitherto only fabulously described'. In the eighteenth century Chinese porcelain, silks, and designs were highly fashionable. So was Chinese art. The Imperial palace in Vienna, Buckingham Palace in London and many rich houses acquired 'Chinese rooms' decorated in Chinese styles. The great German poet Goethe thought the Chinese empire had lasted for thousands of years because of its moderation, morals and propriety.

By the end of the eighteenth century this great empire was beset by domestic problems accentuated by its own earlier successes. Between 1650 and 1800 the population tripled to some 300 million (by 1850 it had grown by another 100 million). The areas available for agriculture and new crops were inadequate and there were food crises, poverty and unrest. Secret societies flourished. The imperial bureaucracy was increasingly understaffed: power accrued to the local gentry; corruption was rife. It was then, in 1793, that Britain attempted its first diplomatic contact with a mission to Beijing led by Lord Macartney. He came with a train of 3 000 coolies, and ninety wagons filled with presents for the Emperor. He wanted to interest the Chinese in British products, to open an embassy, and to have more ports opened to Western trade. But the mission was a total failure.[20] Mutual incomprehension was virtually complete. For the Chinese, given their concept of China's central position in the civilized world, Western ideas of state equality were inherently improper, proposing an unjust system and a disturbance of the proper global order. Moreover, in East Asia the written word had primacy over other forms of communication. An ambassador's written credentials, any messages he might carry from his master, were treated with much greater respect than the ambassador's person. In Western practice, by contrast, an ambassador is the personal representative of his sovereign and partakes, as it were, of the sovereign's personality. In the event, Macartney did secure an audience with the emperor – he even managed, as the envoy of his King, to avoid the customary kow-tow which the British thought impossibly undignified – but his requests were all refused. The emperor gave him the famous answer, noted earlier: 'There are well-established regulations governing tributary envoys from the outer states to Beijing ... the kings of the myriad nations come by land and sea with all sorts of precious things

... [but] We possess all things. I set no value on objects strange or ingenious, and have no use for your country's manufactures.'[21] Macartney
stayed in Beijing, fruitlessly, for some months before returning empty-
handed to England. A Dutch mission in 1795 and a Russian one in
1806 met the same fate as did a second British embassy, under Lord
Amherst in 1816.

Locally, the Chinese minimized contact with foreigners, who
remained very much at the mercy of local officials. European traders
clung to the empire's fringes, and were strictly regulated. But that
created difficulties, for instance regarding radically divergent views on
crime and punishment. The Chinese had a system of collective responsibility for criminal offences. A family, a clan, a village bore responsibility for breaches of the peace by any member. The group was
responsible for identifying the guilty party and could be collectively
punished if it failed. But once identified, the guilty party's trial might
be a mere formality. These principles applied equally to foreigners. If
they interfered with or injured one another, the Chinese were unconcerned, but if a foreigner injured a Chinese, the entire foreign community was held responsible. It was for the foreigners to do the
investigating. The Chinese demanded a victim, or a scapegoat, to make
certain the crime would be avenged.

This was very far from European principles of individual responsibility, or British notions of Common Law, the rights of the accused, trial
by a jury of ones peers. The British were therefore quite unwilling to
subject Britons to a Chinese procedures they thought barbarous and
unjust. One British seaman, for instance, accidentally caused the death
of a Chinese while firing a salute. He was reluctantly handed over to a
Chinese magistrate who unceremoniously had him strangled. This
kind of thing was a major cause of the later insistence on extra-
territorial rights of jurisdiction over British subjects.

There was also the matter of taxes. In China, local officials had
always had powers to vary local taxation, including locally decided
duties on foreign trade. Indeed, the whole distinction between public
revenues and private profit was at best blurred. The British, by contrast,
were quite accustomed to paying taxes; but expected regular imposts at
predictable rates, not demands arbitrarily varied at the pleasure of the
local magistrate. British merchants were also irritated at being unable
to do business freely with Chinese. Instead, they had to deal with
officially approved Chinese merchants associations.

Trade created altogether more important problems. As the eighteenth century went on, demand in England grew, not just for Indian

cottons and Chinese porcelain and silk but for tea. And in spite of the various restrictions, by the mid-eighteenth century Chinese tea had become an important part of the British diet. In 1700 Britain imported some 70 000 pounds weight of tea. By 1800 the figure was 15 million pounds. The trouble was that to be able to buy tea, English merchants needed silver or goods. Silver ran short and the Chinese seemed entirely uninterested in British manufactures. For example the Chinese, used to cotton, said British woollens were too scratchy. What many Chinese did want to buy – in breach of imperial regulations which were ignored by most local Chinese officials – was opium. This was plentifully available from India. The East India Company, with a monopoly of opium growing in Bengal, was, by 1800, holding regular auctions of it; and independent merchants then took it to China. These auctions made major contributions to company earnings, and became important, perhaps critical, to Indian revenue. Not that the British were the only sellers: Americans, especially Philadelphia merchants, cheerfully collaborated with British traders or sold opium bought in Turkey. Meanwhile many Chinese officials took their own hefty cut from the trade. At one stage even the commander of the imperial fleet was transporting opium for a price. While senior officials kept insisting there was no Chinese demand for European products, British and Chinese smugglers stimulated opium demand.

Opium sales became more important than the cost of official Chinese tea exports. These doubled between 1813 and 1833, while opium imports multiplied by four, creating problems not only for Chinese consumers but for state finances. Once opium imports were greater than official exports they had to be paid for in silver, and by 1830 its outflow had become a serious problem. Two parallel channels for currency circulation were therefore created: the imperial treasury earned money from the official tea trade, while ordinary Chinese subjects paid cash for their opium fixes. By 1836 the Chinese empire ran its first overall trade deficit and opium may have accounted for three quarters, by value, of all Chinese imports.

In the decade after 1830 Chinese opium imports doubled. Yet many mandarins still had better things to do than worry about commerce. Such inferior activities must be left to traders at Guangzhou. As its viceroy wrote to one of his merchants in the 1830s: '... the Empire of Heaven appoints officials, civil to rule the people, military to control the wicked. But the petty affairs of commerce are to be directed by the merchants themselves. With such matters officials are not concerned.' Where the foreigners had to be kept in line, administrative pressure would suffice.

Yet there were many signs – if anyone in Beijing had been looking – that it was not just a matter of the British. The Chinese world was confronted by new people and forces. There was the American drive across the great plains and the rockies to the Pacific. By 1778 Captain James Cook surveyed that western coast of North America, reaching the Arctic Ocean. Nine years later the French explorer La Pérouse sailed into the Tatar Strait and looked over the Kuriles. From the 1790s, New England merchants collected furs from Pacific coast Indians in exchange for trinkets, guns and cloth. By 1830 the Russians had dispatched a series of naval expeditions to the Pacific. They started to trade all round that ocean, including Japan, the USA and Hawaii. By mid-century they also began to return to the Amur, at first by infiltration. And what would happen if – or when – Japan emerged from its long self-imposed isolation?

At Guangzhou, Western merchants remained conciliatory. After all, by 1810–20 China controlled Korea, much of Indo-China, Burma, Siam and Nepal; and the merchants trading with China, including the East India Company, remained – much like Western industrialists and bankers two centuries later – keenly sensitive to Chinese susceptibilities. They would concede a good deal to secure their positions in China. During the Napoleonic wars, for instance, when the British government seemed about to occupy Macao, the merchants at Guangzhou advised great caution. Even in the 1830s, new British superintendents at Guangzhou were instructed to avoid any conduct, language or demeanor that might offend the Chinese; and they were to do everything to maintain a good and friendly understanding.

But in England, political and public opinion began to be irritated. Following the brilliant victories over Napoleonic France, the country was in no mood to have British representatives slighted. The failure of Macartney or Amherst to get any response to civil and moderate proposals aroused resentment. British opinion was especially offended that an embassy of the British crown had been treated like barbarian vassals. Chinese arrogance and insulation from normal international dealings were not acceptable. Macartney himself had written: 'Our present interests, our reason and our humanity equally forbid the thoughts of any offensive measures with regard to the Chinese, whilst a ray of hope remains for succeeding by gentle one'; but even he had added that if peaceful methods failed, there would have to be a serious war effort.

Moreover, the reports of Western expeditions refashioned many earlier views of China. The revelations of China's corruption and decadence reversed former opinions. The expeditions reported that the Chinese were childish and had to be educated. A prestigious journal, the *Edinburgh Review*, was scathing. It pictured the Chinese as semi-barbarian; wrote of their submission to despotism, sustained by the terror of the lash; about the imprisonment and mutilation of their women; about their infanticide and unnatural vices; their ignorance of all exact sciences and philosophy; their cowardice, uncleanness and inhumanity. Such views were not confined to Britain. In Germany, the eminent philosopher Hegel wrote: 'The Chinese empire is the realm of theocratic despotism ... the individual has no moral selfhood.' In other words, where the Chinese had once been regarded as among the most civilized of peoples, now they were seen as a kind of anthropological curiosity.

Impatience with Chinese methods and manners therefore grew. Moreover, as the London government assumed increasing responsibility for conducting and promoting trade, and was increasingly committed to free trade, it became more directly involved with the Chinese treatment of British subjects. On the issue of opium, British opinion was relaxed. The drug was freely available in England as a narcotic and pain-killer and the first mild restrictions were only introduced in 1868. Though Liberals like Gladstone fiercely criticized its export to China, that was a minority view. The government, and especially the Foreign Secretary, Lord Palmerston, argued simply that while China could prohibit any import it wished, it was not up to England to deal with Chinese corruption, or to enforce Chinese customs laws, and anyway smuggling could never be stopped, even in England. The real issue was not opium but the point that sooner or later, one way or another, gently or by force, the gates to a regularized China trade would have to be opened. English demand, especially for tea, went on growing, and before 1850 the great bulk of it came from China, not yet India. A British political and economic dynamism confronted intransigence and immobility in China. Two mental universes failed to comprehend each other, let alone to accept each other's point of view.

Matters started to come to a head in 1838, when a Chinese provincial governor named Lin suggested that all drug stocks and equipment be destroyed, all domestic drug dealers lose their heads, smuggling be ended by shutting down any offender's legitimate trade, that sanatoria be set up to help addicts kick the habit but if, after one year's treatment they failed, their heads be cut off too. He was promptly sent to Guangzhou as imperial commissioner. In 1839 he ordered the destruction of 2 000 tons of foreign-owned opium and had foreigners confined to their factories and ships. A British naval demonstration led to shooting and the two sides blundered into war. Chinese weaknesses were at once exposed. At sea, no Chinese vessels could stand up to a modern British man of war. The Chinese army was trained to put down rebellions, not to deal with well-equipped European forces. The British, with their modern ships, soldiers and firepower, prevailed almost effortlessly, both on sea and on land. In August 1842 peace was signed on board the British flagship, perhaps foreshadowing Japan's 1945 surrender, also staged on a battleship, this time an American one.

The Chinese called it the 'first opium war', in which foreign aggression forced opium on China. The British, however, called it the first Anglo-Chinese war, which opened the Chinese empire to normal, international commercial intercourse. The 1842 Treaty of Nanjing[22] provided for an opening of the ports of Canton, Shanghai and three other places, for British consular representation in China, for stated and invariable tax rates (instead of the old ad hoc imposts) the cession of Hong Kong to Britain, and equal treatment for British and Chinese officials. Similar treaties with the French and Americans followed. Here were roughly the concessions which Britain had sought for half a century. The Treaty did not mention opium, except for one aside; but demand and trade continued to grow. Between 1840 and 1859 the opium trade from India to China increased from around 20 000 to 60 000 chests of the drug. By 1860, under Western pressure, the trade was legalized and not finally ended until 1917, after the fall of the empire.

But the war had significance going far beyond opium or even trade. The ignominious defeat, and China's obvious inability to deal with the intrusion of the modern world, began the disintegration of the Qing empire. Though the old empire was an unconscionable time a-dying, this period from 1840 to 1860, culminating in another lost war against the West, marked the beginning of the end. China's very weakness produced protective elements in British and other Western policies. The British had called for trade but did not, at Nanjing or later, demand preferential treatment. In formulating its terms, the British government said it sought 'no exclusive advantages and [we] demand nothing that we shall not willingly see enjoyed by the Subjects of all other States'. It was what the Americans, fifty years later, were to call an 'Open Door' policy, and remained a principle of British policy in China. The British, and the French as well, had become convinced that China needed free trade, Christianity and Western medicines. It was believed with much the same fervour as America's promotion, in the 1980s and 1990s, of 'free trade, democracy and human rights'. In the

1860s the British even helped the empire to suppress the Taiping rebellion. But one of the most important consequences of the war was long-lasting Chinese resentment. A century and a half after the 'opium wars', the Chinese education system seemed intent on continuing to stoke the resentment of successive generations.[23]

Meanwhile, in Japan two and a half centuries of Tokugawa shogunate had seen remarkable domestic developments. Society was organized into four classes. At the top were warriors and rulers, not scholar-bureaucrats, as in China. The division between commoner and *samurai* warrior, the Japanese version of sword-swinging *house-carls*, was strictly maintained, though lower orders were allowed to acquire mere wealth. The basic social unit was the family, which carried both status and property rights. Over time, though, the regime began to need competent administrators more than *samurai* – war became theory more than practice and its modern, technical arts were largely ignored.[24] Gradually *samurai* values became formalized into a code including unquestioning loyalty to one's lord, fierce defence of one's honour and strict fulfilment of obligations. Later still that became the 'way of the warrior', or *bushido*, and the *samurai* a hereditary caste.

The seventeenth century also saw the rise of neo-Confucianism, and re-emergence of shintoism interpreted through nationalist and authoritarian principles. Concepts of a secular society gained ground, one organized by the state and administered by an educated and upright bureaucracy. A strongly national sense developed of Japan as a special society. So did pressures for conformity, a stress on self-discipline, strict codes of conduct and a strong sense of duty and honour. It also produced the intense personal drive which would once more characterize the Japanese business elite after 1945.

This Japan had isolated itself at the very time when change was gathering pace in the West, not least with enormous advances in science. Consequently Japan fell behind Europe. Not that isolation meant barbarism: the Tokugawa regime brought domestic peace after decades of conflict, and saw a great cultural flowering, with marvellous work in painting, woodblock printing, gardening and theatre arts. There was an explosive growth of commerce, lubricated not only with coinage but commercial paper. The house of Mitsui became banker to the shogunate in 1691, and Sumitomo began in iron and drugs. Shortly after 1700 the rice markets of Edo (Tokyo) and Osaka were dealing in futures, much like the twenty-first-century futures markets of London,

Chicago and Amsterdam. Cities and towns grew rapidly, the population more slowly. But by the first census of 1721 it was already some 30 million: larger than any West European country. Well before 1800, Tokyo probably had over a million inhabitants. And by the middle 1800s perhaps 45 per cent of Japanese men and 15 per cent of women could read and write.[25]

By then, after prolonged isolation, the system had weaknesses. A money economy had loosened many older bonds. The military effectiveness of the *samurai* had declined. Loyalty to the system had superseded attachment to local lords (*daimyo*). There was growing emphasis on merit rather than hereditary status. There were also growing worries about the military and naval power of the great Western nations, whose might was alarmingly evident in Asia and the Pacific. The Japanese were especially impressed by the effectiveness of Western arms in China. Russian and British ships had already penetrated into Japan's own waters. The United States was even more interested in opening up Japan. But an improved capacity to resist foreign intrusion was likely to require radical domestic reforms.

By the middle of the nineteenth century, then, European culture and industrialized power – including the Spaniards in the Philippines – were affecting that entire world from Bombay to Nagasaki. Local reactions to these pressures were confused and ineffective. The Indian Mutiny was one. The willingness of Indo-Chinese rulers to accept Western help while warding off Western influence was another. In China, Western power had provoked serious disruption. In Japan, growing unease about the West was about to produce revolution.

In the meantime Europeans, encouraged by the long nineteenth-century continental peace, continued to focus on their own needs – and their own ultimate benevolence. The ascendancy of Western ideas, technologies and industry was growing. France's interest in colonial expansion was beginning to revive. The Dutch remodelling of their East Indies empire was satisfying Liberal opinion at home. The British governed India and had compelled China to open its ancient doors. Further imperial expansion loomed. Within three or four decades the Europeans would reach a high-water mark of empire, and that would produce more far-reaching reactions, at home as well as in the colonies themselves.

5

Imperial Apotheosis

The primary aim of Europe's statesmen after the Battle of Waterloo had naturally been the reorganization and stability of the continent. From that base, the century which followed can be seen in separate halves, divided by the decade 1860–70. Before that time, there was growing emphasis on free trade while the impetus for imperial expansion weakened. Afterwards came the high tide of imperialism.

In Europe itself, the post-Napoleonic settlement confronted two linked problems. One was to crush or contain revolution. The other was to create an international security system. The first meant assuming that the major sovereign states would assure their own domestic order, though mutual support might be available in case of need. The second meant replacing the unstable eighteenth-century balance of power by a Concert of Europe whose maintenance was, itself, a principal interest for each major power.

The 1815 Congress of Vienna, for all the magnificence of its balls and dinners, or the delicious in intrigues in its boudoirs, quite failed to suppress revolutionary and especially nationalist agitation, or the growing belief in national self-determination, representation and plebiscitary voting. The threat of revolution was therefore very much alive; it simmered below the surface and was not confined to German or Italian nationalism. It erupted in France in 1830, 1848 and 1870. Indeed, in 1848 it burst out all over the continent, and the Austro-Hungarian empire had to be rescued with the help of Russian troops. 1832 and 1867 saw major extensions of the franchise in Britain. In the Netherlands, the south was one of the first regions of Europe to follow British industrialization which, together with existing educational and religious differences, encouraged both liberalism and separatism. Meanwhile the northern regions of the United Provinces continued to seek wealth through trade.

External peace and fears of domestic unrest naturally made colonial competition less important and colonies less vital as military or diplomatic counters. In the imperial countries, enthusiasm for expansion therefore declined. Colonies often did expand, but under local initiative or for defensive reasons. Expansion could even flow from individual enterprise. After all, individuals could go where they pleased: government had no power to stop them, or to smother public emotions about their exploits. So the British, apart from expansion in India, extended their claims in Australia in the 1830s, New Zealand in the decade that followed, over Hong Kong in 1842, Natal a year later, Sarawak in 1846 and Lower Burma in 1852. Meanwhile the French conquered Algeria in the 1830s and 1840s, expanded into Senegal in the 1850s and moved into Indo-China from 1858. Their occupation of Tunisia and appearance in Tahiti and the South Pacific in the 1850s were mere extensions of long-standing French 'Eastern policies.'

But with pieces of empire scattered around the globe, the dilemmas – in principle highly traditional – between continental commitment on the one hand and naval and overseas effort on the other, became even more acute for France and especially for Britain. Where the continental focus had always been primary for France, the British situation was more complicated. The basic dilemma had been understood since Elizabethan times, and remains fundamental to England's security debates into the twenty-first century. In the late 1500s the old seadog, Sir John Hawkins, had wanted to blockade Spain, and for England to have '... as little to do in foreign countries as may be (but of mere necessity) for that breedeth great change and no profit at all'. Yet the Queen's Council and Sir Francis Knollys thought that 'the avoiding of Her Majesty's danger doth consist in the preventing of the conquest of the Low Countries betimes'.[1] That view was still axiomatic for William Pitt in 1805, for Sir Edward Grey in 1914, or the British air defence staff in 1940.

The post-1815 European Concert depended on Britain's full-time participation. That would also, *inter alia*, prevent other states from challenging Britain's dominance in commerce and finance. Not that a European balance stopped Britain worrying about French naval rivalry, or the impact of Russian expansion, especially through Afghanistan and Persia on India. Efforts also continued to deny Russia control of the Straits of Constantinople. In other ways, too, London found it impossible to stay aloof. Palmerston, who could quite see the dangers of revolutionary unrest, nevertheless made use of it, as in the case of Belgium, in ways Francis Knollys would have entirely understood. And nations struggling to be free continued to appeal to British opinion with Gladstone and Russell, for instance, becoming strongly pro-Italian. Yet some Cabinet members questioned a strong commitment to continental affairs. Britain dissented when Czar Alexander I of Russia and Prince Metternich of Austria wanted to intervene against popular – i.e. revolutionary – movements in Piedmont, Portugal, Naples or Spain. The Foreign Secretary, Lord Castlereagh, put the point forcibly in a state paper of May 1820: the quadruple alliance of powers which had unseated Napoleon was not intended as '... an Union for the Government of the World or for the superintendence of the internal affairs of other States'.[2]

On the economic front, by the 1830s the philosophic radicals, Adam Smith and the Manchester School of Economists had destroyed mercantilism. To be sure, protection often continued for rising industries and farming; but Britain's lively trade with the Americas now demonstrated that economic success did not depend on overseas possessions or political control. Politicians having accepted that manufacturing and trading countries would become prosperous by freer trade and cutting tariffs, Britain was an open market until 1832 for colonial products, even while self-governing colonies could impose tariffs on British exports and have access in London to capital on favourable terms. Only after that was the empire more tightly governed; though even imperial preference taxed British consumers to help producers, including the colonies. It was the Conservative government of Robert Peel that reduced both customs duties and colonial preferences in 1842. Between 1846 and 1852, when the Liberals were in office, Britain removed almost all remaining duties and preferential arrangements, including imperial preference.[3] From all these points of view, colonies became much less important, even a burden. By 1852 Disraeli remarked curtly that 'the colonies are millstones round our neck'. Accordingly, around the middle of the century Britain began to allow the colonies of settlement increasing control over their local affairs. Indeed, by the 1860s colonies were treated, for economic purposes, like foreign countries. Even much later, in 1880, Gladstone's electoral success rested on his anti-expansionism. In Paris, too, as late as the 1870s the Chamber of Deputies resisted proposals for expansion in Indo-China.

Of course, Liberalism was Janus-faced. Even in purely economic terms, gains are never equal between trading partners. Freer trade always favours the strongest, which is why Britain in the nineteenth century and the USA in the twentieth have been its strongest advocates. Trade in commodities, in which colonies like Australia, Canada and Java specialized, is not the same as exporting or importing jobs. In any case, the comparative advantage enjoyed by any society is not fixed but can move in favourable or unfavourable ways. People do not always respond in timely or effective ways to market signals. Cultural differences are also critical, which is why freer trade also implies growing pressures on a weaker culture to accept uncongenial, even damaging change.

After 1860–70 things changed. There were waves of industrialization, urbanization, changes in lead technologies and demographic patterns. The Concert of Europe altered its shape, especially following the Franco-Prussian war of 1870 and the unification of Germany. Disraeli saw it starkly and at once. 'This war,' he said, 'represents the German Revolution, a greater political event than the French Revolution of the last century ... the balance of power has been entirely destroyed ...'[4] For France, *revanche* against Germany became the core of policy. With her resources of men and weapons, of industry and technology, declining relative to her European competitors, the main role of overseas involvement became the strengthening of French power. Meanwhile, for Britain, the nineteenth-century naval competition with France was followed at the start of the twentieth by an even more dangerous German push for naval power. The 1904 Franco-British entente was clearly a defensive arrangement against Germany. It followed the 'Fashoda incident' of 1898, in which France had to accept British primacy in the Nile valley and the Sudan. While the entente involved France abandoning opposition to Britain in Egypt, in return, Britain undertook to support French claims in Morocco. There was more. While the Ottoman and Austro-Hungarian empires were growing more decrepit, the modernization and territorial expansion of Russia continued, causing growing fears in both Germany and Britain. Indeed, between 1900 and 1905, the British thought Russia was the most dangerous enemy; and concluded a 1902 alliance with Japan to strengthen the position in the Far East, and avoid possibly simultaneous naval campaigns in the Pacific as well as the Atlantic. Yet the growth of Japanese power further complicated the international balance.

The German problem was only part of a larger difficulty. In the absence of a continental hegemon, all the European powers were about to be overshadowed. The fear – Jules Ferry, Chamberlain, Salisbury and others, even John Ruskin, all shared it – was that the world would soon be dominated by great empires of global significance, like Russia or the United States. Britain might join the group, but only if the resources of the entire empire could be combined into some federal union. In the words of the historian John Seeley:

If the United States and Russia hold together for another half century, they will at the end of that time completely dwarf such old European states as France and Germany and depress them into a second class. They will do the same to England, if at the end of that time England still sees herself as simply a European state, as the old United Kingdom of Great Britain and Ireland such as Pitt left her.[5]

In Paris Jules Ferry, replying to parliamentary critics of his expansionist policies in Algeria and Tonkin, marshalled over the first half of the 1880s all the academic arguments about superior civilizations having a mission to civilize inferior races; about an industrial nation needing colonial markets; about merchant and fighting navies both needing coaling stations; that it was Africa where France would regain European prestige and create the basis for *revanche* against Germany. If France abstained from empire, she would 'descend from the first rank to the third or fourth'. In Germany, too, writers like Friedrich Naumann argued that she should become the centre of a European bloc. German *Weltpolitik* (global policy) after Bismarck, and especially after 1897, was clearly designed to gain a leading place in the emerging global pattern. The theme was reiterated in Germany's war aims in the First World War: she would create two empires, one at the centre of Europe, the other in Africa.[6] Japanese ambitions in China, Korea and the Pacific were similar. The victories over China in 1895 and Russia in 1905 were followed by the seizure, in August 1914, of German concessions in China and the German-owned islands in the Pacific.

Imperial expansion therefore became part of the new forms of global competition. It was a defensive necessity, a means of self-protection and the maintenance of national prestige, even of moral regeneration. Asquith, for one, came to argue that European expansion was normal and necessary: indeed, an inevitable sign of vitality. And Ferry wrote at the start of the 1890s: 'An irresistible movement drives the great European nations to conquer new territories. It is like a steeple chase moving headlong towards an unknown destination.'[7] Domestic social reforms would equally promote national strength and unity in an era which would be dominated by world powers, the need for greater social and administrative efficiency being sharply underlined, for Britain, by dramatic inadequacies in the Crimean and Boer wars.

The yeast in the loaf was Social Darwinism. Joseph Chamberlain, Cecil Rhodes, Jules Ferry, Gambetta, not to mention Theodore Roosevelt, all believed in its principles, which were widely, if not universally, accepted. They held that human progress, history itself, depended ineluctably upon a struggle for mastery between races, nations and empires. War was a mechanism of evolution. Only the fittest and strongest would eventually survive. Furthermore, if the leading global powers had been selected by evolution itself, the Europeans owed it not just to politics or religion, but to civilization and even to science, to govern other continents. Nor were such views confined to one party or group. Indeed, some socialists were quite willing to envisage the harshest treatment of inferiors. Marx and Engels even called for the extermination of backward peoples, almost a century before Lenin, Stalin and Hitler did it. Even George Bernard Shaw, in certain moods, wanted someone to invent a humane gas to dispose of undesirables.[8]

Around the 1880s and 1890s the rise and decline of empires was almost universally seen in such terms. In England, Salisbury spoke of living and dying nations. He was prepared to acquiesce in German primacy on the continent as long as Germany did not challenge Britain at sea. But others also wanted to neutralize the growth of French and German power. In France, Ferry argued that the nation had a simple choice between abdication and rebirth. These evolutionist views of international relations also called for national unity and discipline, military preparedness and readiness for sacrifice. The creation of a united Germany by war carried powerful lessons. 'It was too easy for a generation which had seen its nation founded by military strength, after centuries of division and impotence, to believe that military strength must be the chief factor in its preservation, and the military class, in consequence, the chief element in its society.'[9] The same mind-set sent not just the military but the general Western public into the 1914 war well aware that there would be vast loss of life.

There was more. In both France and Britain nationalist pride underpinned imperial motivation. For the British, Queen Victoria became an imperial symbol in a nationalist spirit much like that which had fuelled England's efforts against Spain under Elizabeth I. For generations, English people who settled abroad did so as loyal subjects and members of the British family, not to found new nations. Until almost the end of the nineteenth century, Canada and Australia were little more than geographic expressions while elsewhere, national flags were often hoisted as a kind of competitive sport. Furthermore, a period of small colonial wars gave the public all the usual emotions men experience when their country is fighting foreigners. So, while capitalists did promote imperialism, it was the nationalistic masses, with their growing political clout, who really made it possible and most vociferously backed it. It was not the thought of gain that moved the people, but the lure of the primitive and tales in the popular press of far-off adventures and battles to come. It was exciting to hear of English explorers becoming native chiefs, or the Brookes family becoming rajahs in Borneo, or of Laborde becoming a Malagasy prince and Lagarde an Abyssinian duke. Imperialism was a vast competitive game in which one cheered the home team. Urbanization and the new popular newspapers encouraged this populist nationalism everywhere. Moreover, representative, let alone democratic, government always carries the danger that once the public gets a set idea – even a bee in its bonnet – it becomes hard for government to resist. And neither the British nor the French governments encouraged resistance. Joseph Chamberlain and Disraeli in Britain, Jules Ferry and others in France, were excellent politicians and could see that the home public was patriotic and literate.

Economic motives played surprisingly small roles. For all the rivers of ink spilled on this subject, most of the debates about it have been at best inconclusive. That most major political decisions have some economic elements is obvious. To say that economic considerations played a role in the history of empire is merely trite. But they are rarely the whole story. In the affairs of nations, as of individuals, economic gain is more often a means than an end. Its precise role varies from one situation to the next and from one period to another. Moreover, anti-imperial writing is often based more on visceral opposition to capitalism and colonialism than on numbers and evidence. Lenin and A.J. Hobson, for example, in arguing that the real force behind expansionism was overseas investment and territorial acquisitiveness, largely abandon analysis for dogma and programme. Charges in India by 1900 that Britain was merely draining India's wealth had little to do with economics and much with the desire for political leverage. This is not to deny that trade and finance were important in Europe's calculations of comparative national power. Especially the global search for raw materials following industrial expansion, or the European depression of the 1880s and 1890s, largely caused by overproduction. But in the entire period from 1815 to 1939 very few colonies were annexed by any major imperial power just because of their assessed economic potential. British colonies relied mostly on local taxation and transferred almost no revenue to London. Nineteenth-century imperial governments did not receive anything by way of loot, least of all the British. Arguments about commodity exploitation will not wash, either. Since the colonies were not economically insulated and the empire was not a monopoly – most remaining controls being disman-tled by the 1860s – Britain could not rig the terms of trade in its favour. It is true that British exports rose from 10.3 per cent of GDP in 1870 to 14.7 per cent in 1913.[10] It is also true that, by the latter year, the empire took some 37 per cent of British exports and supplied one quarter of imports. But that had to do with Britain's natural dom-inance of global trade at this time, rather than with empire. Before 1914, the empire was simply not essential to the British economy.[11] Moreover, it was the skills, capital and demand provided by outsiders which gave colonial resources their value; and all industries created by such outsiders paid local wages and taxes and built roads and commu-nications. Not only that, but the economic elements in British, Dutch and to an extent even French motivation were in place well before the 1870s upsurge of political imperialism; and throughout, both state and business regarded expansion in the established markets of Europe, the United States and the white colonies as much more important than economic involvement in less secure regions.[12]

The figures seem conclusive. By 1914 cumulative British capital exports amounted to some £3.9 billion (£186 billion), of which £2.5 (£119) were invested in foreign countries and £1.5 (£71.5) in the empire, two-thirds of it in the Dominions.[13] Trade figures tell the same story. Measured in dollars, British 1913 imports from Europe alone were some $1548 million, well over twice the imports from Asia and Africa put together: $678 million. Exports to Europe were $917 million, compared with $868 million to Asia and Africa. French figures are similar: imports from Europe $880 million; from Asia and Africa $340 million. Exports to Europe $937 million, to Asia and Africa, $317 million. For the Netherlands the contrast is even starker. 1913 imports from Europe were $624 million and from Asia and Africa $288 million; exports to Europe $1131 million and to Asia and Africa $87 million.[14]

Indeed, the costs of empire were considerably greater than any profits, and many colonies turned out to be sheer white elephants. Whatever may have been the economic arguments for promoting empires, nowhere were they actually profitable to the imperial power. As Karl Marx saw long ago in the case of India, in most cases the administrative and military costs of imperialism, including the costs of pacification and imperial defence, were much higher than the tax rev-enues obtained plus the private profits from colonial investment and trade. For example, French net spending on colonies, some £4.4 million (£189 million) in 1875, had grown to £22.3 million (over

£1 billion) in 1913. To be sure, there may have been profit for pressure group(s) of capitalists able to sway their home governments. However, while some individuals and groups undoubtedly grew rich – though others lost their shirts – few grew rich because the enterprise was colonial. Commercial empires like that of Cecil Rhodes in Africa were very much the exception.[15] Profitability depended on movements in the general international economy.

After the loss of America, early Victorian England regarded its colonial heritage, as already noted, at best with indifference, while free traders thought it economically irrelevant.[16] As a rule, in nineteenth-century Britain, the Treasury thought colonies should look after their own economies and that overseas effort should be funded privately, or by colonial governments. Still, while the flag did not invariably follow trade, once it was raised, economics undoubtedly did produce greater effort and keener competition among the Europeans. Even in the earlier part of the century, Asia increased in economic importance taking, for instance, 6 per cent of British exports in 1815 and 20 per cent by the middle 1840s. And even while the East India Company was becoming more of a British government instrument for diplomacy and war, India became the largest single external market for British textiles, and Lancashire cottons in particular. By the 1880s some 20 per cent of British exports may have gone to India and perhaps 20 per cent of foreign direct investment,[17] though by 1914 India had rather less than 10 per cent of Britain's overseas assets.

As for France, as late as the 1840s she had barely begun to recover from defeat and dejection. Later, especially after 1870 when the Germans had occupied so many industrial regions, new areas for economic expansion and trade were indeed needed. Yet the French acquired a large colonial empire while home industries lagged and it was not generally profitable until after 1918. Germany only exported significant capital after it had acquired overseas possessions. The political imperialism of the latter part of the nineteenth century was therefore not promoted chiefly by commercial expansion, or to correct for uneven domestic growth. It was not even a strategy for diverting social tensions at home. In fact, it was under way, and became domestically popular, *before* a general resort to protectionism in Europe or a general export of capital.

In sum, empire was not acquired for profit and its value was not measured in money. It was kept in spite of its costs, because its reward was national clout in a mixture of politics and power, security and prestige. Empire was promoted not so much by traders as by politicians and a patriotic public tempted by overseas settlement and beguiled by the prospect of status in the world. It was not the bankers or industry or the Liberals who sponsored the empire so much as Conservative parties and academics, even if they sometimes used economic arguments. Liberals like Gladstone might hesitate to claim that trade and investment should follow the flag but Salisbury had no such hesitations, any more than did Chamberlain or Grey. Nor did Disraeli, who moved to a pro-imperialist position by 1872 and began to talk about a customs union with colonies enjoying 'responsible government'.

> Basically, the new imperialism was a nationalistic phenomenon. It followed hard upon the national wars which created an all-powerful Germany and a united Italy ... and which left England fearful and France eclipsed. Russia, halted in the Balkans, would turn anew to Asia ... Holland displayed a revived pride in the empire(s) it already possessed and ... administered with renewed vigor.[18]

Britain's self-governing colonies of settlement took parallel views: by the 1880s and 1890s they thought closer imperial unity would give them both safety and a larger world role through shared control of the empire.

Opinion in France was much the same. Indeed, after 1870 France's entire self-respect became tied up with *France outre mer* (France overseas). The new imperialists came in all shapes and sizes and included Jules Ferry, Gambetta, Jules Cambon and Théophile Delcassé. They were a loose coalition of soldiers, Catholics, Jews, political philosophers, churchmen and politicians. By the early 1880s French politics saw an upsurge of patriotism in reaction to the searing defeat of 1870, the even more searing civil war of 1871, and defeats in Mexico.[19] Other countries caught the same mood. By 1884–5 even Bismarck was telling the Reichstag that colonies were vital to the economy. It was not true, but it sounded persuasive. By the 1890s Japan and the USA joined in the game. It seems indisputable that from the 1850s, and certainly from 1870 onwards, while the domestic critics of imperial expansion were being disarmed by economic arguments, the main reasons for colonies were national prestige, power and competitiveness. Indeed, the powers took to a cartographic imperialism in which territories and people were treated like monopoly cards, with gains in one place being balanced or swapped for gains in another.

Consequently, between 1880 and 1914 imperial expansion speeded up. France, seeking compensation for European loss in overseas gain, increased her empire by some 47 million people and almost 4 million square miles in the four decades before 1914. Britain could offset her European isolation by enlarging and glorifying the empire. All the major powers expanded their influence in Africa, Central Asia, Southeast Asia, China and the Pacific. Japan wanted industrial supplies and strategic assets on the Asian mainland. The Russians built the trans-Siberian railway to consolidate their hold on the Pacific coast. The Americans took Spanish possessions and Hawaii for trade and naval bases. The competition required new rules of the game, so the 1885 Berlin conference tried to define principles of effective occupation of territory and commercial equality of effort. The result was even faster imperial expansion. In 1800 the Europeans owned some 55 per cent of the land surface of the globe. By 1914 the figure was 85 per cent.[20] Not only substance changed, but style. 'The world is harder, more warlike, more exclusive; it is also, more than ever before, one great unit in which everything interacts and affects everything else, but in which also everything collides and clashes.'[21]

However, interests and power were never the sole basis of effective imperialism. While altruism was hardly a dominant motive, self-interest was often linked to a liberal sense of duty to the peoples in one's charge. Social and cultural intervention often stemmed precisely from Liberal or Christian high-mindedness, even self-sacrifice. One element was the enthusiasm of the evangelicals and Methodists whose activities ranged from a sense of national mission at home, to missions abroad and the abolition of the slave trade. They were soon joined by others, like the Oxford Movement. The Protestant missionary societies which had been founded in the 1790s, though often distrusted by the imperial authorities as meddlers, won powerful support at home. In France, by contrast, missionary enterprise enjoyed strong official as well as public support. Liberal clergy worried, like their 'politically correct' successors a century later, about cruelty to animals, the evils of drink, the problems of gambling and the condition of poor labourers – in this case in the Congo and South African gold mines. At the same time pious Christian missions often, in practice, promoted imperialism. Their numbers and influence greatly increased after 1850, partly in reaction against materialism at home, partly because of improved transport and communications. And in a nationalistic age, missionaries could easily invoke naval or military protection. Even where they did not directly promote political dominion, they might pave the way for adventurers who did. In any case, their tales fuelled interest and support for empire at home. Imperialism might sometimes be ruthless,[22] but was often cloaked in a perfectly genuine idealism and devotion to duty.

At minimum, it was widely accepted that civilizational superiority conferred duties. That famous humanitarian and iconoclast,

Bernard Shaw, argued acerbically that if the Chinese were incapable of establishing conditions which promoted civilized life and peaceful commerce, it was the plain duty of European powers to establish those conditions for them.[23] Or as Jules Ferry put it in Paris: 'It must be openly said that the superior races have rights over the inferior races.'[24] Lord Curzon saw it in slightly different terms 'In empire we have found not merely the key to glory and wealth ... but the call to duty and the means of service to mankind.'[25] As a French minister put it: 'It is a real empire that we must create ... with free trade, accessible to all ... from which our Christian civilization will radiate ...'[26] The methods might vary from religious instruction to education or administrative order. But the need to justify rule by such duties was inescapable. Liberals could also argue that colonies didn't cost much, British control kept them at peace, stopped settlers from treating natives badly, and could prevent colonies from imposing tariffs on British goods. Thomas Macaulay thought so, as did John Seeley and Charles Dilke, Rosebery and Joseph Chamberlain. Similar French views came from Catholic missions as well as secular support for a *mission civilisatrice*. Everywhere, practicalities suggested similar conclusions. Introducing European skills and industries was pointless without ensuring their proper use. It seemed natural, even a duty, for each imperial power to spread its own civilization, language, literature, customs and laws much as, in the late twentieth century and the beginning of the twenty-first, the US Congress has insisted on 'human rights' and the Treasury, the World Bank and the International Monetary Fund have sought the universal adoption of Western economic and development strategies.

One does not have to believe in original sin to see that such mindsets were likely to produce cultural and racial arrogance. Yet here, too, the muse of history is cloaked in irony. The fact that some became merely arrogant has obscured for later generations the genuine desire of others to do good.[27] Moreover, this very drive to do good, to spread Western religious and moral standards, caused even greater resentment than any arrogance. Western values could be deeply objectionable, whether to Confucian scholars in Indo-China or animists in Borneo or fundamentalist Moslems in nineteenth-century Java or late twentieth-century Iran. European opposition to slavery, for instance, implied notions of souls equal under God, which could infuriate people committed to hierarchy or caste. Colonial administration could be at odds with other local beliefs or grandees. In India, for instance, Western medical practices were very apt to offend local sensibilities. And the administrators tried to ban not only thuggery, infanticide and *suttee*, but the more brutal customs of local rulers. They also thought smaller government and lower taxes would benefit the peasant masses. Furthermore, European rule meant civil peace, predictable laws, roads, railways, medical care and other elements of Westernization. It brought modernization and a style of governance which even many native reformers regarded as enlightened. All of it backed by the West's huge advantages in industrialization and technology.

Even more important in consolidating European rule were the weaknesses of local pre-national and pre-modern social structures. There were fundamental weaknesses of social cohesion, civil and military discipline, of administration and command: in other words, of social efficiency. These weaknesses coexisted with, indeed, even depended on, an ancient and for long quite undisturbed sense of ethnic identity and cultural and religious separateness. In most regions, at least until the later nineteenth century, the kaleidoscopic religions and civilizations of Asia remained relatively untouched by the rule of strangers. Mostly, their political dominance seemed culturally, even socially, irrelevant, except to tiny local elites. Asian societies like those of India and Indonesia did not think in terms of political unity, let alone of coherent social resistance; nor did they understand what might be needed to create such things. In China, especially, the inherited social organization was, by definition, optimal. Rejection of European rule could only become effective once these societies developed their own countervailing 'national' movements and structures.

Under these conditions many Europeans developed a comprehensive and largely unquestioning sense of religious and cultural, as well as material, superiority. The sheer scope of this military, economic, administrative and cultural power, its duty of dominion over the 'stagnant' lands of the East, were facts too obvious to require discussion. For the French and the British, even more than for the Dutch, the pride and prestige of being the citizen of an imperial power became dominant. To be a British subject was to possess the power and pride of Rome: '*Civis romanus sum*' (I am a Roman citizen). It was, for long, a personal, cultural and national sense of self-confidence, and religious certainty, so complete as to seem unassailable. It was this moral ascendancy, supported by social distance on one side and deference on the other, which governed, whether in India or Indonesia or Vietnam or even China. As with all Western colonizers since the fifteenth century, dominion ultimately rested on moral ascendancy, based on a mixture of morale, character and self-assertion.[28]

To be sure, many wiser heads understood its fragility. 'The supremacy of the English', wrote Dilke and Wilkinson in 1892,

> rests only to a limited extent upon their superior force ... to a great extent our ascendancy is 'moral' resting, that is, upon character and self-confidence. To this confidence the natives bow ... For a century the Englishman has behaved in India as a demi-god. He accounts himself a superior being ... and the majority of the inhabitants take him at his own valuation. Any weakening of this confidence in the minds of the English or of the Indians would be dangerous ... If he [i.e. the Indian] sees that his Englishmen are uneasy, he may interpret it as a sign of their coming doom ...[29]

Jan Smuts who, having fought the British in the Boer War, became a revered empire statesman, saw the importance of moral factors with equal clarity.[30]

The corollary of ascendancy was that if Asians stood lower down on the civilizational ladder, it was the plain Christian duty of Europeans to govern justly and help them climb up. For a minority, that even meant colonial independence as the crowning achievement of the imperial task. Macaulay went to India to draft a uniform code of laws for the country. 'It may be', he said in a famous speech in 1833,

> that the public mind of India may expand under our system till it has outgrown that system; that by good government we may educate our subjects into a capacity for better government; that, having become instructed in European knowledge, they may, in some future age, demand European institutions ... never will I attempt to avert or retard [that day].

Indeed, there might emerge 'a class of persons Indian in colour and blood, but English in tastes, in opinions, in morals, and in intellect'.[31] The day Britain left India, he maintained, would be the proudest day in British history. Some seven decades later, Lord Lugard echoed Macaulay: 'If there is unrest and a desire for independence, as in India and Egypt, it is because we have taught the people the value of liberty and freedom, which for centuries these people had not known. Their very discontent is a measure of their progress.'[32] Insert the word 'democracy' and the speakers might be President Clinton or Prime Minister Blair a century later.

In such a climate, societies for promoting the cause of empire flourished in both France and Britain. In London, the government set up a

Colonial Emigration Committee which helped some 6.5 million people to go overseas between 1830 and 1875.[33] The Royal Colonial Institute in London was founded in 1868 and Sir Charles Dilke, returning from a world trip, published his patriotic and hugely popular *Greater Britain*. In 1870, during the Franco-Prussian war, Froude criticized England for ignoring imperial glories. In 1874 the dean of French political economists, Paul Leroy-Beaulieu, promoted French imperialism in *De la Colonization chez les peuples modernes*. At the University of Berlin, the historian Treitschke was telling his pupils a few years later that 'every virile people has established colonial power'. And in 1882 a frankly propagandist Colonial Society was formed in Germany, while Leroy-Beaulieu declared that 'colonization is for France a question of life and death: either France will become a great African power, or in a century or two she will be no more than a secondary European power. ...' A year later Professor John Seeley published his celebrated lectures on the *Expansion of England*, which quickly sold 80 000 copies and won him a knighthood. In 1883 the imperialistic Primrose League was founded by Tory democrats, followed shortly afterwards by the more moderate Imperial Federation League of national-minded Liberals. In Germany came a Society for German Colonization. In the 1890s came a French Africa Committee, a Madagascar Committee and in 1893 the French *Union coloniale française*. A year later a Ministry of Colonies was established.

Opinions and practices naturally varied. French approaches were derived from Roman law, based on principles equally applicable to everyone in the entire empire. After the 1789 revolution the French thought their nation had special wisdom and a mission to pass on its truths to others, if necessary by force. French territories therefore remained centralized. (The Portuguese took a very similar view.) France and all parts of the empire must, together, form an indivisible whole. All parts of the empire must be assimilated; Asians and Africans must become Frenchmen. There were notions of common citizenship; the colonies would be represented in the Paris Assembly; French laws would apply. Secession was not freedom, but a break with civilization. But if that was the theory, the reality was rule by Paris. It was only quite late in the nineteenth century that the French conviction of their civilizing mission was augmented by the notion, shared by Karl Marx and all major powers, that colonies were a source of economic and military strength. Being logical, the French then sought to make colonies economically profitable. Though they were never of primary economic importance, that involved a strong protectionism.

The British, by contrast, developed a loose and decentralized style, with law and rules growing out of custom. Rule with a light hand was encouraged by the loss of the American colonies, the erosion of royal power at home and, critically, the small size of Britain's volunteer army. The key document was the Durham Report of 1839. Though dealing specifically with Canada, its principles were accepted generally. It envisaged self-governing colonies with their own legislatures, it being widely assumed that self-government would mean eventual secession. In reaction the new imperialists, regarding colonial settlements as an extension of Britain, developed ideas of a loose association of sovereign members. By 1900 much of the old imperial structure had gone and the powers of governors waned as those of local ministries and officials grew. In 1907 came the new term 'Dominion' and by 1917 the British were formally committed to the gradual development of 'responsible government' and self-governing institutions everywhere. The path for nationalist leaders was clearly marked out.

The colonies of settlement retained a special place: they were family. In 1917 a British government committee could still declare that 'the man or woman who leaves Britain is not lost to the Empire, but has gone to be its stay and strength in other Britains overseas'.[34] Indeed, Canada, Australia and New Zealand and especially the USA, remained desirable destinations for British settlers. In the East was Australia, where each colony, having its own governor, was directly responsible to London and where British garrisons remained until 1870. Until the end of the Second World War, most Australians thought of themselves as British, members of a world-wide British grouping. 'Home' or the 'home country', whether for New Zealanders, Canadians or Australians, meant Britain. (The Irish, with their often anti-British sentiments, were an exception. They were also a minority.)

There were early signs of local assertion nevertheless. Free immigrants and released convicts pressed for British-style representative institutions. New South Wales got a Legislative Assembly in 1823 and similar developments followed elsewhere. Gold discoveries in the 1850s encouraged economic and demographic development but underlined security worries. Volunteer associations for defence against the French had already formed in New South Wales in 1801. The Crimean War in the 1850s again prompted enrolment of volunteers and the construction of coastal and harbour defences against the Russians. Furthermore, as early as 1857, a committee of the Victorian Legislative Assembly argued that Australia's political disunion invited aggression from foreign enemies and defence was a major reason for creating the Commonwealth of Australia. Defence was not confined to Australian soil: Australians took part, enthusiastically, in British actions in China and campaigns in the Sudan and South Africa.

Expansion into the Australian interior also stemmed from local initiative; and the authorities moved early to restrain local brutalities against natives (aborigines). Protectionism was a lively issue. So was immigration, given fears that Indian or Chinese immigrants might depress Australian workers' living standards. By the 1880s Australians had begun to see themselves as one people, wanting to look after themselves more effectively. The result was a remarkably thoughtful debate in the 1890s, leading to the drafting of the Australian constitution as a fascinating mixture of ideas from Westminster and the US constitution. The federal state, with its own parliament and government, emerged in 1901.

By then, while the British talked about a more unified empire, the white colonies wanted greater autonomy. London was willing to pay for imperial defence and foreign policies, and hankered after trade preferences within a unified grouping. But urgent pressures drove the colonies of settlement in the opposite direction. As early as 1882, with French control in New Caledonia and the Germans in New Guinea, Australia and New Zealand complained that London was giving Europe priority over their own Pacific interests. Five years later New Zealand claimed the right to negotiate its own commercial treaties with foreign states and at the 1894 imperial conference the Australians demanded freedom to impose differential duties on imports. The French had their own worries about colonial competition and some folk called for discriminatory tariffs. Shortly afterwards the Canadians claimed freedom of external action and the Australian Labor leader, William Lane, said in characteristic political style that Australians did not care 'whether Russian civil servants replace the British pauper aristocracy in Hindustan offices'.[35] Though Prime Minister Asquith in 1911 denied the idea of Dominion independence in foreign affairs, Canada had already sent a mission to Japan and the Australians had already decided to establish their own navy, shortly followed by Canada. The role of the Dominions became even more clearly independent in the First World War.

Indian political development was different. A modern system of central government was created, with the Indian Civil Service continuing to govern in what it saw as the interests of India and its peoples. A unified code of law was introduced, blending British law and Hindu custom. Westernization and economic and technical progress continued. The electric telegraph reached India in 1850.[36] Postal services were introduced and the cost of sending written material dropped by 97 per cent. Illiterate people could hire letter writers, and schooling was promoted.

Much teaching was in local tongues but English was emphasized. Physical communication also quickened. Calcutta was linked to Peshawar and Bombay by a trunk road, uniting northern India as never before. In the 1860s came railways. All this helped to relieve famines and gave India the best system of roads and railways in Asia. Communications, including the Suez canal, developed production and foreign trade. Capitalist ways were introduced and by 1870 half the Indian debt of some £200 million (£8.6 billion) was in railway bonds. 'Railways may do for India ... what the genius of Akbar the Magnificent could not effect by government ... they may make India a nation'; and if it did, Britain would have to leave.[37] Together with that came improvements in irrigation and health which contributed to a striking population increase: according to the first Indian census in 1872 the population was now over 206 million.

Westernization also brought a substantial transfer of power from Moslems to Hindus. So much so that the assumptions of the Mogul era faded. India ceased to be thought of as part of the Moslem world; and the British, who until 1870 stood for change, became more concerned to defend the structures they had created. They became even more conscious that, while control of India conferred power, it needed care. The more so because India was ruled not by London but by a governor-general with only about 1000 members of that Indian Civil Service. Beyond that, government was still exercised through local men and institutions. So the ICS continued trying to improve the life of the peasantry, and to defend it – and its land rights – against middle-class claims to power and profit. Yet the Mutiny had had a lasting impact on British feelings. Few any longer agreed with Macaulay that Indian independence was desirable, or envisaged leaving the Indians to look after themselves. Attitudes hardened, while distance encouraged arrogance. But for Indians, deference began to give way to resentment. By the 1870s there were growing numbers of Indians who discovered that education did not create equality. Private relations cooled, too. Back in the eighteenth century, relations between English men and Indian women had been common. That fell away, not just because of the Mutiny but because steamships brought out English women with pronounced views of such matters. There was also that fervent Protestant evangelicalism.

Other regions were no less affected by improved shipping and imperial reorganization. The Suez canal enhanced the importance of the Malay peninsula, and particularly of Singapore as port and entrepot. But development was hampered by constant strife among Malayan sultanates, not to mention rampant piracy in the waterways. So, after 1867 the Colonial Office took over the British Straits Settlements, and concluded treaties with the rulers. The British went on to improvise indirect rule, creating the base for the late twentieth-century creation of Malaysia. British 'Residents' took effective control of much of Malaya. Police and law courts were created, slavery abolished. From 1896 the newly federated Malay states came under direct rule, with the capital at Kuala Lumpur, eventually the capital of Malaysia. By 1909 there was a federal council, with the British Resident-General as secretary; soon afterwards Malaya was run as a single unit, with the unfederated Malay states strongly influenced by British officials. Major economic expansion followed. For instance, tin production was so encouraged by the abolition of tin import duties in 1853 that half a century later Malaya – mostly through local Chinese – produced nearly half the world's tin exports. By 1910 Malaya also had 100 000 acres of rubber trees. The new prosperity tended to swamp political resentments.

In Singapore, by contrast, British residents were few. The city's strategic importance was recognized very early and underlined in the 1930s by elaborating the defences of its great naval base. No one yet dreamed that it would prove hopelessly vulnerable to air power and landward assault when the Japanese attacked in 1942. In the meantime, the Chinese ran its commerce. There was also colourful private enterprise, as in northwest Borneo where the Brookes family established themselves as rajahs of Sarawak. They ran their own civil service and army, and kept as much law and order as the locals would tolerate. Some were even persuaded to give up head hunting. The Brookes' reign lasted until the Second World War.

Nowhere did commercial interests stand alone. The British also wanted to balance French rule in Indo-China. In all of Southeast Asia only the Siamese (Thais) were adroit enough to survive as an independent power, partly by playing off larger powers against one another. They even obtained a Franco-British guarantee of their territorial integrity.

France's recovery of confidence after 1815 being slow, it was not before 1848 that vague but powerful memories of Napoleonic glory led to government by another Napoleon – the Third. In the meantime, France had taken Algiers in 1830, occupied parts of Polynesia, established a protectorate over Tahiti and encouraged exploration. But from 1850 France was once again concerned with prestige and a world role, though metropolitan enthusiasm for empire remained erratic. Imperial

aims still had to be justified in relation to Europe; after 1871 most especially to that overriding need to regain Alsace-Lorraine, lost to
Germany in the Franco-Prussian war, as well as the general imperative
of keeping France in the front rank of world powers. But the drives to
spread political liberty and France's civilizing mission also remained
active. French territorial organization still had to do with centralization, rationality, uniformity and the legal precisions of the *Code
Napoleon*.

French colonial enterprise ranged widely. It became intensive in the
Middle East after 1860. It explored the Pacific and acquired New
Caledonia in 1853. In the East, the most important area of expansion
was Indo-China. By 1850 Christian missionaries and converts were
being persecuted there; it was this as much as anything that prompted
the decision to move in, in 1857. Between 1858 and 1860 the French
occupied the Saigon delta and went on to control Da Nang. By 1862
they controlled much of the south (Cochin-China). Two years later
Cambodia was a French protectorate. Four years later again, all of
Cochin-China was in French hands. A decade and a half of military
action and diplomatic manoeuvre followed, to complete French
control of Vietnam. The treaty extending French authority over the
entire country – making Tonkin and Annam into protectorates – was
signed on 25 August 1883, though followed by some fourteen years of
pacification.

China, which continued to claim suzerainty, tried to oppose the
French advance. Chinese irregulars checked one French force but were
defeated in 1884. There followed Franco-Chinese border negotiations,
confused by the behaviour of local commanders on both sides. By the
middle of 1885 the Chinese accepted a treaty recognizing French sovereignty over Tonkin. (In the same year, the British Indian Army occupied Upper Burma, though the Burmese had hoped for French
support.) At that point the Vietnamese monarchy retained limited
authority only in Annam, on the coast and the Red River region of
Tonkin, while Cochin-China was fully a French colony. Two years later
the French union of Indo-China formally came into existence.
Throughout this period, Paris had usually opposed expansion, but
yielded to pressures from missions and merchants, as well as from local
officials worrying about security. In 1893–5 the French extended
further, by annexing Laos.

An administrative structure for this Indo-Chinese Union was gradually devised and consolidation came with the governor-generalship of
Paul Doumer in 1897. He established direct French rule over all of

Vietnam. Henceforth the governor-general would sit in Hanoi while kings, approved by the French, ruled in Cambodia and parts of Laos and an emperor, equally approved by the French, reigned over Annam and parts of Tonkin, the remainder of Tonkin being under direct French rule. The centralist and cartesian style of French government was much the same everywhere. Not only did it bring significant material benefits to the colonies, for instance in public works programmes, but at least 10 per cent of the Indo-Chinese population became Catholic.

Once again, Western success was only partly due to military superiority. The local reaction to the French was confused and indecisive. Some Vietnamese argued for modernization, not just of the army but of society, wanted Vietnam to study science, develop commerce and the economy, make fundamental administrative and financial changes and, not least, seek diplomatic support against the French, possibly from Germany or Britain. But the old Confucian ruling groups continued to be paralyzed by their own sense of cultural superiority. They refused to adopt Western methods and technologies. Consequently, nothing effective was done. Not until 1885 was a relatively coherent, albeit traditional, resistance effort made, to be crushed by the French eleven years later. Sporadic and poorly organized anti-French efforts, based on traditionalist beliefs and loyalties, would clearly achieve nothing.

That experience underlined the weaknesses of Vietnam's Confucian system. Western material superiority, and the weaknesses of monarchy and court, undermined public confidence in Confucian and governmental traditions. The West obviously had much to teach. But if modernization and social change were to come, new men would have to work to novel principles. The French themselves being inconsistent about promoting Western models, the tasks of innovation and transformation in Vietnam were left to a small class of Vietnamese more familiar with European civilization.

In the Dutch case, the imperial metropolis itself had undergone radical change under French governance during the Napoleonic era; and after 1815 matters were confused by the differences in wealth, outlook and social structure between the North and the French-speaking South which led to the 1830 Belgian revolt, when southern resentment received reinforcement from the infectious revolutionary liberalism of Paris. In January 1831 the great powers, under the influence of Britain's pro-Belgian Foreign Secretary, Lord Palmerston, demanded economic and political partition, and the creation of an independent Belgium. A protocol was devised partitioning the country and guaranteeing the security of the new entities. (Eight decades later, the violation of these Belgian borders would propel Britain into the First World War.) Partition was finally accepted in 1839 by the Dutch in the North, where liberalism and constitutional reform had also gained ground. These came to a head, in company with the general 1848 European conflagration, with the creation of a constituency-based popular franchise for the Lower House of the Dutch States General.

In the meantime, the Dutch state faced growing problems in the Indonesian archipelago. For several decades after 1830, when the struggle against local princes ended, Dutch-controlled areas were governed by hereditary native 'regents' grouped into residencies under a European officer. In time, European supervision became tighter and by 1900 Java had 'indirect rule': centralized residencies responsible to Batavia; a system only slightly loosened before the Japanese attack of 1942. However, the Dutch preserved Indonesian juridical independence, with many states having courts which were entirely Indonesian-run. A different system operated for Europeans.

The period up to 1830, which emphasized Dutch military weakness in the East Indies, also led to the creation of an East Indian army.[38] This pacified most of Sumatra by 1845 and in the later 1870s campaigned against the strongly anti-Dutch ruler of Aceh. The war continued for almost thirty years. Even then the final treaties could not prevent occasional reassertions of Aceh separatism lasting into the twenty-first century.

Indonesian economic development was slow. At first, the Dutch took taxes in money, a system introduced by Raffles. That led to crisis when world commodity prices fell. So, from 1830 to 1870, they tried the 'cultivation system', taking land rent from local rulers, or tribute in nominated crops and spices. Java provided things like coffee, indigo and sugar. The trouble was that under this forced delivery system peasants cultivated only, or chiefly, crops which happened to be in demand in Europe. Which brought misery once demand patterns in Europe changed. Moreover, as Dutch demand and hence company profit margins rose, so did pressure to grow commercial crops rather than food, with more intensive land use but less money for the peasants. It was a system open to exploitation by officials.

By mid-century, the Netherlands themselves had problems. Dutch cemeteries were overcrowded by epidemics. The working-class diet was poor, yet the industrial working day was fifteen hours, women worked like men and industrial hazards reduced life expectancy to some thirty years. Unsurprisingly, Europe's 1848 liberal storm gave the Dutch, too, a more liberal political system and by 1860, these liberals began to attack the East Indies cultivation system. Agrarian reform concentrated on developing plantations by private capital, and stopping exploitation of the peasants' own rice lands. Instead, peasants would now keep their own land, with plantations depending on government leases. Production grew and by the 1880s and 1890s Europe's industrialization sharply increased the demand for timber, tin, rubber and oil. There were other reforms, including abolition of slavery. The new system benefited the Dutch, too. As Indonesian trade boomed, and more exports even went to markets outside Holland, the Dutch merchant marine revived. So did the Amsterdam spice market.

The Dutch introduced other medical and social changes. The previously strong peasantry was weakened. Javanese social organization became more authoritarian. By 1870 there was some reform of forced labour. But improved health and sanitation also increased a population which quadrupled in a mere seventy years from 7 million in 1830 to 28.4 million in 1900, rose to 41 million thirty years later and reached 70 million by 1940. Economic development could not keep pace. The standard of living in Java declined and conflicts of interest arose among the Dutch themselves. Many became uneasy about declining local living standards, while private businessmen wanted to take over export crop production from the colonial administration.

Towards the later 1870s reforms went much further. So far, the government had directed cultivation and reaped taxes in both land and labour, in the process discouraging enterprise. Now that changed. Interference in the internal affairs of native states would cease. Financial surpluses would no longer go to the Dutch Treasury but be used locally, especially to promote native culture. In consequence, the pre-1877 flow of money from Batavia into the Dutch budget ceased. Indeed, sometimes the Netherlands subsidized the colonies instead, paving the way for the introduction, in 1901, of the 'Ethical policy', officially recognizing Dutch responsibility for Indonesian welfare. That produced an increasing Dutch interest in Indonesian social issues, expansion of education, road and rail construction, agricultural advisory services and some shift of the burden of taxation from Indonesians to the wealthier Europeans. Nevertheless, the chief economic sector remained the plantation economy. By 1928 some 4 million hectares of land in Java and Sumatra were held by non-Europeans, growing chiefly sugar, tobacco, rubber, tea, coffee, copra, as well as producing oil and tin.

Developments in China were slower and more painful than elsewhere. The years 1840–60 saw a build-up of foreign communities in the newly opened ports. They, and especially the missionaries, brought influences the locals often found obnoxious. Meanwhile the political condition of China deteriorated. The population growth and prosperity of the eighteenth century was replaced by slump. Government degenerated. From the middle 1850s there were three contending forces on the political scene: the entrenched Manchu dynasty; a growing popular nationalism; and the Western powers. Since none of them could establish control, tensions among them paralyzed the country. In the process, the weaknesses of the Chinese polity were more and more pitilessly exposed.

In the 1850s and 1860s China endured a series of rebellions and famines costing tens of millions of lives. Starting in 1849 came the Taiping rebellion. Its young peasant leader, Hong Xiuquan, had had some contact with Europeans. He acquired some understanding of their technological superiority and a rudimentary grasp of Protestantism. He insisted that his followers observe the Ten Commandments and banned alcohol, tobacco and gambling. In 1851 he proclaimed himself emperor and 'King of Heaven'. Millions of Chinese followed him. He soon controlled eleven of China's eighteen provinces and even attacked Shanghai. Ironically, it was the West which, for the first but not the last time, rescued the Manchu empire, starting in 1861 to supply weapons, ammunition, advisers and even soldiers to the empire. By 1864, when the King of Heaven killed himself and the rebellion was crushed, it had caused some 20 million deaths.

In the meantime, in 1857 mutual irritation led to another armed clash with foreign powers. Gladstone might plead in parliament that justice was on the side of the Chinese, but the government was adamant. Next year an Anglo-French fleet compelled the Chinese to agree to another 'unequal treaty'. The British envoy, Lord Elgin, privately condemned both sides. The Chinese officials, he wrote, were fools to bring such calamities on themselves by their pride and treachery; yet British policy merely consisted of 'resorting to the most violent measures of coercion and repression on the slenderest provocation'.[39] Further armed conflict followed. Tientsin was captured, some English and French negotiators were tortured and murdered, and British, French and American troops entered Beijing in October 1860. Then, in revenge for the killing of European prisoners, the invaders were turned loose against the Summer Palace. An Anglo-French army sacked and burned, even destroying the replica of Versailles designed long before by French Jesuits. The plunderers were stunned by the riches they could now loot.

At least some Europeans were appalled. Victor Hugo in Paris wrote that 'We Europeans are civilized, and to us the Chinese are barbarians.

Here is what civilization has done to barbarism! History shall call one of these bandits France, the other England ...'[40] The trauma created in the minds of Chinese was to have long-lived and highly political consequences.

These feats of arms led to the Beijing Conventions. Together with the 1858 Treaty, they laid China open to Western trade and influence. Russia and the USA claimed their share. Kowloon was added to Britain's Hong Kong. Additional 'treaty ports' were opened and foreign trade concessions became autonomous. Western warships were authorized to sail 600 miles up the Yangzijiang. Permanent representatives were exchanged, with Western ministers resident in Beijing. The Chinese were forced to pay an indemnity and a Westerner was put in charge of the Chinese customs service, whose revenues guaranteed payment. Opium imports were legalized. Christian missionaries were allowed to settle in China and to preach freely. They would be protected by law and, if necessary, by soldiers. This had at least three important consequences. For many Chinese, the foreign missionaries were imported by military force and were therefore the agents of foreign powers; that tended to harden resistance. The Chinese attacked and burned missionary establishments with great regularity, though Christianity became attractive for some and a few tiny Christian communities did develop. Third, and by no means least, the missionaries became significant in shaping opinions about China in their home countries. The profound sympathy for China which marked American opinion for many decades had much to do with the influence of missionaries and their families.

The British, especially, were now anxious to be more generous to China. Their major demands had been met. Trade was now open, and an increasingly important part of total British commerce. They were therefore ready to help the Chinese, for instance with administrative problems. Sir Robert Hart, the Irishman who ran the Chinese customs service with impeccable honesty, earned lasting Chinese gratitude. Visitors once more brought back admiring reports of Chinese culture and manners. Altogether, the British were more successful than some in dealing with the Middle Kingdom. As John King Fairbank has put it, there was a

> tacit community of interest between the British and Ch'ing [Qing] administrators. Each side represented a conquering power that had learned to rule its conquests by qualities of moral commitment and administrative skill ... China's aim was ... to appease the British with trade concessions but to set precise treaty-based limits to their activities and to keep them under control through material inducements.[41]

In the meantime, Russia loomed. It had become a continental land mass covering the region from Poland to the Pacific, in the process absorbing the Ukraine, the Crimea and Siberia. In 1858 China ceded Amur province and two years later the Russians took the maritimes. Russia also moved into the Kazakh steppe, absorbing the Islamic khanates of Bokhara and Kokand. By 1870 the Russians stood on the borders of Afghanistan and after 1880s encouraged millions of migrants to move to Siberia and the eastern provinces. As France and the Americans, too, began to concern themselves more with China, the pressure for trading and other privileges grew more relentless.

Paradoxically, therefore, in the last half century of its existence, the Qing regime depended on the props of foreign power. So long as the empire was not past praying for, the outsiders were jealous of each other's advantage and worried about possible chaos in China. No one wanted China partitioned, either. In 1895 Russia, France and Germany intervened to limit Japan's profits from victory over China. The powers would accept an informal division of spheres of influence, but neither undue influence for any outsider nor the empire's effective partition. However, that did not prevent the Russians from eyeing Manchuria in the 1890s, or the British from angling for exclusive interests in the Yangzi basin, or the French from claiming a quarter of China, including Yunnan, Sich'van and Guangxi. And by 1900 the USA, Japan, Russia, France, Germany, even Italy acquired rights to trade and invest in the so-called 'treaty ports'; to live in international settlements free of Chinese courts; to maintain bases and spheres of influence and missions, not to mention confining duty on their imports to 5 per cent.

Still, British aims in China were limited to commerce. After all, Britain was the world's dominant industrial and commercial power, and because trade between China and India was so important, it was Britain that commanded most of the trade with China. But the composition of that trade changed. By 1880 the chief sales to China were no longer opium and raw cotton but cotton goods made in England. With the rise of tea plantations in India – promoted if not introduced by the British – the demand for Chinese tea diminished. Instead, the market demanded products like soya beans, vegetable oils and pigs bristles (for brushes). As early as 1863 a senior Chinese official had written to the emperor acknowledging that Britain did not covet Chinese territory or China's people. Indeed, as the Japanese, Russians and French encroached on Chinese territory, Britain became concerned for China. London warned Beijing that the Russian demand for Port Arthur would threaten China and in March 1898 the House of Commons passed a resolution declaring that 'it is of vital importance for British commerce and influence, that the independence of Chinese territory be maintained'. It was a view echoed by the United States in the 1930s and again in the late 1960s, when President Nixon and Dr Henry Kissinger, at the height of the Cold War, told the Russians that China's territorial integrity was of vital interest to the USA.

For the Chinese, and especially for intellectuals, scholars and officials, these developments were shattering. China, obviously central to human civilization, to whom all other societies owed tribute, had been humiliated. The introduction of standard Western diplomatic practices meant that the established world order had been turned upside down. How could the foreign inferior now be, scandalously and outrageously, elevated to equality with the rightful Chinese superior? Here were singularly painful and hateful developments.

Yet the reaction was quite inadequate. While Western demands for greater privileges continued, the Chinese engaged in merely passive resistance. The imperial system even accentuated bureaucratic paralysis. Where the Japanese reacted to the Western challenge in this period with wrenching, painful and thorough structural reforms, the Chinese retreated into their shell. The old emperor died in 1861. His successor being four years old, power was wielded by his mother, the imperial concubine Cixi. A remarkable, brilliant and ruthless woman, she was unshakeably convinced of the superiority of Confucian thought, of Manchu superiority over the Chinese and Chinese superiority over the West. She tried, with immense energy, to reorganize the army, to build steam-powered ships, to fight corruption and to introduce Western technology. But she tried to patch up the system, not to change it. The senior mandarins, on whom government relied, wanted to have the least possible contact with foreigners, to insulate Chinese affairs against outsiders, to be left in peace. Nor did ordinary Chinese seem interested in understanding foreigners. Few tried to learn foreign languages (in official dealings, it was usually foreigners who brought interpreters). Only very slowly did the notion develop, even among educated Chinese, that they should learn more about the foreigners, their languages, ideas, science and technology. Very few Chinese travelled abroad. Not until about 1860 were the British asked to build gunboats for China. Only around 1880 was the first ambassador sent abroad; and a Foreign Ministry was set up as late as 1901, at foreign insistence.

By then, though, things were changing. Railways, banking, mining were being modernized, mostly around the treaty ports. A modern press developed: so did education and, with that, revolutionary groups. From the 1890s more students went to study abroad, and absorbed Western political and economic ideas. By 1900 it was widely agreed that thorough reform of the entire machinery of the Chinese state was necessary, with elected assemblies, modernized law and education and modern armed forces. Within a decade many of the reform-minded young had begun to be active in government, education and the army.

The Chinese experience proved, if proof was still necessary, that there was no one in the entire Pacific region capable of confronting the political military, technological and economic power of the West – and, soon, Japan. If that power was to be checked, it would have to be through the mutual jealousies of these nations. The Pacific islands, in particular, were easy pawns, though the strategic importance of these dots of territory was not appreciated quickly, even in London which had most reason to worry about naval balances. Concern only grew during the naval competition of the 1880s and 1890s.

By then the USA was also asserting its Pacific position. American whalers had long roamed the southern oceans, in the process making Boston rich. The US Navy established an East India squadron in 1835 and by the middle of the century visionaries were talking about America's 'manifest destiny' and progress towards a universal empire. But until almost 1900 American expansion concentrated on Texas, Oregon and California. Not until 1890 did Alfred Thayer Mahan, in publishing his sensational work on sea power, argue that the USA must be a two-ocean nation and, for its own security, control the Caribbean, and the Pacific for 3 000 miles beyond its West coast.[42] By 1900 the USA had annexed Midway and Hawaii, ended Spanish rule in Cuba and, with Commodore Dewey's crushing victory over the Spanish fleet in Manila Bay, begun a six-week conquest of the Spanish Pacific empire.

In the South Pacific, French exploration began in the time of Napoleon I. It began from mere curiosity, though in 1840 the British hastily headed off a French claim to sovereignty in New Zealand. But between the 1840s and 1880s the French extended to Tahiti, the Marquesas and annexed New Caledonia, having discovered that such Pacific dots could be useful.[43] The Germans seized parts of New Guinea, the Carolines, the Marshall islands and Guam. They took Samoa while the British were too busy fighting the Boers in South Africa to stop them. By then, the British had been invited to rule Fiji, and used their High Commission there to supervise other Pacific protectorates. They took over the Solomons and Tonga, while the New Zealanders captured German Samoa. They also took Nauru, with its vast phosphate deposits. Some of these island groups became strategically vital in the Second World War. The 1942–5 US Pacific campaign depended critically on the Marshalls, on Guam and the island chain to Okinawa. And the resource problems of the later twentieth century were to be much affected by new rules allowing everyone to claim a 200-mile exclusive economic zone beyond their shores.

By the end of the nineteenth century, then, the trajectory of British, French and Dutch empire-building had reached its apogee. But expansion had undermined the capacity and rationale for imperial maintenance. These empires already contained the seeds of their own destruction; so that some historians have unfairly dismissed them, as 'gaudy empires spatchcocked together'.[44]

To begin with, for all the reluctance of politicians, the entire context of decision-making changed. It did so with developments in industry and technology, transport and trade, of demography, of urban living and of the international balance. First, demography: Europe's nineteenth-century overseas expansion was partly driven by a doubling of its population. In the century after 1820 some 60 million Europeans sailed for the Americas alone, three fifths of them to the USA. But by 1900 birth rates in the industrial countries were declining. Except for Russia, they fell below replacement levels by the 1920s and shortly afterwards the same thing happened in the USA, Canada, Australia and New Zealand. Yet the populations of India, China and Japan rose sharply, helped by the modernization of agriculture, health and sanitation that the West had introduced. It also seems likely that declining birth rates in Europe were associated – together with wars and economic turmoil – with a decline in social optimism, as compared with the energy, passion and rising morale in other regions.

Industrial growth pointed in similar directions. By around 1850 Britain was the only industrial power of any importance and world production of steel was around 80 000 tons. By 1870 the UK was producing some 700 000 tons, Germany and France 300 000 tons each and Russia virtually none. By 1900 world production was 28 million tons; and in 1914 Britain and France produced 6.5 and 3.5 million tons respectively, with Russia producing 4.1 million and Germany 14 million tons.[45] Germany was also producing almost as much coal as Britain, while the USA had become the world's leading coal producer and her pig iron production was greater than those of Britain and Germany combined.

At the same time, new technologies changed all previous economic, trading and strategic calculations. The last three decades of the century brought scientific and technological innovations amounting to a second industrial revolution. Steam navigation changed relations among continents and, together with railways, the electric telegraph and regular postal services, transformed spatial relations for people, goods, services, governments and armies. Railways provided swift and secure lines of communication. They also made countries less vulnerable to seaborne attack. They encouraged the growth of large domestic markets, favouring countries like the United States, Russia and Germany. A host of new inventions also appeared: new kinds of machinery, aircraft, the telephone, broadcasting, new bicycles, chemicals, artificial silk, plastics and the internal combustion engine. Energy consumption shifted from coal to oil and electricity. All this weakened the positions of Britain and, still more, of France. By 1918 Britain was no longer at the cutting edge of technological or economic developments, and not always at the hub of political ones either.

These same developments made it possible to deploy and supply unprecedentedly large armies, while breech-loading rifles, introduced from the 1860s, and improved cannon, vastly increased their killing power. By the early twentieth century military might meant manpower plus railways. In the meantime, navies changed from wood and sail to iron and coal. The American civil war even brought iron-clads, which made all older navies obsolete. Advanced naval power spread, while steam navigation required coaling stations and helped to promote the scramble for Africa. All that led to a competition not only between armies, but between technologies.[46]

The new industrial technologies also changed the political economy of trade, and greatly increased wealth. The period 1840 to 1914 saw a sharp rise in economic globalization, not only of trade but of capital flows. World trade, estimated at US$8 billion in 1860, had by 1913 multiplied by almost five. In the 1840s, the journey from Sydney to London had taken four months or more; by 1910 it took thirty days. The saving in time, plus developing refrigeration technologies, meant working-class access to butter and meat from the colonies as well as tea from Ceylon and India and wheat from the USA. Argentine beef reached Europe by 1877 and the first shipment of New Zealand mutton landed in England five years later. This made a huge difference to food supplies, improving nutrition and standards of life. The pressures for new markets and investments owed not a little to Europe's increasing dependence on overseas food supplies.The new shipping particularly favoured the British, who by the 1880s owned half the world's merchant fleet. Medical care also improved: Britain's death rate dropped sharply in the last third of the century. The same developments also widened the gap with underdeveloped regions and greatly improved the practicalities of exploiting their resources. On the other hand, the new developments were unsettling and uncomfortable for many: as always, some people wanted governments to protect them against foreign influences and dangers, all of which helped to make a new protectionism, promoted by men like Joseph Chamberlain, plausible.

The impact of the new industrialism on domestic affairs was equally powerful. Populations crowded into cities and manufacturing centres. Large impersonal factories replaced older systems of small shops. The resulting alienation of working folk accentuated the split between capital and labour and fed ideas of class war, which were only headed off by active industrial and social amelioration. Information and education became more widespread and made the labouring classes politically articulate. The technologies of mass production, invented by the Americans, changed the price and availability of many goods not just for the rich but for everyone. Indeed, in countries like France and Britain, between 1800 and 1900 per capita income probably multiplied by five.

The voting base of politics broadened. Before the middle of the nineteenth century, voting was based on property, but the new conditions demanded broader suffrage. Significantly, the pace was set by the USA, Canada, Australia and New Zealand, all of which had universal (male) suffrage by 1840. France and Germany reached the same stage by 1871, followed by Britain, beginning with the 3rd Reform Bill of 1884 and the Netherlands in 1896.[47] Moreover, the old forms of representative democracy became unworkable and were gradually replaced by more highly organized party politics to be, in turn, qualified by the twentieth-century growth of administrative law and the media manipulation of a mass electorate.[48]

These trends greatly changed the domestic politics of the European powers. The growing cities and industrial centres created a mass society which was more impersonal yet more malleable by populist leaders. The new urban industrial workforce had new needs expressed through syndicalism, trade unions, political organizations largely based on class, and demands for welfare. Political sensitivities and demands changed. That led to a broader and more activist role for the state, starkly illustrated by the social legislation of Bismarck's Germany in 1883–9[49] followed by Britain, with Churchill's and Lloyd George's National Insurance Act of 1911. Not surprisingly, many people came to regard empire as a distraction from these urgent domestic issues.

The administrative nation-state also grew stronger. Administration became more detailed and required better information. Government started to focus on the new availability of comparative statistics; about demographic trends and expectations of future manpower; about the economic and industrial rise of Germany; about comparative steel and coal production or railway development; about relative tonnages in the century's naval races. Industrial capitalism therefore produced an increasingly national, rather than regional, focus on economic activities and evened out some kinds of regional and social difference. The growth of public sector revenue, expenditure and employment marks the onward march of the regulatory army. Where, in the first decade of the eighteenth century, annual revenue in Britain was £5.1 million (£365 million) and expenditure £6.1 million (£436 million),[50] by around 1750 the figures were £7.4 and £8.8 million (£605 and £719.5 million). By the 1850s the totals were £62.2 and £59.6 million (£3.05 and £2.92 billion).[51] In the public sector as a whole, by the mid-nineteenth century 2.4 per cent of the British and 5 per cent of the French were in public employment. A century later it was 26.6 per cent in Britain and 16 per cent in France. By 1981 the UK figure was 31.4 per cent and the French figure 32.6 per cent. Even more significant are the figures for the central ministries. In France, Holland and Britain alike, between the middle of the nineteenth century and the end of the 1960s their staffs multiplied roughly by ten.[52]

This had major consequences. As government became bigger and more complex, central administration became a more important political playing field. In France the revolution had already strongly promoted central power; furthered still more by Napoleon's stress on rigorous civil service training. In Britain, central power grew in gentler fashion half a century later, especially with civil service reform. It was the Indian Civil Service which decisively influenced reform in Britain. In 1854 Sir Charles Trevelyan, who had served in India, reported on the British service. He recommended recruitment by open competitive examination, selection for high rank by intellectual attainment rather than specialist knowledge, and the creation of a Civil Service Commission.[53] For government, a unified service with promotion by merit made it easier to respond to the social distresses of industrial society. It began to take responsibility for prisons, factories, the poor law, as well as powers over transport and shipping. The age of classic liberalism in Britain therefore coincided with a decisive growth of bureaucratic scope and power which, by 1870 or so, had laid the foundations of modern government.

One of the shrewdest observers of these developments – however faulty his prophesies and programme – was Karl Marx. 'The bourgeoisie', he declared in the Communist Manifesto of 1948,

> has agglomerated population, centralized means of production, and has concentrated property in a few hands. The necessary consequence of this is political centralization. Independent, or but loosely connected provinces, with separate interests, laws, governments and systems of taxation, became lumped together into one nation, with one government, one code of laws, one national class interest, one frontier and one customs tariff.[54]

That was storing up trouble. If one considered the social consequences of these developments,

> the bourgeoisie ... has put an end to all feudal, patriarchal, idyllic relations, it has pitilessly torn asunder the motley feudal ties that bound man to his 'natural superiors', and has left remaining no other nexus between man and man than naked self-interest, than callous 'cash payment.' It has drowned the most heavenly ecstasies of religious fervor, of chivalrous enthusiasm, of philistine sentimentalism, in the icy waters of egotistical calculation. It has resolved personal worth into exchange value, and in place of the numberless indefeasible chartered freedoms, has set up that single unconscionable freedom – Free Trade.[55]

Indeed, as Schumpeter added a hundred years later, capitalism and commercial competition imply neither stability nor democracy. On the contrary, since 'creative destruction' is of the essence of capitalism, the idea of a stable capitalism or capitalist system is a contradiction in terms.[56]

Above all, the balance of global power moved remarkably quickly against the empires. In Europe, the weight of newly united Germany became, for a hundred years, the central issue for the diplomacy of the powers. There were, moreover, fundamental changes from a European to a world balance of power. This had several elements. Russian power grew. Above all, there was the 'Americanization of the world'.[57] It started with the extension of US power into the Pacific with the takeover of Spanish possessions and the 1899–1900 'Open Door' notes of Secretary of State John Hay[58] concerning the inviolability of China. Here were the first US assertions of global rather than merely American concerns. The trend continued with Theodore Roosevelt's brokering of the 1905 peace negotiations between Japan and Russia. American worries about Russian 'imperialism' replaced the previous understandings between Washington and Moscow, half a century before President Truman and Dean Acheson constructed a Western bulwark against that imperialism in Europe. From the middle 1890s onwards, therefore, the Far East became an independent focus of international rivalries.

Now the European imperial powers found themselves suffering from severe strategic over-extension. For Britain and France, global involvement implied increasingly painful resource burdens. For the British, India remained the key. In fact, Britain's global position depended on India rather more than the kaleidoscopic society of India depended upon Britain. As Lord Curzon remarked, without India Britain would become a third-rate power.[59] Moreover, as a 1892 survey of strategic problems pointed out: 'We have undertaken the political and moral education of the peoples which inhabit that peninsula, and we therefore implicitly assumed the duty of guarding our work against interruption. We have made ourselves responsible not merely for the Government, but also for the peace of India.'[60] The security of the Suez canal route to India was the main reason for British interventions in Egypt in the 1880s and 1890s. The Himalayan frontiers did not seem secure; between 1830 and the mid-1880s Russia had advanced some 1800 miles through Central Asia to the borders of Persia and Afghanistan. This brought a first-rate European power close to the Khyber Pass and provoked those British forays to Kabul. By the late 1890s the Czar had a regular army of over a million men, backed by 3 million reservists. Meanwhile, the British Indian Army had some 225 000 men, one-third of them British. It was clear to planners in London and Delhi that defending India against a major Russian attack was quite beyond British means.[61] For London, the 1917 Bolshevik revolution merely changed the threat to one of revolutionary subversion.

Other parts of the empire only needed small land forces, but depended on the navy. Many British efforts in Africa were driven by the requirements of the imperial lines of communication;[62] which meant more than coaling stations. Missionaries in out-of-the-way places and even humanitarian movements needed protection. The struggle against slavery also compelled intervention. Strategic responsibilities multiplied. The Prime Minister, Lord Salisbury, remarked crossly that if his military advisers had their way, they would garrison the moon against an attack from Mars.[63] Britain's resources were therefore spread very thin and her military weakness (and diplomatic isolation) cruelly exposed by the Boer War in 1899. As Michael Howard points out:

It was not of Imperial power that British statesmen were primarily conscious at the beginning of this [the twentieth] century. They were far more conscious of Imperial weakness: of commitments all over the world to be defended, of well-armed and rapacious adversaries who threatened them, and of very slender resources to protect them with.[64]

The glad, confident imperial morning was fading well before 1914. In France there were parallel worries about resentments in the colonies, the limits of French power and the diversion of men and resources into colonial campaigns which, while excellent troop training grounds, could bring no lasting settlement. As early as 1885, while French power was advancing strongly in Indo-China, Jules Delafosse told the Chamber of Deputies that France was dreaming of utopia and within half a century there would 'not be a single colony left in Asia'.[65]

The changed dynamics of power compelled everyone to adjust. Though some British politicians had talked earlier about not holding colonies against their will, public opinion in England had strongly opposed any idea of abandonment. Yet after 1900 Britain's reserves of manpower were barely enough for peacetime garrisons, and political attention was anyway veering back to Europe and the German problem. Canadians, New Zealanders and Australians began to question whether the navy could really meet both the looming Pacific and Atlantic problems. Such doubts were amply justified. In March 1914 the First Lord of the Admiralty, Winston Churchill, considering a German threat in the North Sea, said frankly that Australia and New Zealand could not count on the navy. If the worst came to the worst 'the only course of the five millions of white men in the Pacific would be to seek the protection of the United States'.[66] By 1921 it was largely South African and Canadian worries which brought an end to the Anglo-Japanese alliance. Two years later New Zealand and Australian concerns forced Britain to start fortifying Singapore. Altogether, it became clear well before 1914 that while the Dominions relied on empire unity and mutual support, each had unavoidably special interests; and the kind of imperial union favoured by Joseph Chamberlain or Cecil Rhodes was neither feasible nor desirable.

Together with such practicalities came shifts in political ideas which also undermined imperial principles. By 1900 there was intense preoccupation with competing theories of social organization. Many were socialist or revolutionary, unwilling to tolerate existing ruling classes or the capitalist system, let alone empires. Issues like national self-determination were in the air. Liberals moved easily from the idea that all men are equal to the notion that they are much the same. Socialism therefore meant direct action, at first by peaceful trade unionism, but the two or three decades before 1914 also saw an upsurge of groups reacting fiercely against progressive Liberalism and promoting violent revolution.[67] Johann Most produced his *The Science of Revolutionary Warfare*. Georges Sorel's *Réflexions sur la violence* was published in 1905. More fatefully still, Lenin not only wrote his *What Is To Be Done?*, but invented a new and unprecedentedly powerful form of political organization: the Vanguard Party. No longer did the Party represent the collectivity of the people, it was an avowed elite, leading the people in the direction which, did they but understand the true position, they would recognize as being in their real interests. For such men, invariably willing to sacrifice millions in the name of abstract ideas, real men and women were mere raw material, to be shaped in line with 'scientific' theory.

It was not only theory. In 1890–1914 anarchists or lone assassins[68] murdered the Austrian Empress Elizabeth, a prime minister of Spain, a president of France, another president of the United States, a king of Italy, the French socialist leader Jean Jaurès and a number of lesser notables, not to mention the heir to the Austro-Hungarian throne, whose death triggered a world war. Yet that war also demonstrated that, when the test came, anarchism and socialism would give way to patriotic loyalty.[69] Not that unrest and revolution disappeared; not only Russia but Germany and Central Europe were riven by it in 1918. Leon Trotsky was not far wrong when he said that the war had 'transformed the whole of Europe into a powder magazine of social revolution'.

There was a related debate, within each metropolis, about the true role and justification of empire. Thucydides had long ago raised the question whether a democracy could manage an empire; now democratization made empire less interesting, especially as the costs grew. Not only that, but confidence in the moral justification of empire wilted under the attacks from socialists and internationalists, as well as for religious and humanitarian reasons. This directly undermined just that prestige and moral ascendancy on which, far more than on mere military power, the maintenance of empire had depended.

Asian opinion moved also. Closer metropolitan control of colonies brought changes, sometimes subtle, to their administration. Earlier rulers had, for better or worse, known and been known by the men they dealt with. They had understood local customs, peculiarities, needs, fears. They had known the villages, the forests and streams, the local animals and plants. But the new and distant administrations had different priorities. What had been direct, human, personal, became impersonal, abstract, legalistic. Once such language and abstract measures were used, Asians began gently to point out that when they became 'more civilized', surely they would be entitled to the same rules of self-determination, even juridical equality, as those which increasingly governed European affairs? Surely the brotherhood of man, and the principles of liberty, equality and fraternity said no more about ethnic or cultural differences than had the sermon on the mount?

In many places, Asian resentments could come in more militant forms, and not just in East or South Asia. In the mid-century the Russians fought to subdue the Caucasus. Egyptian resentments flared in Arabia Pasha's revolt of 1882. In the 1880s there were rebellions in Cambodia and Saigon. The Anamite Emperor, Ham Nigh, staged a five-year resistance to the French, followed by more guerrilla war and fresh uprisings in Hanoi and Hué in 1906–8. The British suffered setbacks in the Sudan, fought repeatedly in Burma in the 1880s and 1890s and in 1905–9 confronted terrorism in Maharashtra and Bengal. The Dutch, too, faced a holy war in Aceh in the 1880s, rebellion in Bali in the 1880s and 1890s and peasant protests in Java during the First World War. Chinese nationalism was stimulated by the 1894 defeat by Japan and the subsequent threat of partition. As Sun Yatsen (Sun Yixian) once pointed out, Chinese nationalists saw the 1905 Japanese victory over Russia as 'a defeat of the West by the East'. And in spite of the failure of that year's Russian revolution, its struggle against despotism stimulated revolutionary impulses elsewhere. It probably stimulated unrest in Vietnam and helped spark off the Persian revolt of 1906. By 1908 the Young Turk movement staged a revolt and in 1911 China itself collapsed into revolution.

Such outbursts heralded the arrival of much more clearly political and national resistance movements, increasingly prepared to use Western language and to operate in the Western manner. The Indian National Congress was created in 1885. In 1905 Sun Yatsen founded a revolutionary organization which, seven years later, became the Guomindang. The Moslem League in India was founded in 1906, followed two years later in Indonesia by the vaguely nationalist Budi Utomo and in 1912 the Islamic Sarekat Islam. In 1913 came the Association for the Restoration of Vietnam. They all signalled the development of a sense of nationalism in recognizably modern forms.

6
Imitation and Rejection

But what, more particularly, caused this development, and the eventual success of a modernized nationalist response in the colonies? Several explanations have been offered. One says that resistance to the outsider always existed; and most societies did indeed offer some resistance from the start. Another stresses the role of European liberal and religious ideas in stimulating colonial claims and undermining the European belief in imperial legitimacy. A third emphasizes the imperial achievements in urbanizing and industrializing traditional societies. Another again stresses the encouragement which nationalism in one place gave to its growth elsewhere.

All these propositions have merit, but the phenomenon may be more complicated. What seems to have been decisive was a combination of factors, broadly similar but taking somewhat different forms and occurring at somewhat different times in each colony. In some, the sense of ethnic and cultural separateness was already ancient and fundamental to the social structure, as among Japanese, Vietnamese or Han Chinese. In India it was multiple rather than singular. But what developed everywhere between approximately 1860 and the 1930s, was an assertive political nationalism both in imitation and rejection of the dominant Western power.[1] Typically it happened in three stages. First came a conservative reaction, primarily designed to maintain local cultural and political patterns. It has been called 'proto-nationalism'. There followed a middle-class-led bourgeois movement, but without mass appeal. Only the third stage saw more general political mobilization, with modernized organizations and more clearly defined aims and methods. This third stage became the decisive nationalist reaction, conducted in Western political idioms, allowing local civilizations to imitate Western forms and structures and use them in a successful struggle against rule by the stranger. The more clearly Europe's own behaviour reflected national and nation-state principles, the more others needed to define themselves in similar ways.

That meant developing not just national consciousness but organized mass politics, with each individual no longer a passive subject but in principle an active, even equal, participant in the movement for 'national liberation'. The citizen became a participant in creating a common will, someone to be mobilized in the pursuit of common ends. Correspondingly, dissenters could be treated as traitors to the national cause. Nationally organized political structures grew alongside equally national administrative machines, centralized in purpose, comprehensive in scope, and everywhere largely staffed by newly educated men sympathetic to nationalist ideas. Here was the basis for a government embodying the national personality, able to mobilize all social resources, most particularly so in pursuit of the principal aim of the modern secular state: unfettered sovereignty and independence.

Such patterns are, of course, inherently artificial. Sovereignty has never been absolute and cannot be, least of all in a largely globalized environment. The scope and power of central administration has always waxed and waned over time in relation to ever-changing domestic and external pressures. No change in the scope, incidence or intrusiveness of government is therefore likely to be permanent. Moreover, the very concept of 'nation' has always been problematic. All nations are artefacts of will, as Ernest Renan noted long ago[2] and the twenty-first-century designers of a united Europe strongly believe. Ernest Gellner puts the matter pointedly: 'nationalism is not the awakening of nations to self-consciousness: it invents nations where they do not exist'.[3] Nations became the framework for effective political action as older loyalties dimmed, older beliefs began to fade, established social forms broke down. Marx saw long ago that industrialization and mechanization lead to social fragmentation and declining fraternity or a sense of common purpose. The language of independence struggle may therefore have been that of justice and progress, but the underlying factors were Bismarck's *Blut und Boden* (Blood and Soil): the sense of racial and ethnic difference and desire to control people and territory. The 'nation' therefore became an anthropomorphic entity whose 'liberty' also implied the liberty of the individual citizens. Although that idea may be deeply flawed, most serious political movements since around 1800 have formed, and conducted their affairs, in nation-state terms. For the ex-colonies nationhood and statehood have been the very conditions of independence and the principal way to make themselves heard in the world.

Developing coherent national feelings in Asia was bound to be more difficult than in Europe. It meant inculcating notions of society as an organism, derived from Hegel and, later, from Darwin. It meant accepting that society was malleable, could be designed and shaped. No Asian society started with that intellectual framework. Nation also implied a defined territory. That was a given in Japan, but in East, South and Southeast Asia political territories had usually fluctuated, sometimes wildly. In Europe, ethnic and cultural homogeneity, cemented by language, strongly defined nationality. Belgium was created precisely because the older United Provinces lacked the cement of language and religion. Even in France the first modernized dictionary only appeared after the mid-nineteenth century and the first in England soon afterwards.[4] In these matters, too, Japan was an Asian exception. But neither India nor Indonesia had such attributes. Even China, Vietnam and Malaya had them only in part. To this day, the Chinese authorities are trying to impose a relatively uniform Mandarin on a society with dozens of mutually incomprehensible languages and dialects, and with widely varying religious and social ideas. In Indonesia, the Chinese had no idea they were 'Chinese', rather than members of their dialect group, until the Dutch classified them. In the Philippines, until the twentieth century natives were 'indios', 'Filipino' being reserved for someone of pure Spanish descent; just as in present-day Peru popular usage distinguishes between 'los indios', 'los mesquites' and the 'blanquitos'. As for India, in 1999 a senior newspaper editor could still write that: 'The national concept is so remote that no Indian language, including my native Bengali, has ready words for India and Indian ... Indian ... is not a race at all, but citizenship.'[5]

The growth of colonial nationalism would therefore have been much more difficult had not two other elements been present. One was the weakening of the imperial powers by the tides of world politics. The other was encouragement to nationalism, most powerful when most inadvertent, from the colonizers themselves.

World politics was transformed by the First World War. The Russian, Ottoman and Habsburg empires disintegrated. Even the victorious empires were weakened by exhaustion, disappointment and deep changes in domestic politics. To be sure, one must not forget the sense of fellowship and purpose which fighting soldiers kept to the end. Few of them thought themselves victims of some insane conspiracy by generals and politicians, though some vitriolic post-war writing suggested otherwise. Nevertheless, what had been hope, enterprise and energy before 1914, gave way to weariness and disillusionment. For many, the magic had simply gone out of the old totems of faith, loyalty, patriotism. The 'golden summer' of 1914 seemed all the more wonderful when glimpsed across the great gulf of war by the frenetic 1920s. Too much energy, resources and above all, blood, had been poured out. Yet more effort was now needed to cope with post-war problems, of which no one had any experience.

Two sharply competing visions of world order emerged. One came from Lenin and the Bolshevik revolution, the other from President Woodrow Wilson of the United States. Both understood they were competing for hearts and minds across the globe. Both rejected 'outdated' notions of balances of power, secret diplomacy and trade discrimination. Each proposed to diminish the nation-state in favour of a new international system. Lenin and Trotsky offered universal revolutionary socialism, an end to independent statehood and a classless, egalitarian social order. In contrast, Wilson proposed the self-determination of nations, within a League of Nations meant to end aggression and resolve disputes peacefully.[6] The League was never effective, since neither Russia nor Germany were members and the USA itself ultimately refused to join. Nevertheless, each scheme proved vastly popular; and the conflict between them produced a seventy-year, world-wide ideological and political struggle; followed by powerful after-shocks. But the vision of a new and benign world order was to revive in a variety of forms.

Neither vision succeeded in shackling nationalism. Europe's central issue was still Germany and the disjunction between her inherent geographic, demographic and industrial strength, and the durability of restrictions the victors had imposed. The Germans refused to accept that imposed order, or the justice of the peace treaties. They deeply resented the imposition of reparations, though little was actually paid. The chief French objective being security against Germany, Paris wanted to compel payment and keep Germany down, and spent the next decade trying to obtain guaranteed frontiers, permanent German military inferiority, and a consolidated alliance with Britain. London, too, wanted to keep Germany in check but differed fundamentally about methods. The British thought Germany would be peaceful and cooperative once the injustices of Versailles had been removed,[7] and wanted to conciliate German opinion. These differences suffused Anglo-French relations through the inter-war period and beyond. They deeply influenced France's attempts to secure other alliances, whether across the Atlantic or in Eastern Europe. Meanwhile, efforts to return to pre-1914 conditions of economic activity were doomed, since the global economic structure had anyway been transformed. Yet by the late 1920s much economic recovery had taken place, accompanied by a general shift of emphasis from industrial to finance capitalism, implying yet further changes of economic structures and power. In 1928–9 there followed a stock market boom on both sides of the Atlantic.

In the East, attention and energies also focused on balancing power. Japan's ambitions had been fuelled by military and industrial growth, by wartime acquisitions and by the collapse of China and Russia into revolution and civil war. But the arms limits agreed by the 1921–2 Washington Naval Conference seemed likely to let the Pacific avoid the naval competition that had proved so destructive in pre-1914 Europe. Moreover, a stable and prosperous Japan was moving to liberal and representative government, with fruitful external economic ties, especially to the USA. During the 1920s America absorbed 40 per cent of Japan's exports and US banks provided 40 per cent of its foreign investment. Yet this moderate liberalism was not supported by the bureaucratic and military elites. And Japanese pride was deeply affronted by Australian, Canadian and US bans on oriental immigration and land purchase. But Japan also exercised increasing economic influence in China, where it supplied 90 per cent of foreign investment. Chinese resentment grew, and the Guomindang turned to Moscow. After Sun Yixiang's death his successor, Jiang, adopted a widely supported policy of national unification and liberation. But by 1927 he turned against his communist allies, earning golden opinions in the United States which restored China's tariff autonomy. However, that implied a challenge to Japanese economic interests and inflamed opinion in Tokyo.

Then came economic disaster. The stock market bust was followed by a banking collapse and the unravelling of much of the world network of investment and trade. The Great Depression of 1929–32 followed. Employment and production collapsed, bringing massive social unrest. The USA stopped lending money, called in former loans and liquidated assets. The disaster spread. Britain and France stopped lending, too, and a European financial panic followed. Britain went off the gold standard in 1931, signalling the end of the existing international monetary system as well as of Britain's own financial pre-eminence. German industrial production was halved. In the USA, industrial production and national income dropped by half rendering almost a quarter of the workforce unemployed. One third of the banks closed their doors, and wholesale prices dropped proportionately.

World trade suffered as the USA, France, Germany and others, including the free trade champion Britain, raised tariffs to protect home industries. American imports dropped by two thirds. Throughout Europe, depression and mass unemployment fuelled a cry for protection and state welfare programmes. In Holland, in 1929–30 unemployment multiplied by five. By 1933, while the Dutch were virtuously but disastrously sticking to the gold standard, over one third of their merchant fleet was lying idle. Wages dropped. Similar things were happening everywhere.

These disasters, and the social misery they brought, strongly contributed to the progress of fascism in general and German national socialism in particular. In January 1933 Adolf Hitler became German Chancellor. The new government made short work of French diplomatic defences. In 1934 came a non-aggression pact with Poland; a year later Germany repudiated the disarmament provisions of the 1919 Versailles Peace Treaty, reintroduced universal conscription and by plebiscite returned the Saar territory (under French occupation since the war) to Germany. France and Russia promptly concluded mutual assistance pacts with Czechoslovakia, but a new Anglo-German naval agreement allowed sharp increases in the German Navy. By 1936 the Germans reoccupied the previously demilitarized Rhineland. Neither France nor Britain reacted: Britain, in particular, still hoped that, by conceding Germany's more reasonable claims, peace might be preserved or, at least, time gained for rearmament. Germany went on to assist the military rebellion in Spain which, after three years of civil war, brought General Franco to power. By 1938 Austria had been absorbed. A year later Czechoslovakia was occupied and Hitler opened the European sector of the Second World War by attacking Poland.

In Japan, too, the Great Depression proved devastating. Unemployment rose and exports to the USA dropped sharply. In 1929–30 the price of Japan's raw silk fell by three quarters and silk exports to America by 40 per cent. Lower export income meant less money to buy the oil, coal, iron, rice on which Japan depended. Japan also moved from parliamentary system towards military dictatorship and the idea of a neo-colonial relationship with Manchuria and China looked increasingly attractive. The successful occupation of Manchuria confirmed the army's political dominance in Tokyo. America was cautious and Britain even less willing to antagonize Japan, whose business leaders sympathized with a policy of rearmament which helped to multiply Japanese industrial production by five between 1930 and the bombing of Pearl Harbor in 1941. By July 1937 an accidental clash between Chinese and

Japanese troops near Beijing led to undeclared war. The USA was drawn in after its potentially crippling 1940 economic sanctions against Japan were followed by the Pearl Harbor attack at the end of 1941.

These changes in the Pacific balance relegated the British, French and Dutch to powers of the second or even third rank. The British had long understood that their resources were wholly inadequate to preserve their positions in both Europe and Asia.[8] The Dutch adopted even lower postures while the French, following their 1940 defeat by Germany, were also forced to come to terms with Japan.

It is unnecessary to follow the course of the Second World War in any detail here. Suffice it to say that it ended Europe's role as the arbiter of world politics. By 1945 almost every state of Central and Western Europe had been, in turn, defeated, occupied, despoiled. World-wide some 50 million – soldiers and civilians – had died. Europe was exhausted, economically ruined, politically an object rather than a subject, and effectively divided between the spheres of influence of two superpowers newly dominating the world, the Soviet Union and the United States. The Europeans' will and capacity to rule overseas, having already declined for half a century, dropped to vanishing point. The First World War had already exhausted the desire for imperial expansion and governments had accepted far-flung responsibilities and burdens in a spirit of weary resignation rather than in hopes of great advantage. Now, after a war so clearly fought for national preservation and independence, as well as ideological purpose, most colonial claims to independent status were likely to find even less resistance.

Since the beginning of the century, then, the colonial powers had seen a steadily increasing gap between their powers and responsibilities, between resources and commitments. Not only that but they faced an insoluble dilemma. Whatever strategy of governance or modernization they adopted turned out to undermine their rule. Intervention in the colonies could not help being a solvent of the local social order. The increasingly detailed and technical decision-making of modern governments, not to mention changes of economic structure, demanded an educated administrative class. This had two paths to power. One was a 'long march through the institutions' of administration. Alternatively, bright young nationalists could help transform local or inchoate resentments into more powerful and organized forms of dissent, eventually leading to the formation of Western-style political parties. Where the colonizing power developed or cooperated with such Westernized elites, it strengthened them at its own expense and that of traditional rulers. Where it supported local rulers, they tended over time to become discredited. Western interests and duties alike demanded local economic development, yet local businessmen wanted to monopolize local markets, if necessary under nationalist flags. Altogether, the Europeans found themselves triggering developments which they could neither stop nor reverse. However well-meaning their strategies, against local vitality and ingenuity, and the growth of local nationalism, they ultimately had no defence.

Modernization and westernization were critical. Western law and sanitation, medical services and irrigation, produced large and frequently unmanageable population increases. Indonesia had 28.4 million by 1900, 41 million thirty years later and over 200 million by the end of the twentieth century. India's population grew between 1900 and 1930 from 294 to 353 million, and growth accelerated further through the 1930s. Governance became vastly more difficult. The colonial powers could not increase agricultural production enough to keep pace with population growth; or to satisfy the increasing land hunger in the villages. The resulting unrest created a stronger base for populist and national politics. Western industrial capitalism and local nationalism reinforced each other in various ways. As early as the 1840s, when Palmerston forced China, Egypt and the Ottomans to open their empires to trade, commerce and foreign loans, that had brought changes which none of these societies or governments could cope with, while the resulting dislocation of local economies and the shortcomings of local institutions stimulated xenophobia. But the British, French and Dutch brought more than a wave of industry and technology. Improved communications broke down localism and tribalism. Manufacturing and mining produced urbanization, an industrial proletariat and other changes in class structures. European rule produced fundamental economic and social changes, in many cases ruthlessly. As Marx had pointed out, the British drove Indians, sometimes brutally, through unavoidable stages of material and intellectual development, and did so in less time and with greater effect than Indians could have achieved for themselves.

Westernized education created a modern educated class with new political and religious ideas. Christian evangelicals and secular liberalism alike undermined the belief in Europe's right, let alone duty, to rule. They fostered notions of the brotherhood of man which differed sharply from, for instance, some of the central elements of Hindu civilization. The concept of *dharma* or that which is established, provides a context in which social relations are defined as duty and where one caste, Brahmins like the Nehru family, have a duty to govern. Western ideas of rights, and equality, therefore infuriated groups committed to hierarchy or caste. Nevertheless, for many young administrators, clerks, teachers and businessmen, equality became a synonym for modernization, and modernization a path to power. Nationalist and revolutionary leaders, often scions of the old ruling groups, learned Western techniques and arguments.[9] They welcomed principles of equality and self-determination, of the rule of law and representative government. Not that they immediately demanded independence. What the *evolués* wanted was to enter a power structure they admired. Quite soon black 'Frenchmen' sat in the Paris parliament. Spain had, even earlier, transformed Inca scions into Spanish aristocrats. In the British colonies they began by wanting to be 'brown Englishmen'.[10] They had a friendly enough reception in Europe, but back home in the colonies a socially highly stratified officialdom tried to 'keep them in their place'. Only then did the drive for power extend from middle-class persuasion into the search for mass appeal. Only then did the strategies of men like Nehru in India or Hatta and Sjahrir in Indonesia become a drive for national independence. In the process the nationalists seized the very governmental machinery created, in India and Vietnam by the colonial power and in Japan by the reformers of the Meiji restoration which is discussed below. The absence of that effective machinery in China before the advent of Mao Zedong may have been critical in delaying what his era termed China's 'standing up'.

If you want to make God laugh, goes the old saying, tell Him your plans. Secular Liberalism's focus on modernization, social amelioration and reform could only mean more interference with local customs and beliefs. By a process which seems ironic only in retrospect, it was just these cultural interventions which especially stimulated a resistance increasingly defined in nationalist terms. If any one element was decisive, it was surely this. The imperial powers inevitably brought their political ideas, administrative structures, education systems and legal codes with them. Local customs which offended Western morals were suppressed. Western soldiers, administrators and wives tried to impose European social customs and habits as the gift, or assertion of a superior civilization. It was all incomparably more important in stimulating resistance than the poverty or injustice or oppression which had always been facts of local life, or economic exploitation, real though that often was. Stability, even if oppressive, could be endured, as for centuries it had always been. But cultural invasion was an affront to the very identity of local societies, which a casual imperial paternalism could only make worse. Technological change, industrialization, and the upsetting of immemorial customs, were bound to arouse strong reactions.[11] Here, too, 'India, with a large class of men educated in European principles, with strong religious and cultural traditions and social changes reflecting a century and a half of British rule, [became a] pioneer and pace-setter for the modern tropical empires. ...'[12]

Groups, like individuals, cling to identity and custom, and yearn for recognition. Nationalism has everywhere sprung from just these desires for the maintenance and recognition of a self-determining culture and society. Once Asian elite groups understood European ways, they saw all this clearly, and said so. They seized on the contagious notions that each culture has a natural right to political autonomy and, hence, that the idea of the nation should be tied to that of the state. It was from this perspective that Rabindranath Tagore, in his presidential address to Congress in 1908, charged that the British '... are behaving as if we [i.e. Indians] do not exist ... as if we are huge cyphers', and added 'The only real gift is the gift of strength; all other offerings are vain', for without strength there could be no equality or justice. As long as India remained weak, she would continue to be ignored and humiliated.[13] As noted earlier, Soetan Sjahrir, the first prime minister of independent Indonesia, made much the same point some forty years later about Indonesia.

The First World War greatly stimulated colonial economic development, urbanization and social change. Colonial industries expanded, both to help supply the armies in France or the Middle East with everything from weapons to food, and to replace the manufactured goods which metropolitan industries, now devoted to war, could no longer supply. By 1918 Australia, Canada, India, some parts of Latin America and, of course, Japan, had developed industrial sectors well able to compete with European exports. Many colonies had also begun to look to Japan or America for supply. Japan took a major slice of Britain's former textile markets while the development of coal and oil in the USA, India and the Middle East slashed foreign demand for British coal.

Even more important were the political and intellectual consequences of the war. In Britain and France, the public mind began to come to grips with the globalization of international politics and changed dynamics of power; with the growth of Liberalism and anti-imperialism; with the rise of labour as a political force, based on trade unions which distrusted overseas effort, and begrudged the resources it needed. The rise of organized labour even implied a potential for fraternal alliance between the oppressed at home and the downtrodden in the colonies. In the eyes of the old order, it was all deeply subversive.

By 1918 the tectonic plates of politics had therefore shifted. For London, Paris or The Hague, the centrality of problems in Europe made the affairs of Vietnam or Ceylon or Indonesia, even of India, into minor orders of business. Except, perhaps, for the global dangers posed by the Bolshevik revolution and its agency, the Communist International (Comintern), established in 1924. Yet the trend towards national independence was becoming general; even local rebellions, previously so divisive, were now more likely to unify colonies. It was all an unpleasant surprise to those colonizers who had thought of nationalism as an essentially European phenomenon.

It became increasingly difficult to resist in the colonies the ideas of liberty and equality which had dominated European politics since 1789; or those of 'national self-determination' which became one of the organizing principles of Europe after 1918. Yet they rendered empire and nationalism inherently incompatible. Four empires – Russian, Ottoman, Austro-Hungarian, Hohenzollern – had just been dissolved. The West's own pronouncements hailed equality and self-determination. As Woodrow Wilson told a cheering US Congress on 11 February 1918, the '... peoples may now be dominated and governed only by their own consent ...' ; and Europe was duly carved up in terms of his fourteen points programme.[14] The British Prime Minister, David Lloyd George, declared in 1918 that self-determination principles applied to the colonies as much as to Europe. Yet 'national self-determination' was bound to be a political time-bomb.

These principles, the invention of the League of Nations, the mandate system for ex-enemy colonies, the new British emphasis on Dominion status, reduced the whole concept of imperialism to something temporary and limited. So did the denunciations of empire from Woodrow Wilson and Lenin. So did the example set by the new Soviet Union's at first admirably egalitarian nationalities policies, though its founding commissar, Joseph Stalin, soon changed tack. These ideas limited British, French and Dutch freedom of movement, while the fun, the pleasure and most of the pride had anyway gone out of the business of running empires. It no longer offered a great and glorious destiny. Novel ideas about trusteeship and service to the colonies might impose fresh obligations, but these were minority preoccupations.

Much of this was absorbed by colonial troops and civilians returning from Britain, France and the Middle East. Sailors and soldiers from dominions and colonies, from African members of the French Union to Moslems from the Punjab or farm boys from the Australian outback, had fought in France or the Middle East or at sea. They came home having learned much more of European ways and ideas; and familiarity did not increase admiration. The war's conduct had starkly displayed the fissures in Western and Christian cultures and the fierce hatreds of Christian civilization. European claims to superior wisdom, not to mention goodness, were less and less plausible. Moreover, the Europeans actually fanned colonial nationalist fervour as a weapon against one another: the Germans stirred up the Mahgreb against the French, as the British and French stirred up Arab feeling in Syria and Mesopotamia against the Turks. It was largely to prevent similar Turkish or German subversion in India that London issued the declaration of 20 August 1917 promising 'the gradual development of self-governing institutions' there. The Allies used the same weapon against Austria-Hungary throughout the war. After 1917 the new Soviet Union went on stirring up such feelings, as the Japanese were to do in Asia, with huge effect, between 1930 and 1945. From an Asian point of view, therefore, colonial contributions to the allied war effort deserved a handsome reward. And if the Turkish and Austrian empires could be replaced by self-determining nations, why could the same not happen elsewhere? What was sauce for the European goose could hardly be denied to the Asian gander.

In other ways, too, the war weakened Europe and created new centres of power. Demography itself strongly encouraged the British, French and Dutch withdrawal from colonial possessions. Indeed, it continued to change the whole global balance of power. Europe's population increases and emigration rates had populated many overseas possessions but after 1900 increasing birth rates in Asia and declining ones in Europe, together with the bloodletting of the First World War and devastating post-war epidemics,[15] changed that. Twenty years earlier the German Kaiser William II had sounded the alarm about the 'Yellow Peril'. By 1901 the Australians, perennially conscious of the weaknesses of their thinly populated continent, adopted 'White Australia' legislation, followed by similar enactments in New Zealand, Canada and the United States. All were worried about Asia's 'teeming millions'. After 1918 such fears grew. American restrictions on Japanese immigration and land-holding accentuated trans-Pacific tensions. And as late as 1951 a senior Australian politician, R.G. Casey, remarked that 'Unless Australia doubles her population, in a generation our children will be pulling rickshaws.'[16] By 1953 the Chinese census figure was 583 million people. Forty years later, the number had doubled.

The empires had economic problems, too. The 1920s saw increased production in Europe, while declining prices for their raw materials and food diminished the colonies' ability to buy European manufactures. Then came the turmoil of the Great Depression. This virulent economic downturn was especially hard on primary producers as the economic 'complementarity' between colonies and metropoles broke down. Moreover, much European technology and capital had by then been transferred overseas, eroding Europe's earlier technical and industrial advantages. Hence the industrial nations became even more anxious to protect domestic employment, which meant less buying of colonial products and smaller sales overseas. Which allowed massive export-led growth in Japan in the 1930s, largely through commercial penetration of Europe's Asian empires.

The patterns were complex. After 1918 the British found themselves depending much more heavily on overseas investment income and debt servicing by the Dominions, whose London-held reserves supported the continued role of sterling as an international currency. The 1929–31 crisis brought a strong sense of imperial solidarity. But by the 1930s British overseas investment flows had declined sharply compared with 1914, as did trade with the empire. After 1929 the Dutch East Indies experienced both declining imports and diminished local purchasing power as many Dutch, paid from home, had their civil service salaries cut. Various colonies imposed duties even on imports from their own metropoles. Students rioted in Jakarta and Rangoon while Malay peasants, faced with a collapse in the rubber market, went back to subsistence production. In such circumstances urban workers and colonial peasantry alike became radicalized and the political and social collaboration of locals with the colonial power, on which the British and Dutch had especially relied, broke down. Trust in the wisdom and benevolence of European government was further undermined, the loss of support in rural society being especially significant. Not everyone found this surprising. Back in 1915 Lenin had argued that the war would produce new extra-European power centres and a colonial awakening, and European power would be decisively weakened.

The trend towards imperial dissolution was therefore set well before 1939. But the Second World War accelerated it decisively. Pearl Harbor, the fall of Singapore, the Japanese occupation of Hong Kong, Malaya, Indonesia and Burma, all demonstrated that the West was not invincible. European prestige and power in Southeast Asia were destroyed. While the Germans made a cardinal error in Russia by oppressing groups that had welcomed the *Wehrmacht* as liberators, the Japanese in Asia knew better. From the beginning, their conquests were under the banner of 'Asia for the Asiatics' and the expulsion of the Europeans. Except for India, all Europe's Asian colonies fell to a Japan which strongly encouraged anti-colonialist and nationalist passions. Local governments were created, based on national movements: in 1942 in Burma and in 1945 in Indo-China and Indonesia. The Japanese also created Indian, Indonesian and other nationalist militias as their allies. As early as 1941–2 the British in Malaya and Singapore were astonished to get so little local help against the Japanese invader; and even more surprised that, though 2 million Indian volunteers fought with Britain, the Japanese recruited an Indian nationalist force to fight on their side. The four years of Japan's 'Greater East Asian Co-Prosperity sphere' confirmed national consciousness in Asia and encouraged local national movements. Certain economic factors pointed in similar directions. As economic exchanges between Europe and the occupied Asian colonies ceased, local production was encouraged, further eroding imperial links. Even in India, relations with an embattled Britain were transformed. Nationalist leaders there and in Ceylon prudently secured a firm promise of independence after the war.

A further and irresistible challenge to the European empires came from the greatest of the allied powers. For America, the war was a moral crusade against German and Japanese imperialism and for democracy, not for a restoration of the colonial system. Washington's support for anti-colonial nationalism was outlined in the 'Atlantic Charter', signed by President Roosevelt and Prime Minister Churchill in August 1941. It said that Britain and the USA 'respected the rights of all peoples to choose the form of government under which they live'. Together with a later statement of war aims, this meant that little room was left for imperial constructs.[17] By 1945 international opinion expected everyone to be a citizen of some sovereign state which was a member of the new United Nations Organization. This would safeguard separate and legally equal nation-and-statehood, under law, for the world's peoples.

Colonial nationalist leaders were further encouraged by each other's example, beginning with the early assertion of self-determination in the white colonies of settlement. Gandhi's successes in India were a signal to to other parts of the world, including Africa. Pan-Islamic movements developed, stretching from the Indonesian archipelago across South Asia and the Middle East to North Africa. By the time of the Afro-Asian conference at Bandung in 1955, the whole arc of Asia from Japan to Persia was occupied by independent states, conscious of their power and, often, solidarity *vis-à-vis* the West.

Naturally, the ways in which Asian societies developed national forms varied greatly. The earliest and most dramatic – even explosive –

adjustment came in Japan. It became the outstanding example of the adoption, under Western pressures, of economic and political modernization, and nation-state forms.

By the middle of the nineteenth century the Tokugawa system displayed significant weaknesses. It was coping poorly not only with domestic change but with external threats. To be sure, Japan was insulated and never colonized. But by the middle 1800s, developments in Asia and the Pacific clearly brought threats, actual or implied, from the great imperial and military powers (by then including the United States). Retreat into isolation was impossible. The combination of domestic problems and fears of external pressure forced a modernization programme: for government, education, industry, the military and for society itself. It produced a modernizing nation-state revolution, which enlisted many traditional social values in the service of reform.

By the 1830s and 1840s foreign ships, notably American, came to negotiate for trade. The Japanese refused, but it was clear that foreign naval power was becoming much too great for Japan to resist. American intrusion finally proved decisive. On 8 July 1853 Commodore Matthew Perry anchored his armed squadron in the mouth of Tokyo Bay, inducing the Japanese to accept a letter from the US President to the Emperor. The Japanese saw they could not resist Perry, let alone the much larger British Far Eastern squadrons. Tokyo itself, with a million people, relied entirely on food supplies carried by water, and was therefore open to blockade. When Perry returned in 1854, the Japanese agreed by the Treaty of Kanagawa to establish a consulate, to open up two small harbours and to accept some limited trade. Within a year, similar treaties were concluded with the British and Russians. Commercial treaties proper followed, with the British and then the USA. The Japanese deeply resented these 'unequal treaties' and their impositions on Japan. These included special treatment and extra-territorial rights for foreigners, and limitations on Japan's right to tariff protection. The country's rulers worried fruitlessly for a decade what to do about them. Worst of all, they brought a number of Westerners to Japan – whom the locals regarded with great hostility.

After much domestic turmoil, the great break came in 1868. Shogun Tokugawa Keiki resigned, and modernizers took over. Not that their slogans threatened modernization: on the contrary, they claimed that they merely wanted to restore the Emperor's ancient powers, to expel the foreigners and abrogate certain treaties signed under foreign pressure. It was a revolution apparently led by the Emperor himself.

Furthermore, the Emperor Meiji, though only sixteen when he came to the throne, was an unusually able and intelligent man. The leaders of the revolt were equally intelligent, with little emotional commitment to the old order. Themselves *samurai*, they were also remarkably young. Of the three or four most powerful, the oldest was forty-one and the youngest a mere twenty-seven. Once in power they quickly saw that their original programme would produce disaster. The fifteen years since Commodore Perry's arrival had shown that the foreign barbarians were too strong to be simply expelled. Moreover, the last thing Japan needed was to retreat into ancient habits. The country must be modernized to match foreign strength. Feudalism had to yield to a centralized modern government, able to make drastic governmental, economic and social reforms. Only then could Japan hope to be secure.

A year after the collapse of the shogunate the four greatest western feudal lords – who could see that feudalism had had its day – surrendered their fiefs in return for financial compensation, thereby also relieving themselves of the expense of running estates. They stopped being rulers but became millionaires. Within a couple of years others followed their example. Feudalism gave way to a central bureaucracy operating through a system of prefectures. Modernization turned out to be explosive. Internal stability was assured, taxes were reformed and there was a sound currency. Railways were built to connect towns and cities, which were given a regular water supply. Streets were paved. Ships were bought, reverse engineered, and more of them built at home. Modern banks were created. So, too, were great trading houses; although the two greatest, Mitsui and Mitsubishi, had started in the Tokugawa period with rice merchandising. Feudal restrictions on domestic trade were abolished and quality controls imposed on exports. Modern industry was encouraged, especially in fields useful for military power. Private manufacturing developments were encouraged with easy credit, technical assistance and subsidies. Here were the very methods of government support destined to yield similarly brilliant results for Japan after 1960. To be sure, many new ventures went bankrupt, partly because the Japanese were unfamiliar with industrial machinery and importing foreign technicians was inordinately expensive; but modernization went forward.

However, real power was closely and centrally held. At its core, political clout was confined to a mere one or two dozen men from two clans close to the throne. If there were manoeuvres, disputes, resignations among these groupings, the public was given no inkling of them. In a country which, by 1870, numbered some 31 million people, the job of the general public was simply to pay taxes, develop the country, serve in the armed forces and obey orders.

Of course things were not quite so simple. The new regime created a bureaucracy with recruitment and promotion systems comparable to those of France and Germany. From 1900 this was increasingly staffed by graduates of Japan's new universities. But Japanese were also urged to study abroad, to become teachers, engineers, scientists. As the young men of the Meiji revolution had said from the start: 'Knowledge shall be sought throughout the world so as to strengthen the foundations of imperial rule.'[18] Returning students were likely to have important careers as intellectual, economic and political reformers. Foreign experts were imported as well. Starting in 1871, German doctors gave Japanese medicine a German cast while English and American scholars were important in other fields: all of which also meant learning foreign languages, reading foreign books, absorbing foreign ideas[19] and better educational organization. Japan already had high literacy rates, but by 1871 a ministry was created to run nation-wide education. Within thirty years, it catered for nine tenths of Japan's school-age children. Initially, children of both sexes received sixteen months of compulsory schooling; that was extended to three years in 1880 and six by 1907. Many of these medical, economic and social reforms no doubt also contributed to the sharp increase in Japan's population: from 35 million in 1873 to some 55 million in 1918.

In the process Japan learned that foreign cultures, like those of America or Britain, encompassed very different political systems. The Meiji revolutionaries also learned from the French Revolution, and the contemporary backwardness of Russia, what happened to regimes which remained too autocratic for too long. They therefore considered representative politics. As early as 1868 they issued a document saying that 'deliberative assemblies shall be widely established and all matters decided by public discussion'. The idea caught on. Within ten years, and in spite of some repression, many Japanese agitated for an elected assembly. If the Emperor was by definition above criticism, his senior officials were not. Imprisonment and fines notwithstanding, people continued to criticize. Eventually, the rulers saw that repression might weaken Japan, not only at home but internationally, in a world which believed in democracy.

Consequently, in 1881 the Emperor declared he would grant a constitution. It would provide for an elected assembly, and come into force in eight years, in 1889. Within a mere twenty years from 1868, Japan would move from feudalism to a parliamentary system. But the constitutional model was Germany: until very recently a patchwork of principalities, now forcibly unified under an imperial ruler; also, a martial people who valued military power. Only a few years ago, in 1870–71, they had won the Franco-Prussian war and become the greatest military power in Europe. Given that model, the Japanese oligarchy was determined to hold on to effective power. The constitution looked democratic, but in practice allowed the emperor and the ruling clans to retain control. There was an elected Diet, but it lacked substantive power, including over finance. All it could do was debate, and send an address to the throne: that, at least, was the form. In practice the Diet, where a political party system had formed almost immediately, clamoured for greater powers. It also wanted Cabinet made responsible to it. When the real rulers refused, the Diet held up Bills. Frequently, there was deadlock with the governing groups trying to dissolve the House. However, actual supreme government was organized under the emperor whose imperial line, it was now claimed, was descended from the Gods. Cabinet ministers were not responsible to the Diet but appointed or dismissed at his pleasure. Alongside Cabinet, a new governing council was created, composed solely of senior members of the oligarchy and the court. It was the inner fortress of real power, advising the throne in secret. And once the emperor made a decision, all debate had to stop. In sum, the constitution was a gift from the emperor to the people; and gifts can be revocable.

Japan's leaders also understood that military power mattered both for defence against the West and for government control over the nation itself. In January 1873 a new conscription law made all men liable for three years active military service, followed by four years in the reserves. This universal conscription may have been the single most revolutionary step in Japan's modernization. For 300 years no commoner had even been allowed to possess a sword. The entire social system had depended on a demarcation between *samurai* and commoners. Suddenly, the demilitarized masses became the foundation of a huge, modernized and centralized military machine whose officers came from among the 400 000 prestigious armed *samurai* retainers of the erstwhile feudal lords. Those who did not become officers could enter the new bureaucracies of the modernizing state, or were simply turned loose – but allowed to engage in business, trade and agriculture, hitherto forbidden to *samurai*. A new navy was also created. More yet, it was established that in matters of military and naval command – as distinct from administration or finance – the chiefs of staff were independent of the civil government. They were solely responsible to the emperor who was, directly, in supreme command of the army and navy. This made the armed services doubly independent from the civilian government.

A new kind of state had clearly emerged. Centralization, the administrative state, national enthusiasm, the capacity for mobilization had been achieved. Educational and technical advances were pursued with remarkable energy and single-mindedness. Yet the creation of this new national state also heralded an age of Japanese militarism and expansion. The country's *samurai* traditions had prepared it well; and the military were now free from civilian control. Moreover, foreign conquest and colonial acquisition were as popular as they were in other countries. Imperialism was admired and imitated everywhere. Japan's rulers could see that Western nations were scrambling for parts of Africa and Germany was loudly claiming a 'place in the sun'. Obviously, if Japan wanted to be recognized as a major modern power, she would also have to have possessions.

At the start of the 1870s an expedition made Okinawa part of Japan. Nine years later the Ryukyu islands became a Japanese prefecture. In 1875 Japan completed acquisition of the Kuriles. Japan also became embroiled over Korea, where Beijing insisted on its sovereignty, which Japan refused to recognize; and there was repeated friction in the 1880s. Indeed, one reason why China yielded Vietnam to the French in 1885 was that the Japanese threat was much nearer and more urgent than French dangers in the distant south. However, much the most urgent and emotional issues for Japan were at home: those 'unequal treaties' imposed by the Western powers in the 1850s, which the Japanese, like the Chinese a century later, deeply resented. Yet simple xenophobia was no answer and the new rulers were cautious about relations with Western powers which were unwilling to give up their treaty rights. Indeed, the Japanese could not agree among themselves on the specifics of treaty revision, and no faction would let another have the sole credit for any changes. Whatever treaty amendment might be negotiated by one group was immediately denounced by the others as inadequate.

Some of these problems came together in 1895, when Japan went to war with China over the issue of Korea. The government wanted the war and the public was enthusiastic. Japan was totally successful, acquiring Formosa in the process, but the Western powers intervened to limit Japanese gains. The effects were twofold. One was to cement the oligarchy's power and increase the influence of the military. The other was to give Japan a bitter grievance against the West, especially the Russians. The trouble was, however, that while Russia might pose immediate dangers, she was a great power. To have any hope of revenge, Japan would have to be even stronger, her citizens more heavily taxed, the armed forces further strengthened.

The Diet would have to cooperate: so party politicians were brought into the Cabinet, and the Diet bribed. The army and navy secured an imperial rescript of critical importance for the future workings of the whole government. It laid down that only serving generals and admirals could act as Ministers for War or the Navy. Consequently these officers, being on the active list, remained subject to the orders of the commanders in chief of the two services, not the orders of whoever happened to be prime minister. If the service chiefs disliked Cabinet policy, or wanted ministerial changes, they could order the Ministers of War and Navy to resign, and refuse to nominate successors. Such control over service representatives in Cabinet meant essential control of the whole government while the Diet could do nothing.

This system ensured that, for most of the time up to 1945, the military remained in effective control. Initially, Japan's power and influence were hugely increased. The 1905 victory over Russia astonished the world and brought Japan immediate great power status. In 1910 she annexed Korea. Although some elder statesmen counselled caution, others wanted more expansion. Japan being poor in agricultural resources and raw materials, with a vital need for security of supply, her leaders concluded that the alternatives were expansion across the Pacific, in the face of US opposition, or on the Asian continent while keeping the USA acquiescent. Expansion into China looked like a low-risk strategy.

The First World War offered opportunities. France and Britain were willing to buy Japanese friendship with Pacific concessions while Russia and Germany were wholly committed in Europe. Japan took charge of Germany's – now defenceless – Pacific island and Asian possessions, including the formerly German area in Shandong, Fujian and Manchuria, thus doubling the size of Japan's overseas empire. By 1915 Tokyo demanded further concessions from China, including land, railway and mining rights in Manchuria. China was even asked to accept Japanese political, financial and military advisers and to place the Chinese police under Japanese command. The war in Europe benefited Japan in other ways. Japanese industry grew apace as Japanese conglomerates took over Asian markets and greatly increased commercial penetration of the USA. Japan became a major importer of raw materials and exporter of manufactures and her gold reserves multiplied by one hundred.

Domestically, military ascendancy grew stronger still and by 1918 the army seemed almost willing to act independently. In spite of more democratic trends in the 1920s this made the domestic political history of Japan for most of the first half of the twentieth century as uninteresting as its foreign and military policies were tragic. Japan had indeed been modernized and shrugged off foreign influence in an upsurge of national passion. But the hundred years following the Meiji restoration proved yet again, if proof was needed, that modern socio-economic ideas often cohabit uneasily with older customs and beliefs. For all the modernization, Western liberal and secular assumptions remained foreign to much of the Japanese polity. As late as the 1980s, brand-new Japanese factories built in Europe or North America could only be opened with the aid of ancient rites and geomancy. And, as the 1930s painfully demonstrated, neither modernity nor the administrative nation-state guarantees peaceful behaviour.

Apart from Japan, it was the colonies of European settlement that set the pace in self-assertion. In England, men like Lord Milner had seen the empire's future as one of states which, domestically independent, were nevertheless developing a common civilization. But the practical interests of the colonies and the metropole rarely marched in step and the desire for imperial unity dissipated under the pressure of events. In their own urgent interests, Canada, Australia, New Zealand and South Africa moved – were driven – towards separatism, self-determination and protectionism. They would not allow Britain to decide local defence issues nor accept automatic defence commitments abroad. They followed, reluctantly and for very different reasons, the American example by becoming new national states: Canada between 1867 and 1873, Australia in 1901 and South Africa in 1910, following the Boer War. In 1914 they fought under their own flags and the war produced an upsurge of national feeling and a demand for equality with the UK. These claims were asserted, sometimes raucously, by the diminutive Australian Prime Minister, Billy Hughes. By 1918–19 Australia, New Zealand, Canada and South Africa had to all intents and purposes become independent countries: they demanded, and obtained, independent roles in the peace conference, signed the peace treaties independently, developed independent views and interests in foreign affairs and became separate members of the League of Nations. So did India.

The 1931 Statute of Westminster, giving a legal basis to the (British) Commonwealth, merely confirmed that these countries and Britain enjoyed equality of status; that they had full parliamentary autonomy but continued to rely on Britain for military protection and, in an increasingly protectionist post-Depression world, for markets. Yet Britain also saw them as an essential prop for the UK economy. The

Ottawa trade deal a year later established a system of imperial preference, while the UK continued as banker to the sterling area. But for Australia, New Zealand and even Canada, the power politics of the 1930s, when logic might have suggested common policies, actually emphasized how their needs diverged from Britain's. The British worried about depression economics, about relations with the USA, and especially about the economic and military recovery of Germany. But the Australians and New Zealanders, while also worrying about economics, focused on the rising military, naval and export threats from Tokyo; and became more assertive about their independent interests and wishes, which included strong support for the appeasement of the fascist powers. The Japanese attack on China in 1937, followed by Pearl Harbor and the collapse of the Franco-British positions in Indo-China, Malaya and Singapore, confirmed the Pacific focus of all their interests, not merely of their security. It also confirmed their reliance on the United States. Australia was, and would remain 'primarily a Pacific nation and every question of national policy' would have to be considered in a Pacific context.[20] It was a reality which various Australian governments were to rediscover, apparently afresh, fifty years later.

In India, nationalist developments were altogether different. British control from the middle of the nineteenth century made the sub-continent for the first time into a single political entity. That fact, combined as it inevitably was with the *mores* and philosophies of Britain, carried the seeds of destruction of imperial control. Political and administrative unification gradually produced a psychologically effective sense of 'Indianness' which in time arched over the kaleidoscopes of opinion, caste, locality and ethnic grouping, creating a national identity 'molded out of the pressures and opportunities of power, often by active gerrymandering of the boundaries of individual and collective selves',[21] which became a counterfoil to the nationalist consciousness conveyed by Europe. It created a 'national' forum within which Indian, and potentially separatist, pressures could be built up. Once that process was under way, the writing was on the wall for British rule, whatever the liberal imperialists in London might say and however humane and selfless many British officials might be.

Unavoidably, the British promoted this, sometimes in contradictory ways. The very scale and complexity of India continued to compel a mode of government with, not against, local views of what was politically proper. Yet the processes of modernization and industrialization destroyed traditional habits. By the 1880s many traditional beliefs had been weakened and many of the independent institutions of Indian political life had effectively broken down. In place of Indian law and administration came British administrators, legal codes and a modern judiciary. New property rights in land established, among other things, a new class of land owners. The system favoured modernized professional groups and, naturally, its own employees. The economy was remoulded. Its context was a commitment by Delhi to impose no barriers to imports from the UK; to continue to meet India's obligations in London;[22] and to maintain the Indian Army, at India's cost, while making it available for imperial missions elsewhere.

The British also, both officially and privately, insisted on social, class and racial differentiation between themselves and the Indians; which undermined that identification of local political elites with the imperial power which is always a precondition for imperial stability. It also encouraged the idea that Indians might be considered as a single grouping. Equally unsettling were the implications of Britain's own expanding franchise. A special Indian ruling class which happened to be British was one thing. One alien ruling class had followed another for much of India's history. But once authority resided in the entire British people, permanent governance by that people was something else. Thus defined, a right to rule could only rest on a claimed superiority of race, not just of class or culture; hardly a proposition which British liberals, or the churches or even the trade unions, would support or the Indians accept.

The Indian reaction went through the classic three stages of developing national assertion. For twenty years, beginning in 1885, there developed a grouping, mostly of upper class and educated Indians, who sought greater Indian participation in the new system. That was followed by some fifteen years of demands for independence by bourgeois groups working over the heads of indifferent and supine masses. Only then came the change to a mass movement, and the organization of a party structure capable of managing it.

In India, as elsewhere, the – at first, tiny – educated elite was the driving force. The early Indian politicians, many with a Western education, were strongly pro-British. But they wanted equal opportunities and by the later 1870s educated Indians, often involved in local self-government, found it hard to secure equal treatment from the British, or to join the governing class. They formed societies in Bombay and Calcutta to discuss problems and created the beginnings of European-style political parties. Indeed, the British themselves helped to create and even lead the political group that would later mobilize the country and demand independence. The Indian National Congress first met in 1885 in Bombay, its formation made possible by the new train and telegraph services criss-crossing the country, and supported by British members of the ICS, notably A.O. Hume. A year later Congress met in Calcutta. At this stage, it concentrated on equal treatment for educated elites, rather than general political activity. Congress meetings were conducted in English. Some of the British suspected this would lead to nationalism, but the administration thought it a helpful safety valve for Indian opinion. British power continued to depend on a popular acceptability, which largely continued. Indeed, many Indians thought British rule was better than rule by the princes or soldiers who would dominate after independence. 'The people of India submitted to British rule because it was infinitely better than that which obtained in India at the end of the last century [i.e. the 18th] ... and better than any other rule which it is possible to have at the present day.'[23] In any case, for most Indians the organizing principle of life was not yet politics but religion.

Still, by 1900 more Indians felt they might be a nation. The growth of Congress, improved communications and a single, India-wide administration, had other consequences. In focusing on the educated, Congress proved more attractive for Hindus, who were interested in education, than for Moslems. Consequently, as government became more bureaucratic, Hindus carried greater weight. The British, however, distrusted the educated, allegedly subtle and devious, Indian 'babu' and admired the soldierly Punjabi Moslems of the best Indian Army regiments. In time, just as Congress underestimated Moslem political consciousness, the British underrated the force of Tagore's search for power and the growth of Indian nationalism.

Hindu-Moslem relations continued to be difficult. Curzon's 1905 attempt to partition Bengal between them produced mass agitation. Moslems felt Congress did not understand them and in 1906 launched the Moslem League. In 1909 another viceroy, Morley, legislated for expanded regional councils and suggested a separate Moslem electorate. But Congress suspected that Moslem separatism stemmed from British encouragement. Also, by 1908–09 Congress was making nationalist claims and moving towards demands for independence proper, so when the capital moved to Delhi in 1911, nationalists saw this as an abandonment of Calcutta's political activism, as well as a claim to Mogul-like pre-eminence. Indians could also see that British administrators disliked the – frequently Hindu – money-lending class whose numbers had tripled over thirty years and against whose demands the

ICS wanted to protect peasant lands. The service was still giving priority to 'native interests', meaning local customs and social patterns, as against India's own modernizers. Suspicions on such varied grounds persisted through the rest of Britain's time in India.

The first Congress generation, then, did not seek a transfer of power. They thought control of the masses unachievable. What they desired was acceptance by the British ruling groups. That began to change during the first decade of the twentieth century and changed more sharply still during and after the First World War in which India responded to Britain's need. But the stimulus then given to national feelings by the war was not confined to Indian regiments returning home. Even more important were the beginnings of India-wide political organization. Two events were especially critical. One was an agreement, in 1916, between Congress and the Moslem League. The other, a year earlier, proved truly revolutionary.

Much of the twentieth century was decisively shaped by a few politically gifted individuals. What might the history of the world have been but for personalities like Lenin, Hitler, Mao or Roosevelt? History has always been a matter of personalities and character quite as much as of deep forces. In India, too, one man was destined to cause a political earthquake. He was a small, wiry lawyer, given to asceticism, a man of immense political cunning and something of a sanctimonious prig.[24] He was also a moral force and an empire-breaking revolutionary leader. His name was Mohandas Gandhi. In 1915 he returned from South Africa to India and started to involve himself in social and political causes. He became an immensely adept convert to populism, his preferred weapons being, always, moral pressure and non-violent methods which the British could not counter. But his issues were pragmatically specific, dealing with the actual conditions of workers and peasants. On such grass-roots issues he began to build a nationalist alliance, while also linking nationalism with traditional Hindu ideas and values. He was joined by Motilal Nehru and his son Jawaharlal, whom Gandhi converted to nationalism.[25]

These second-generation nationalist leaders were not initially much concerned with how power should be used after independence. They respected Britain and the British example: they wanted to run their own affairs while maintaining strong links with Britain, rather like the Canadians and Australians. They continued moving towards 'Dominion status', which Congress had sought as early as 1908. But they also turned Congress into a mass party; and Britain obviously lacked the means, let alone the will, to suppress such a truly mass movement. Moreover Gandhi, the greatest of these Congress leaders, enjoyed growing renown throughout India not just as politician but as a holy man. In accepting his politics, his followers also bowed to his religious standing. For the British, dealing with a politician was one thing, opposing a holy man quite another.

In India, as elsewhere, much had changed by 1918. Having been a producer and base for the war against Turkey, India now possessed 'infant industries'; and a few large-scale capitalists, like the Bombay textile magnate J.N. Tata. Almost 70 per cent of all cotton workers were in Bombay province. Much of India's steel production came from Tata Iron and Steel. As local production grew, India absorbed more Indonesian and Malay rubber and Burmese wolfram. The working class grew and cities expanded. So did a mature and bureaucratically-oriented middle class. In 1917 the British decided that their aim in India was 'responsible government'. Two years later they created provincial councils and a representative government in Delhi, and an assembly with some powers of taxation and legislation.

In the meantime, the 1918–19 influenza epidemic killed millions, prices rose, trade was disrupted and unrest grew. The Viceroy was heavy-handed in using his emergency powers, creating easy targets for Congress. Gandhi organized *satyagraha*, or non-violent mass protest, a tactic he had first developed in South Africa for use against race laws. But then, in the city of Amritsar, troops under British command shot down crowds of peaceful demonstrators. Many died. Resistance stiffened. By 1920 Gandhi controlled Congress, whose structure and constitution were reorganized to make it a truly mass movement, with his people concentrating on civil disobedience and a boycott of British goods. In 1922 he was gaoled. Protest was non-violent but other difficulties fed into the mass non-cooperation movement. For instance, Moslems were deeply offended by the Allies' post-1918 treatment of their spiritual head, the Turkish sultan. They now sought redress of such iniquities, as well as self-government. Meanwhile Hindu-Moslem divisions were exacerbated in communal riots or over matters like provincial elections. The government temporized and tried to pay more attention to Indian opinion. It was not just politics: the British had learned that the entire social fabric depended on established beliefs and social practices more than on modernization. As Beloff has put it: 'The missionary gives way to the anthropologist.'[26] But it also depended on economics. Though India had fiscal autonomy, tariffs were introduced to protect Indian cotton, iron and steel, in spite of ICS arguments that tariffs would burden poor consumers.

By the mid-1920s India was a member of the League of Nations, would shortly have its own chair at imperial conferences and was effectively recognized as an international power. But Congress, politically strong, could also be unrealistic. For example, Indian leaders thought that if Britain left, defence costs would disappear, since India had no quarrel with anyone. Such illusions persisted well into independence. Moreover, some Indian revolutionaries were in contact with Moscow; and the British expected the Comintern to use Chinese communists to stir up trouble in South Asia. There was unrest in Bengal, Madras and the northeast. A group of Indian radicals, headed by Jawaharlal Nehru and Subhas Bose, wanted Congress to be more forceful. Yet no alternative to British rule was in sight: Congress was internally divided and unable to speak for all Indians, especially Moslems. Nevertheless, in 1929 Congress decided to seek complete independence, while the Viceroy countered that Dominion status was the 'natural issue of India's constitutional progress'. In 1930 Gandhi staged his 'salt march', challenging the ancient salt tax and starting a civil disobedience movement for total independence. His campaign profited from the unemployment brought by the Great Depression. Gandhi was arrested, but had to be invited to London to confer with ministers. Elsewhere, too, the British were giving ground: in 1931 they started to Indianize the Indian Civil Service and in the same year came a new constitution for Ceylon.

In 1935 the Government of India Act gave India 'responsible government', but without powers of war and peace. It provided for an all-India federation and provincial self-government by elected legislatures. Some 35 million would have the vote, with separate electorates for communal groups. The British retained checks and governors could suspend the constitution. Though Congress objected strongly to these reserve powers (which were nevertheless continued later by the independent Republic of India under the name of 'President's Rule') it did not refuse cooperation, for everyone understood that representation at provincial levels would soon be followed by representation at the centre. Congress won a substantial victory in national elections in 1937. The Moslem League, led by a chain-smoking, London-trained lawyer, Mohammed Ali Jinnah, failed to get a majority even in seats reserved for Moslems, which convinced them even more that Congress was just a Hindu monopoly. The League adopted the slogan 'Pakistan', claiming an independent Moslem territory which would have 90 million people. So unrest continued. By 1937 some 50 000 troops, even tanks and aircraft, were active in the northwest.

In 1939 the Viceroy declared war on India's behalf. He was legally entitled to do so, but by a foolish bureaucratic bungle[27] did so without consulting the Indians. Congress Party ministers resigned. The party decided not to participate in the war[28] and staged a 'Quit India' campaign against the British, although that was not universally supported: as noted earlier, some 2 million Indians volunteered for military service. The British treated civil disobedience as wartime rebellion and arrested Congress leaders. By November 1940 around 100 000 Congress supporters were in gaol. The party now claimed to be the sole nation-wide popular political force. In 1942 a UK governmental mission to India failed to settle matters and there were widespread Quit India disturbances. Although the Indian Army stayed firm and many Congress leaders were interned, the British had to agree to leave India once victory was won. Following Japan's surrender, London sent another Cabinet mission to try to secure Hindu and Moslem agreement on a path to independence. But Moslems had long ceased to have confidence in the Hindus or the British or faith in Congress nationalism. Jinnah had committed the Moslem League to partition as early as 1940 and by 1944 consolidated its hold in the north.

By the time the war ended, the Indian economy had also developed further. Before 1939, India manufactured little more than consumer articles. During the war chemicals, light tanks and capital goods began to appear.[29] And in 1945 Britain, having financed its war effort largely by issuing government bonds, owed some £2.5 billion (£59 billion equivalent in 2000) to the colonies in so-called 'sterling balances': India had become one of Britain's major creditors.

The links between British interests in India and those in Burma and Malaya, also continued. Britain's control of Burma, finally achieved in 1885, made it part of British India until the 1930s. That control was partly in reaction to growing French power next-door, in Indo-China. Indeed, Siam (Thailand) remained independent largely because the British and French found a neutral state between them useful. But administering Burma was difficult, encountering resistance on both religious and national grounds. Burmese Buddhism fended off Christianity as it had earlier resisted Islam, its cultural strength reflected in occasional national responses to official intrusion and anti-European outbreaks. By 1935 Burma was separated from India and given limited responsible government. But it was a country in which the modern nation-state, insofar as it was made at all, was arguably made by the army. Revolutionary nationalism was greatly stimulated by military experience and by military training received from the Japanese in 1942–5.

Indonesia's approach to nationhood was different again. Until after 1945 there was no agreed definition of what Indonesia actually was. The literature on this subject has been '... colored by the pervasive but elusive idea of the nation'.[30] But Indonesians, with their 300 languages and dialects, had always been deeply divided by religious and other differences. Village Moslems in hundreds of islands had eclectic versions of Islam, greatly influenced by old Hindu and even older animist ideas. City Moslems, by contrast, were more influenced by religious ideas from the Arab world. There were Buddhist, Hindu and even Christian strains as well.

As in many other colonies, notably in Africa, the boundaries of the new 'nation' were set by the colonial power, the idea of 'nation' being for a long time quite malleable. It was Dutch activities that welded the East Indies, especially educated upper-class Indonesians, into greater unity. The very term 'Indonesia' seems to have been coined only around 1850, by English scholars seeking a single term for a disparate grouping of islands. At various times Indonesia was simply regarded as a multi-cultural or multi-regional phenomenon. The nineteenth-century Aceh that fought the Dutch for thirty-five years regarded itself as a nation. Insofar as an Indonesian national sense existed, it was cultural rather than political. As late as 1945, when the Japanese allowed Indonesians to select their future state boundaries, only a minority defined 'Indonesia' as the Dutch East Indies; most also wanted to include the Malay peninsula, east New Guinea (now Papua New Guinea) and north Borneo. What influenced the independence movement to act for a unified Indonesian nation was Dutch boundaries, supplemented by the racial competition between white and brown.

The rise of political nationalism was associated with rapid population increase, Dutch discrimination, increased local education, and the declining power and prestige of traditional leaders. It was also associated with religion: Islam came to symbolize resistance to the alien. The population, as noted earlier, reached 28.4 million by 1900, and some 41 million thirty years later. Although the Dutch had long accepted the primacy of native interests, social, political and administrative discrimination against Indonesians continued. However, the Dutch respected religion and its links to politics. They helped Moslem pilgrims to travel to Mecca, which was the religious and perhaps even the political focus of the Indonesian world. In 1859 2 000 pilgrims were assisted. By the mid-1920s it was 50 000 a year.

In 1901, when the century was still young, The Hague formally declared the 'moral duty of the Netherlands towards the people of the

Indies'. Local and religious education was supported, and secular education gradually encouraged. By one count, in 1903 there were 1700 schools and 18 000 in 1940. In 1907 came separate education for ethnic groups. The Dutch also saw the need to Westernize the literate classes and to break the Islamic hold on rural education. And yet, though there were two native technical colleges as early as 1866–7, the Dutch did not establish a modern Westernized technical college, or law and medical schools, until after the First World War. As late as 1940 a mere 640 Indonesians were going to college.

In spite of the 'ethical policy', which also brought larger economic shares for Indonesians, much social discrimination remained. Dutch and Eurasians were given job preference, especially in government. Judicial administration was tilted against Indonesians. Native rulers became mere civil servants. Almost all the few educated Indonesians held low-ranking government jobs. By one calculation, as late as the end of 1940 Indonesians only held 7 per cent of higher civil service posts.[31] Others could not find jobs at all. Yet they had absorbed Western concepts of individualism, efficiency and impersonal action, and learned about Western ideals of equality and nationalism. They could also see the Europeans treating modernized Japanese as equals. Not surprisingly, modern, educated and dissatisfied young Indonesians were receptive to nationalist appeals. So the Dutch, who by the 1920s feared nationalism as much as communism, sought to develop indirect rule further. Army and police remained officered by Dutchmen and much of colonial society, especially the Chinese and Eurasians, favoured the status quo.

The economy was also divided largely along racial lines. One part, a modern sector linked to trade and investment, was mainly foreign-controlled, while the Indonesian sector was labour-intensive, traditional and largely self-sufficient. The Dutch-Indonesian imbalance persisted into the 1930s. Indeed, Dutch private business wanted to take over exploitation of Javanese export crops from the colonial administration, while traditional Javanese farmers continued to expect help, advice and care from their rulers.[32] Still, by 1910, Indonesia had an efficient economy. There were, of course, periodic disruptions. The growth of export products from the outer islands after 1900 came together with decline in Java. During the First World War trade with the Netherlands was suspended, though trade with other regions, including the United States, blossomed. After 1930, global recession plus that growing population resulted in shrinking per capita incomes.

The first leader of post-independence Indonesia, President Sukarno, once said that the Indonesian nationalist movement – partly inspired by Japan's earlier modernization – had three main streams: the nationalists, the Moslems and the Marxists. But national consciousness stemmed largely from cultural factors: a Javanese cultural revival, an Islamic movement throughout the archipelago and a national movement among the Chinese who, by 1930, numbered 1.2 million, with strong cultural ties to China. National concepts began to be active from roughly 1912 onwards. By 1916 there was a partly elected consultative assembly in Batavia. But for many Javanese intellectuals, nationalism still concerned Java, not Indonesia, their views fuelled by resistance to the all-Indonesian political framework which the Dutch had established. It was, therefore, the Dutch who fused local nationalisms into an inclusive Indonesian concept; partly by giving a single foreign focus to local grievances, and partly by replacing peasant communal relations with the individualist social organization of city and business. The first organized national movement seems to have been launched in 1908 by the 'Pure Endeavour' group. In 1912 came an Indonesian nationalist organization proper, the Sarekat Islam, which grew to 2.5 million members within seven years. It wished to strengthen ties with the Islamic centres of Mecca and Cairo, and to promote commercial enterprise and mutual support among Indonesians. It also called for complete independence, if necessary by using force. By 1921–2 the Dutch accepted that the future lay with self-government and within five years Indonesians were a majority on the National Council (Volksraad) in Batavia.

The original Sarekat Islam leadership sought nationalist unity. But after the 1917 Bolshevik revolution communist ideas began to ripple through the islands and by 1920 a Communist Party (later the PKI) had been created. Like other communist parties it obeyed Moscow. Some Marxist groups merely sought Westernization, but hard-liners followed Lenin in using nationalism to promote revolution.[33] The moderate Marxists developed a radical nationalism. From this base came Sukarno's later appeal to the people: 'I am a convinced nationalist, a convinced Moslem, a convinced Marxist.' Meanwhile, Sarekat Islam and the communist party, the PKI, struggled for leadership. At first the PKI gained ground, only to see revolutionary efforts fail in 1926–7. At that time, too, the Indonesian Nationalist Party(PNI) was founded, chaired by Sukarno, then a young engineer. Many other nationalist leaders sprang from the 'Indonesian Union', formed in 1922 among Indonesian students in Holland, and influenced by European nationalism. Though the PNI originally wanted to be a comprehensive national movement, in practice it was based on the white-collar class, with no support in the peasantry. All these groups were tiny, and further constrained when Sukarno and other leaders were deported or gaoled.

By the time of the economic depression – which brought a collapse of the sugar market and the halving of Javanese wages – Indonesia also had a quarter of a million Europeans, few of them much interested in local customs or linked with Indonesian society. In 1936 an Indonesian 'Peoples Council' called for a ten-year plan of political development and a year later a new left-wing party was formed, the Indonesian People's Movement. Yet the nationalist groups were urban, whereas Indonesia's basic social grouping remained the village. As late as 1930 only 4 per cent of the population lived in sizable towns. Capitalism remained underdeveloped and the working class small. Before 1939 much nationalist sentiment tended to have anti-commercial and therefore also anti-Chinese foci. The larger political organizations of the 1930s derived their strength from localities; so when, despite the imprisonment or exile of many nationalist leaders, a broader nationalism developed, it was stimulated by events elsewhere in Asia. This contrast between localism and a national view persisted; and although a larger federation of national organizations was formed in 1939, even by the time of the Japanese invasion of 1942, 'Indonesia … was less clearly or consciously a nation than most colonies'.[34] There was certainly a very low level of political mobilization. By the early 1930s probably only around 50 000 Indonesians and 25 000 Europeans were politically organized. According to one Indonesian observer, even in 1940 only one Indonesian in 300 was 'politically and socially conscious', these few being deeply influenced by Europe in their approach to society and politics. 'For me,' wrote Soetan Sjahrir, 'the West signifies forceful, dynamic and active life … the West is now teaching the East to regard life as a struggling and a striving … not for plunder … this is what the West has taught us, and this I admire in the West despite its brutality and coarseness.'[35] Indonesian leaders rarely sounded more Western than in railing against centuries of Dutch domination and deploring Indonesian sufferings.

After Pearl Harbor, Japan's lightning campaign in Southeast Asia brought a quick Dutch collapse, followed by an occupation that strongly encouraged ideas of a unitary, independent Indonesia. The Japanese made gestures of Asian solidarity and emphasized everything anti-Dutch and anti-Western. They promoted Indonesians in the administration, and ran the region on a loose rein, which encouraged more local dynamism. They encouraged pre-war radicals and nationalists. Sukarno petitioned them for Indonesian independence, and they gave him and his associates jobs, as links with the populace. By 1943 they enlisted Indonesians into a home defence force, which numbered some 120 000 by 1945. From late 1944, Sukarno was built up as a 'man of destiny'. In June 1945 he announced the principles on which 'we will establish an Indonesian national state'. By now the nationalists were using the term 'Indonesia' to describe the archipelago, but there was still disagreement about what its boundaries should be. Sukarno himself wanted both sides of the Malacca Straits (including parts of modern Malaysia) in Indonesian hands. By August 1945, the Japanese were willing to promise independence. Immediately after their surrender Sukarno declared it and proclaimed the Republic. By this time, the veterans of unitary Indonesian nationalism had a substantial following of revolutionary youths. Naturally, they were all denounced as unprincipled Japanese collaborators by those groups which welcomed the returning Dutch as liberators.

The Indo-China story is even more complicated. Laos and Cambodia initially welcomed French protection, partly as security against Vietnam. There, surprisingly given the country's history, the court initially failed to mobilize resistance to French incursions. Some Vietnamese opposition to the French emerged at local levels, but it was sporadic and disorganized. The earliest national movements, from the 1860s onwards, were led by mandarins and scholars with Confucian loyalties. They sought to re-establish the old imperial and mandarin order. Naturally, that was diametrically opposed to French principles of uniting the colonies into a single, centralized polity; and making Vietnamese, like other members of the empire, into *français de couleur* (Frenchmen of colour). It was even more opposed to the civilizing mission which millions of Frenchmen regarded as the primary justification of colonial rule: the obligation of the advanced peoples to bring modernity and civilization to primitive societies. Which also tallied with French commercial interests in bringing Asian societies into world markets, not only to make money but to promote modernity and representative government.

Many Vietnamese could see that Western culture offered alternative paths to self-assertion and social fulfilment. Ideas about transforming Vietnamese institutions and practices along Western lines were discussed from about 1900. A Westernized elite developed which, like similar movements elsewhere, imitated French ways and admired Western technology and principles of government. But it was confined to the urban middle class, educated in French schools and engaged in pursuits encouraged by French rule. Government based itself on these Francophone Vietnamese officials, and was involved with the growing Europeanized bourgeoisie in the professions, teaching, commerce and manufacturing. Yet in Vietnam, too, European education and Western ways sharpened frustrations when men, taught to believe in Enlightenment notions of progress, nevertheless found the colonial system blocking access to influence and wealth. Ideas of separate nationhood were encouraged, especially among the young.

By 1918 active propaganda movements had appeared throughout the country. They did not shake the French empire, but they did express nationalist resentment against the Chinese commercial classes as well as against the French. Tension also continued between Indo-Chinese nationalism and the particularistic nationalisms of Vietnam or Cambodia. The first fully nationalist groups, appearing in the 1920s, spoke in Western terms and adopted Western-style forms, which had little relevance to a local society which remained agrarian, largely Confucian, and quite unaccustomed to popular political participation. Religious groups and communist ones appeared somewhat later. The French reacted strongly. By the later 1920s some organizations wanted total independence but these were local efforts, mostly by young urban radicals, with no rural base. Discontent among peasants concentrated, not on nationalism, but on mandarin corruption, taxes and prices. Similar economic motives fuelled labour activism in the factories, coal mines and shipyards created by the French. A short-lived nationalist movement at the end of the 1920s, inspired by the 1911 Chinese revolution, was suppressed.

Economic conditions were difficult. By 1918 Vietnam was a source of raw materials and a tariff-protected market. But between the world wars most Vietnamese were too poor to buy French goods or participate in the French-sponsored coal and ship-building industries. Too little of the profit from new industries benefited Vietnam's economic development. It did not even benefit the French state. It went to large, French-controlled enterprises like the Bank of Indochina. The French did finance public works such as roads and (underused) railways. There were large irrigation and land reclamation works, too. But they aroused complaints that rural life was being disrupted, that commercialization of agriculture was more disruptive still, that much new land was going not to peasants but to speculators and that taxes were much too heavy. Modern economics seemed inherently foreign and the growth of a property-owning middle class was limited. Yet constraints on civil liberties limited the rise of parliamentary-style political parties; which stimulated illegal political organization and a revolutionary mentality.

Then came Nguyen Ai Quoc (meaning Nguyen the patriot), known to twentieth-century history as Ho Chi-Minh (He who Enlightens). Of mandarin stock, he was educated at the prestigious National Academy in Hué, knocked about Europe, settled in Paris and in 1920 joined the French Communist Party. He went on to Moscow to be trained as Comintern agent and by 1924 returned to China to organize exiled Vietnamese radicals. In 1930 his group became the Indo-China Communist Party. This became, little by little, the leader of anti-colonialist sentiment. From the beginning, its aims included both the overthrow of French rule and revolution against local land-owners. Ho's timing was lucky. In 1930, world depression led to serious disturbances in Vietnam as prices dropped, plants closed and peasants rioted. Encouraged by communist activists, some local soviets were set up and communal land distributed to the poor. Yet by the middle of 1931 most of the unrest had been quelled and most communist leaders were in prison. Some were executed. Ho escaped and was condemned to death *in absentia*. For three years he studied in Moscow and from 1936 to 1941 in China.

Back home, resistance to the French faded, though the Communist Party began to revive in 1935 with active support from Moscow. Young nationalists trained there and gradually returned to rebuild the party. The French learned that gaoling revolutionaries only made prisons into 'schools of Bolshevism'. By 1936 the stress on civil rights by the Popular Front government in Paris relieved pressure on the Vietnamese communists. As their own 'front' arrangements flourished, and bourgeois nationalist groups declined, they became the core of resistance. Their members were strikingly similar to the young nationalists in almost all other colonial resistance movements. They were disappointed job-seekers, students, clerks, journalists, teachers and petty bourgeois. Much the same, actually, as those flocking to similarly charismatic right-wing leaders in Germany, Italy, even Japan. In Vietnam's case, the leaders came, like Lenin, Mao and Zhou Enlai before them, or the Nehrus in India or the Meiji reformers in Japan, from the middle and upper middle class. Educated in the French system, they were drawn to revolution when denied the status they thought they deserved. They absorbed Lenin's ideas about a nationalist alliance of all 'progressive' forces, Mao's about using the peasantry to make revolution, and ideas about using nationalism to expel the French and build 'socialism.' Here were the beginnings of a party-led, nation-wide movement. Its growth was helped by French passivity, especially in rural administration. Village structures were left alone, yet

Vietnam's French-led transformation into a major rubber producer and rice exporter greatly worsened the conditions of the rural proletariat.

In the meantime, Japan's interest in Southeast Asia began to revive, especially after northward expansion from Manchuria was blocked by the 1939 German-Soviet pact, which allowed Stalin to concentrate on Siberian defence. Japanese planners, determined not to be at America's mercy for essential supplies, thought about incorporating Southeast Asian resources into Tokyo's new 'Greater East Asia Co-prosperity Sphere'. In 1941–42 Japan seized control of the region. From September 1940 to August 1945, Vietnam was a *de facto* Japanese possession, albeit formally still under the control of the Vichy French government.[36]

Here, as in Indonesia and elsewhere, Japan's 1940–41 victories were a decisive turning point. Most Vietnamese nationalists were confused by the Japanese occupation. Some wanted to oppose both the Japanese and the French. Others cooperated with the occupiers, accepting Japanese promises of independence. The communists were more clear-headed. To Ho, returning from exile, it was obvious that both the Japanese and the French had to be opposed. Japan, he predicted, would fight America and be defeated. That would create a vacuum in Vietnam, which the communists could use before European forces returned.

The party devised a new strategy to seize power after the war. In May 1941 it formed the League for the Independence of Vietnam, or Vietminh. Formed in China's Guangxi province, it was a united front of refugee groups wanting to defeat the Japanese by cooperation with the Allies. In promoting a moderate social programme but insisting on independence, the Vietminh would cooperate with anyone, not least the Americans. 'All the Indo-Chinese people,' they declared, 'beg the great powers and, above all, the United States for assistance to their movement ...'[37] Together with that went 'People's War' guerrilla action and mobilization of the peasantry on the march to power. Tightly controlled by the communists, the Vietminh established guerrilla bases in remote regions; some near the Chinese border, able to get arms from China to fight the common Japanese enemy. By 1945 the Vietminh held considerable stocks of weapons and ammunition.

There was more here than military cunning. The communists offered three kinds of appeal which proved irresistible. One was the persuasive Marxist alternative to a Western capitalist democracy which seemed strange and foreign, especially to the peasants. Its approach to social problems stressed popular mobilization, centralized leadership and a coherent system of thought. As early as the 1920s Marxism had become a familiar element of intellectual discussion as an attractive alternative to the less coherent democratic systems. Adding to the appeal was the Leninist party's combination of leaders chosen by merit, wielding a Confucian-style moral authority, with the sense of equality and active individual participation in a party where membership was itself an honour. The party's centralized control system also echoed, for all its differences of form, the glories of the imperial past. A third element was the party's rough way with opponents of its benevolent system.

In March 1945 the Japanese interned the remaining French. They left the issue of future control open, but armed those groups likely to resist restored European authority. In mid-August, as the Japanese surrendered, the Vietminh – with only a few thousand poorly armed guerrillas – seized power in most cities and villages, including Hanoi, while President Ho Chi-Minh announced the formation of the Provisional Democratic Republic. In September, Allied occupation troops began to arrive but the Vietminh had established themselves firmly in the north, though not in the south. Nationalist Chinese forces in northern Vietnam agreed to withdraw. The French signed agreements with the Vietminh; and France recognized the Republic of Vietnam as a part of the Indo-Chinese federation and the French Union.

The evolution of a modern national system was a still more confused and lengthy business in China. Between the 'first opium war' and the early 1860s, China changed from an empire resisting foreign importunities to a helpless giant whose formal independence was only maintained by the mutual jealousies of stronger powers. Even that hardly dented China's profound disinterest in the outside world, though it did develop Chinese resentment leading, eventually, to modernized nationalism. Once again, that evolved, roughly, in three stages. The first saw reform attempts within the Manchu framework. A second opened with the creation of Sun Yixiang's revolutionary grouping in 1905. The third stage lasted from the 1926–7 split between Sun's heir and the communists, until Mao Zedong's triumph in 1949.

Initial reactions to the humiliations inflicted by foreign barbarians were highly traditional. Many Chinese took humiliation as a sign that their rulers had lost the mandate of heaven. Popular reactions to foreign devils and their pretensions were compounded by resentment of domestic corruption, social immobility, and the pressures of population increases. By the 1850s there was a remarkable spread of secret societies. Many of them, patriots of a sort, started to use Western weapons, the most formidable of them being the Taiping movement.

Other reactions were less dramatic but more intelligent, and for a time looked like being more effective. The Chinese had always assumed that they were supreme practitioners of the art and science of government, and disillusion came hard. But when foreign legations opened in Beijing, officials had to be trained to deal with them. That meant importing knowledge of the West, its people and ideas, into the very city where thousands of China's best scholars normally prepared for civil service examinations. China also had to send officials abroad to deal with foreign governments. Influential scholars lived and learned. The first Chinese official in London was Minister Guo who, Gladstone said, was the most urbane man he had met. Guo returned to China saying 'Confucius and Mencius have deceived us', meaning that other forms of government were evidently possible. He confided to his diary that 'Western states have been established for two thousand years, and their principles of government are entirely civilized and rational'. When he published his diary back home, it was banned.[38]

Meanwhile China was developing legal codes to regularize relations between state and citizens, alongside increasing numbers of binding regulations under foreign treaties. Also, by the 1880s the first students returned from foreign studies. From the USA they brought ideas of 'government by the people, for the people', and from England notions of universal education and widening franchise. Above all, there was the pervasive Western notion of constant change, compelling reform. Mission schools reinforced new ideas and some children even went abroad to be educated. One youngster who went to live with his elder brother in Honolulu was Sun Yixian, destined to become the first president of the Chinese Republic. Numbers of Chinese labourers went to Java, Malaya and the Californian and Australian gold rushes. Though some were abominably treated they, too, glimpsed a different world. Also, there were young army officers, later led by men like Chiang Kaishek (Jiang Jieshi), who trained in Moscow and Japan, or Zhou Enlai after his return from France.

This did not mean early change in Beijing. The experienced mandarins around the Dowager Empress Cixi had no wish to make way for new men, even while foreign pressures on China became less and less bearable. In the 1895 war even the despised Japanese prevailed over the empire. Korea became independent. Taiwan and the Pescadores islands went to Japan. Russia got a sphere of influence in Manchuria, the French the right to intervene in provinces bordering on Tonkin.

The Germans obtained a concession in Shantung and the British trading rights on the Yangzijiang. The Chinese government responded by looking for allies, and with cold pragmatism they approached Russia, the very neighbour who had given so much trouble on the Amur. (The 1950 Sino-Soviet treaty would partly rest on the same geographic realities.) The move was a red rag to the British, who had fought in the Crimea, and considered Russia a major menace. London, while continuing to feel protective about China, reacted with consular posts in Chinese Turkestan, an expedition to Tibet to observe developments on the approaches to India, and a naval base at Weihaiwei to offset the Russians at Vladivostok and Dairen.

However, as defeat by Japan destroyed the prestige of China's rulers, the country declined into weakness and revolution. With hostility to foreigners growing, there were attempts to reform the country and its technology base. Efforts were made to improve the armed forces. For a brief hundred days, in 1898, a new young Emperor tried to force innovations rather like those of Japan's Meiji restoration. Beijing university was founded, more young people were sent for study abroad, a national budget was published. Ministries of Trade, Technology and Agriculture were established and uncultivated military land distributed to peasants. The courts were overhauled and political journalism was encouraged. But the old Empress, Cixi, declared the Emperor feeble-minded, confined him and had the reformers executed.

By now China was in a state of nervous excitement. A wave of political and religious hysteria swept the north. The Empress and parts of the oligarchy encouraged anti-foreign rebellion, even the xenophobic village militias, including the so-called 'Boxers'. In June 1900 Cixi declared war on the foreigners and appealed for popular support. There was a mass rising and some missionaries and diplomats were slaughtered. Western forces were quickly brought in. Beijing was occupied, and duly pillaged, by an international force.[39] But popular unrest, even against foreigners, was a huge problem for the empire itself. Paradoxically, therefore, the West's suppression of the Boxers also rescued the imperial regime, prolonging China's social and political paralysis. Chinese debates about what to do continued without coherence or leadership: some wanting to reinterpret Confucian values for modern conditions, others wanting to use Western techniques but maintain established structures (rather like China's reformers of the 1980s) and others again seeking a break with tradition altogether.

The diplomatic tides continued to ebb and flow. As Russian influence in China seemed to grow, the British countered with the 1902 alliance with Japan. The British merely wanted to check Russia, but in Chinese eyes Britain was now aligned with Japan, which was China's enemy. Indeed Japan, after her 1905 victory over Russia, looked like the most dangerous power in Asia. When she acquired control of Korea, agreed with Russia on spheres of influence and sought greater control of Chinese affairs, it looked as though Tokyo was also threatening a chief element in Britain's Asian policies, the maintenance of China's territorial integrity.

This entire ten years' crisis of 1895–1905 also greatly stimulated Chinese nationalism. It taught all Chinese the necessity of serious structural reform. Revolution from below and resistance from above were no longer in balance. In 1905 Sun Yixian founded the group which would become the Guomindang. There were rebellions in 1906, 1907 and in 1908, when Cixi died. The empire passed to a three-year-old boy, Puyi, the actual regent being his uncle. Unrest continued. Provincial assemblies were convoked in 1909, and a (national) consultative assembly a year later. A year later again, almost by accident, an uprising began in the Russian concession at Hankou. This time, revolution spread like wildfire. Sun Yixian's republic was officially inaugurated in 1912, with himself as President. But what might have been the culminating point in creating a modernizing nation-state was in fact, merely the start of four decades of warlordism, turmoil and civil war.

At first, China's external problems became, if anything, even more acute. To be sure, China was still partially protected by mutual distrust among foreigners. That led to the so-called Open Door policy which, devised in Britain, was promulgated by the United States Secretary of State, John Hay in 1899–1900. It appealed to all powers to respect China's integrity and to maintain trading rights for all. The US China lobby was pleased and Hay became its hero, since for the Americans, as earlier for the British, a market of 400 million Chinese seemed one of the world's great commercial prizes. The policy also affected investment in Northeast Asia. In an era of railway building, the Americans seemed especially interested in Northeast Asia's communications. However, a Russo-Japanese agreement partitioned Manchuria and shut the door to outside investors, while Japan made huge gains in China during the First World War.

A detailed account of East Asian problems in the two decades after 1918 would be superfluous here. Suffice it to say that by the 1920s Tibet and Mongolia made themselves independent of China; that Japan was never able to achieve secure command of the supplies and commodities needed for its industries and people; that the USA was unable to combine its preferred Pacific power balance with the non-involvement its electorate demanded; and that China not only failed to defend itself against Japan but was unable, amid much domestic chaos, to make an effective choice between the alternative paths to nation-state modernity which its factions developed.

Clearly, reform was essential. But there was no agreement on specifics, or even many generalities. Running through the jigsaw of groups and parties, as so often before and since, was the dispute between those who desired, like the Japanese before them, Western industries, institutions and ways, and those who resisted 'running after foreign things'. To counter warlordism and political disintegration, Sun Yixian organized his party on a mixture of Western-style democracy, Marxist ideas, Leninist party structures and ideas about modernization, as well as expelling foreigners and their ideologies. Hence the post-1918 Allied decision to hand Germany's former Chinese possessions to Japan produced fresh uproar, culminating in the revolutionary 'Fourth of May' movement of 1919. It was another milestone in the Chinese revolutionary saga.

In the welter of ideas that followed, the Chinese Communist Party was formed in Shanghai in 1921, while Sun himself courted Soviet aid. Moscow pursued its usual dual strategy: maintaining normal relations with the Chinese government, while simultaneously supporting the communists. By 1927 the Guomindang staged mass arrests and executed communist and left-wingers. The communists were reduced to a few wandering bands, one of them led by an obscure Hunanese named Mao Zedong. The Gwomindang occupied Beijing, and claimed to form the first legitimate government of China since the fall of the empire, and the only entity properly dedicated to expelling foreign imperialists. But turmoil continued. In 1931 the Japanese occupied Manchuria. Seven years later they had occupied most of central and north China and most of the chief ports and industrial centres, which were also the Guomindang's chief political bases. Meanwhile, the communists had retreated from both the Gwomindang and the Japanese into the interior and were waging guerrilla war.

By the 1930s, therefore, these were two central issues of Chinese politics. The first was not whether, but how, to change the former empire into a modern Chinese nation-state; and what the precise mixture of modernization and tradition should be. That meant structural reform – economic, administrative, above all psychological. Some reforms happened. Chinese pig iron production, a mere half million tons in 1928, reached almost 6 million tons by 1937. In the same period coal production rose from 25 to 124 million tons and steel from 30 000 to 5 million tons. The remaining issue was which of the two contending groupings would provide the new social and political patterns: the Guomindang or the communists. For all their differences, both were nationalist reformers, determined to make China 'stand up'. For the next two decades, however, all solutions were delayed by their dual wars: that between them, and that against Japan.

Though the details and timing of these developments varied greatly in the different colonial regions, certain common themes emerge. They have to do with newly 'national' self-identification, new structures of political representation and organization, of society, and rule-making. They also have to do with the establishment, or capture, of increasingly potent government institutions and, not least, new attitudes to the internationally and politically appropriate distinctions between 'us' and 'them'.

Given such developments, the general patterns of decolonization seem to have been more or less set by the beginning, and certainly by the end, of the Second World War: this is clearer in retrospect than it was at the time. Even in 1939, for the British, much of the map was still coloured pink and in 1933 the French empire included almost 110 million people. In that decade, few of the colonies looked like modernized nation-states: whether in France, Britain or Holland, few statesmen thought independence for the colonies was imminent. Wise policy could limit or channel local unrest and, in any case, the advantages of closer imperial links would make themselves felt in time. In Britain, the pre-war appeasers of Germany, Italy and Japan argued that the imperial system might not survive a global conflict; and most of the elites were confident they could finesse local nationalisms. People responsible for India, for instance, still looked forward to its self-government, but not to an end of Britain's role in India. Even after the Japanese surrender, the first impulse was imperial reassertion. The British also thought for some time that careful diplomacy could maintain the empire in its revised form of a commonwealth. The French even more clearly thought their colonies of increasing, not declining, importance, whether for their resources or as a basis for France's global influence. A single, if geographically scattered, political union was feasible. The Dutch, too, persisted.

In the event, of course, the pressures for independence could not be contained. The Second World War did break the mould. Colonial political demands, often forcible, became irresistible. The costs of empire became intolerable. In the metropoles, popular enthusiasm for empire finally disappeared. The future was likely to be, not the next movement of a grand symphony, merely a coda.

7
Decolonization as Aftermath

There is, then, a sense of inevitability, of epitaph, about the great era of decolonization after 1945. Not that the full force of the political *tsunami* was immediately obvious. In 1945 Britain, France, even Holland and Belgium, were ranged with the victor powers. By 1950 they were richer than ever before. They freed most of their colonies well before anyone might have forced them to do so. Yet, between 1945 and 1960 some 800 million people in forty countries became independent; and by the mid-1960s the empires had ceased to exist. The Philippines became sovereign in 1946; India and Pakistan followed in 1947; Ceylon, Burma and Israel followed in 1948; Indonesia in 1949. Laos, Vietnam and Cambodia became sovereign in the same year but remained in the French Union until 1954. Two years later Tunisia and Morocco left that Union, Britain evacuated the Sudan, while Malaya became sovereign a year later still. The French Union was finally dissolved in 1960. Two years later again, a long and cruel North African war ended with Algerian independence.

Why were the changes so sudden? Because colonial claims to independence and armed nation-and-statehood had become more strident and violent, and the global environment had radically changed. The meeting of Russian and American troops in the middle of Germany in April 1945 dramatically symbolized the eclipse of Europe as a centre of power. As Tocqueville had foretold over a century earlier, it had become dominated by the two great powers on its flanks, the USA and the Soviet Union. The USA, in particular, enjoyed unparalleled economic and industrial ascendancy. Moreover, global security affairs changed shape, with collective arrangements becoming dominant. The United Nations Organization, created in 1945 to succeed the League of Nations, provided an accepted forum for expressing international opinions and stronger machinery to restrain aggression. There, the old imperial powers could be put further on the defensive. Especially since the two new superpowers, hostile to one another on everything else, agreed on anti-imperialism.

Western Europe itself was weakened, even shattered, by war and occupation. The most urgent task for every state, including the colonial metropoles of Britain, France and Holland, was domestic reconstruction. (Complicated, in countries like France, by powerful tensions between resistance groups and wartime collaborators with Germany.[1]) While security was provided by US protection, some European unification seemed essential to make future continental wars impossible and to fend off Soviet pressures into the bargain; also, eventually, to rebuild global clout, if not for any single European country, then for 'Europe'. The process began with the Marshall Plan of 1947 and the Organization for European Economic Cooperation (OEEC) (later the global Organization for Economic Cooperation and Development (OECD)). Belgium, the Netherlands and Luxembourg were collectively designated as Benelux. In 1950 came a plan to integrate French and German coal and steel industries. The European Economic Community followed after 1957 and would develop into the European Union of 1992. Only the British, conscious of being a major victor power, spent two post-war decades concentrating on domestic reform; and torn between a desire to remain a party principal in world affairs, reliance on US support, resentment at the occasional American veto and the generally elegant management of decline.

Nevertheless, the first post-1945 instinct of the colonizers was to recover old possessions. Perhaps even more so in France than in Britain. As usual, motives were mixed. The habits of dominance are not easily shed. Winston Churchill's wartime claim that 'I have not become the King's first Minister in order to preside over the liquidation of the British Empire' represented widespread views. The empire remained critical to UK trade and payments until the 1960s. Moreover, there was a feeling, only too justified in many cases, that most colonies were simply not yet capable of establishing stable and sensible governments. Although Hitler had given a very bad name indeed to ideas of inherited or genetic differences, even a committed left-winger like J.A. Hobson – the very man who had so influentially condemned imperialism in 1902 – had written only shortly before the war that 'a situation like the present in which lower stocks and races displace higher races and higher stocks would denote a human retrogression'.[2] The obligations of care for local minorities also suggested caution. So did the thought that it might be better for everyone to be part of a power-ful empire than to be in small, vulnerable, independent states. Many smaller or island territories were patently too small to be indepen-dently viable anyway. The problems of multi-racial and/or multi-religious societies in Kenya, Algeria, India, Ceylon and Malaya could not be solved by simply having the colonizer go away, though some colonial nationalists sounded as if that would solve everything. Still less could the colonies' links with the old metropoles be easily replaced as sources of ideas, technology or aid.

For these and other reasons the situation was often ambiguous. The forms of colonial rule had, after all, varied greatly. No colony was uni-formly hostile to the colonizers and no European state whole-heartedly resisted 'liberation', or used its whole power to do so. For the British, as early as 1839, the Durham Report had outlined principles of eventual self-government, thereby avoiding American-style revolution as the solution to colonial problems. Moreover, though some colonies had strong communities of European settlers, clinging to old loyalties, European rule elsewhere often had shallow local roots and its removal would cause no great cultural traumas. Of India, Khilnani has written of a '... slow but irresistible erosion of the sandcastles of the British Raj, washed by the rising tides of India's ineffaceable past: a revival of pas-sions of community, religion and caste ...'.[3] Even so, in most places parliamentary forms and political structures were more or less main-tained. In India especially, the customs of Westminster and the rule of law would survive remarkably, despite severe social difficulties. Half a century after India, Pakistan, Sri Lanka, Kenya and Vietnam became independent, special links with former colonizers remained at levels ranging from governmental bureaucracy to business and finance. Other, more sentimental links did not evaporate either. Customs of empire often survived and there were old men who would talk nostal-gically of imperial days. Not that sentiment always affected policy: by the end of the 1960s it was a British Labour government which made Commonwealth immigration restrictions effective.

Unsurprisingly, conflicts between reassertion and burden-shedding, between impatience with colonial distractions and the attractions of imperial status, were at first disguised. Various expedients were tried. Whether for Britain, France or Holland, they were meant to manage change by policy, not enforced by weakness; meant, indeed, to make decolonization look more like liberal constitutional reform.

The aim was to avoid complete separation, by securing the collab-oration of moderate nationalists, and undercut the irreconcilables.

In the British case, the Dominions were already sovereign states, closely linked with Britain and each other in ways that avoided antagonizing local nationalisms. The net was extended and loosened in creating the 'Commonwealth'[4] as a new way of grouping Britain and the former colonies; the British slowly abandoning a series of old wishes, even interests, to retain ties that would not push the colonies into total independence. The group gradually expanded from the independent white Dominions to include other countries as they became independent. Most critical was India's decision to became the Commonwealth's first republic. Pakistan followed, as did Sri Lanka (Ceylon) in 1972. Burma did not join. The Irish Republic left in 1949 with no fuss, though both London and Dublin were careful to let Irish citizens continue to enjoy the rights and privileges of British subjects. A decade later a raft of African states joined also: Ghana, Gambia, Malawi and others.

From the start, the group had no constitution, no common programme and no necessary obligations. It evolved into a club whose members could discuss and cooperate at will, give one another a measure of preference, even mutual help in finance, education, sport and other matters. It even developed political qualifications for membership – for instance in human rights. In such an atmosphere nongovernmental links naturally also flourished.

The way of the French was different. Where the British don't like plans based on abstract theories, the French love them. Where the British like proceeding step by step, the French, with Cartesian logic, prefer to work from first principles and by detailed programmes. Before the war the French empire, for all its theoretical centralism, had embodied variety. Most colonies had councils to be consulted, but effective power remained with governors. Yet administrative patterns and practices, in theory more or less uniform, varied in practice in dealing with differing local cultures and traditions. The empire distinguished clearly between citizens and subjects; would conscript non-Europeans for overseas military service; and produced a small but thoroughly assimilated native elite. That principle of assimilation into what later decades would call multi-cultural groupings was one of the chief characteristics of the Francophone empire. Yet assimilation was resisted, not only by many in Indo-China but by Moslems in North Africa.

But in 1940 France lost control of most of the empire and in 1942–3 control of North Africa as well. By 1945 many or most French possessions had been transformed and the political struggle in the major colonies no longer concerned nationalism versus colonialism so much as competing versions of the proposed new socio-political framework. Once French control had been re-established after 1945, therefore, Paris attempted to bring its many colonial relationships into a single, progressive constitutional system: a single republic from Dunkirk to Brazzaville, in the Congo. Some of the colonies were even brought into the home constitutional system, thus avoiding issues of 'independence' altogether.

The first of these attempts was through the *Union française* (the French Union), created after 1946. The second was the 'Community' twelve years later. The French Union was essentially about assimilation. This came in two parts. The old colonies were declared overseas *départements* of France. Their inhabitants were declared citizens of the Republic and expected to adopt a French way of life. France now 'forms a union with its overseas peoples which is based on equality of rights and duties without distinction of race or religion'. This constitutional unity between France and Algeria and New Caledonia became for hundreds of thousands of Frenchmen a national fact, like the unity of Normandy and Brittany. Colonial deputies joined the National Assembly in Paris. The text of the new constitution was sub-edited by a Senegalese teacher of French grammar and literature, Leopold Senghor, who later became president of his African nation. Paris voted development funds. The other part of the Union consisted of 'Associated States', like the protectorates of Tunisia and Morocco and the Union of Indo-China. These states, whose ex-officio head was the president of the French Republic, were to have full autonomy, except for control of foreign policy. Here was part of the larger plan to bolster France's post-war international position, especially *vis a vis* the Anglo-Saxons.

In the end, all such expedients failed. They were defensive, stemming from weakness, designed to avoid separation, or at least to lessen its psychological impact at home. None of them provided real shelter from the storms of national self-assertion.

Two critical turning points for post-war French colonial affairs were the defeat at Dien Bien Phu and the loss of Indo-China in 1954 – discussed below – and the Suez débacle of 1956. If there was a single catharsis for the British, it was at Suez. Egypt's nationalization of the Suez canal, apparently threatening Europe's trade and oil supplies, led to conflict with Britain, France and Israel. A Franco-British invasion failed to reoccupy the canal or, for Paris, to end Egyptian support for Algerian rebellion. Decisive in that failure were the delays and confusions of British planning, and the American threat to end market support for the pound sterling. Washington had become worried lest the Egyptians, and general Arab nationalism, should be driven into alliance with Moscow. The West's overriding Cold War strategies must not be jeopardized, even for two major European allies. The affair carried important lessons. London and Paris had to accept that their capacities for overseas action would henceforth depend on American goodwill. In spite of great bitterness on the political Right at America's 'betrayal', all subsequent UK governments sought to cement the US alliance. And London began to hustle other colonies towards independence.

The French, by contrast, were embittered by British hesitations, failures and yielding to American pressure. Once more, France had been betrayed. In 1914–15 the British had left France to bleed virtually alone. In the 1920s they had failed to support France over German reparations. In the 1930s they had forced appeasement and the dismantling of restraints on Germany. They had abandoned the French in 1940, belittled their role in and after 1945 and failed to cater for France's European concerns in the late 1940s and early 1950s. From this standpoint, Suez was the final straw: there had to be a fundamental redirection of French policy.

These resentments also fed into the drive for a (French-led) European union. Beginning in the mid-1950s, and continuing under President De Gaulle, Paris concentrated its energies on Europe, the European Economic Community, and especially on a Franco-German alliance. French armed forces were told to forget colonies and become modern, nuclear-equipped and focused on the European continent. This mood also produced the 1963 French veto on British membership of the EEC: Britain might challenge French continental leadership, and anyway had too many extra-European links and interests.

The Suez affair highlighted something else. Most of the strategic reasons for acquiring and keeping colonies now fell away. The very connections which had once promoted colonial expansion now encouraged decolonization. Indian independence in 1947 itself made possession of the Suez canal less imperative, and evacuation of that canal base undermined Britain's interest in Southeast Asia and East Africa. Moreover, much the most important strategic relationship was now that with the stoutly anti-colonialist United States, which made colonial claims and complaints an even greater nuisance for foreign policy makers. Economics pointed in the same direction, since Western Europe's post-war economic dependence on the USA was all but absolute. The less developed world remained a source of oil, raw materials and other commodities. But, provided only that ex-colonies had stable governments – which most of them did with more or less authoritarian administrations – modern transport and communications made it much easier and cheaper to obtain these by trade, rather than administering empires. It was equally evident that the costs of holding on, always considerable, were still growing. Even before 1939 most colonies had received aid. After 1945 the newly independent states treated aid as an entitlement. Even if, as Peter Bauer once pointed out, most aid meant taking money from poor people in rich countries and giving it to rich people in poor countries. Not only were colonial costs now clearly far greater than any likely benefits, but such obligations distorted reform and welfare at home.

And in most of the West European countries, far-reaching economic reforms included social expenditure which grew sharply for a quarter of a century after 1945. Most states increased general public spending, but especially welfare and redistribution payments.[5] Indeed, following depression and war, the welfare state became indispensable to social stability.

> With the structural transformation of the state, the basis of its legitimacy and its function also change. The objectives of external strength or security, internal economic freedom, and equality before the law are increasingly replaced by a new raison d'être: the provision of secure social services and transfer payments in a standardized and routinized way ...[6]

By the mid-1970s the nations of Western Europe were spending almost 25 per cent of their national resources on public social expenditures.

Once such attitudes to welfare dominated home politics, colonial expenditure was bound to decline. Some continued to argue that colonial progress still depended on taking responsibility for societies not yet

Table 7.1 Comparative public social expenditures[7]

	Total public expenditure* 1950–75	Social expenditure# 1962–75	Social transfers* 1950–75
Britain	30.4–46.1	NA–19.2	5.7–11.1
France	28.4–42.4	16.3–22.7	11.1–20.0
Netherlands	27.0–54.3	13.7–28.3	6.6–26.1

* Percentage of GNP
# Percentage of GDP

ready for an independent place in a competitive world, but most people accepted that independent societies should look after themselves.

Yet it was intangible factors which, as so often in politics, were decisive. After 1945, and especially after 1956, the imperial powers lost all serious confidence in their own ability to manage. Not only that, but colonialism was increasingly condemned as morally undesirable, not just as a fiscal burden. Indeed, since victory has a thousand fathers but defeat is an orphan, opinion in the metropoles moved towards a historical revisionism which said empires had always been wrong. As Macaulay had said a century before, colonial administration was '... tainted ... with all the vices inseparable from the domination of race over race'.[8] The political Left became especially hostile, while the Right was resentful of never-ending demands for aid and pessimistic about the economic capabilities of the new states. The broad middle classes, especially in Britain and Holland, simply no longer wanted to know about colonies, especially after barbarism like that of India's partition or of the Mau Mau in Kenya. Before the war, defenders of empire had cited humanitarian policies of liberalization and development to fend off attacks from the political Left. Now, they stressed that colonial independence actually fulfilled colonialism's civilizing mission.

All that dovetailed once again with shifts in the intellectual temper of the times. Some of these seem abstract and theoretical, but had vital practical results. Between 1950 and 1970 popular consciousness absorbed the notion, largely from modern science, that the appearance of the universe, and of life, were mere accidents, their lack of design proof of their absurdity and pointlessness. More important still, science seemed to reveal huge conceptual gaps in the whole Enlightenment promise of eventual human omniscience. Modern physics, with notions like Heisenberg's uncertainty principle or the question whether light is wave or particle, or the fundamental problems of observation and measurement, was placing question marks against the very notion of everyday physical reality; while evolutionary psychology was saying disturbing things about the revolutionary impact of the imagination. Multiple uncertainties encouraged philosophical movements like existentialism and deconstructionism, from which the new tertiary educated classes drew important practical conclusions. It was all promoted by a remarkable cast of characters. Its high priest was Jean-Paul Sartre, small, brilliant, ugly, indomitably selfish, subtle, voracious for praise and women,[9] whose egoism illustrated much of his philosophy. There was also Albert Camus from North Africa, handsome, dashing, marvellously gifted, whose novels painted a deeply pessimistic picture of the modern condition, and with whom Sartre had furious quarrels; and Simone de Beauvoir, even cleverer than Sartre, whose brilliant writings made her a feminist icon while her practice made her Sartre's servant. Sartre's views, especially, sowed seeds of distrust of almost all accepted standards of measurement and judgment; taught that, confronted with an uncaring universe, the individual was unavoidably and wholly alone, without external rules or fixed points of reference. In a world without certainty, with only probabilities, the individual could never escape total responsibility for his own judgments and decisions.

For many Europeans, especially for the rebellious young, the implications for unfettered individualism proved hugely attractive, especially after the regimentations of wartime. A little later, deconstructionism even questioned the meaning of meaning. It argued that no social or political judgment could be demonstrated to have stronger external and 'objective' validation than any other (except, presumably, the view that no judgment could be thus justified). Consequently all such judgments were personal and subjective.

The intellectual atmosphere produced by these movements encouraged a fierce individualism. It created deep distrust of rules as not merely subjective, but as self-interested interpretations of the world. The honourable position was to strip away the universal mendacities and hypocrisies of society, to understand the tawdriness of all power, all claims to knowledge, all pretence at virtue. Of course, that created practical dilemmas. It justified resistance to external authority, since no claim to authority could ever be more than someone's attempt to gain personal – mainly material – advantage. On the other hand, the rigorously individualist and self-centred life was especially dependent on a strong state to make it possible, let alone safe. Consequently, politics and social relations became even more clearly a battlefield for power and privilege.

At roughly the same time came a model of 'deliberative politics' with important effects on the relations between colonies and metropoles. For the old, nationally communal whole, the model substituted what Habermas has ponderously called 'anonymously intermeshing discourses'[10]: a shifting of normative expectations towards procedural democracy. A traditional emphasis on social cohesion, homogeneity of descent or institutional stability, gave way to one on the procedures to which consent was deemed to have been given. The meaning of 'nation' and 'nationalism' therefore also tended to change.

For example, in the new post-1949 West Germany, while the *jus sanguinis*[11] continued to apply, the Basic Law (i.e. constitution) laid down that every resident would enjoy its protection, have the same duties, entitlements and legal rights as full citizens, would even enjoy almost identical economic status. This increasingly dissociated citizenship from all inherited ideas about national identity. It emphasized a constitutional patriotism of citizens of different ethnic and cultural backgrounds, socialized by choice into a common political culture.

These developments accommodated the pluralism of the post-war world. Pressure groups proliferated. National economies meshed more closely with one another. Governmental administration became increasingly complicated as well as more directly important to citizens and groups, and more costly. Its agencies, managing an increasingly complex network of regulations, acquired hugely increased administrative discretion, while also becoming more closed off and self-referential.[12] This made colonial policies, and their cost, yet more clearly an element of domestic administrative politics, even when administering more elaborate programmes of overseas aid. It meshed more closely with multi-national and multi-cultural interests and paved the way for an anti-racist and pro-multi-cultural orthodoxy. It was, therefore, also an outlook which emphasized abstract administrative categories. It had room for policies which were often sentimental. But then, as Carl Jung reminded us: 'Sentimentality is a superstructure covering brutality.'

The end of empires may be foreseeable and foreseen, but is almost always violent. Ruling ideas also die hard. These things are major convulsions. The empires of France, Britain and the Netherlands were not immune, any more than the beliefs which had sustained them.

Developments in India were among the more traumatic. Various ideas and structures for a new nationally based government had emerged before the war. When Japan surrendered, Britain's departure from India was no longer an issue of principle, merely one of modalities and timing. The ICS and London still hoped for a united India. But Moslems insisted that continued British rule was preferable to incorporation in a Congress-ruled India, which would be a religious tyranny. The winter of 1946–7 saw violent communal riots. Early in 1947, the British government concluded that no single, central Indian authority could be created. The effective choice was between transferring power to several independent provinces, or continued British rule for a decade or more. But British public opinion was now entirely unwilling to contemplate indefinite rule by force over unwilling local populations.

Indian divisions hardened as politicians manoeuvred for position. Nehru and Congress retreated from their insistence on all-Indian power and accepted partition as the price of governance; the more so as they thought no independent Pakistan would prove viable. Difficulties continued and London adopted shock tactics, simply announcing that Britain would depart in June 1948, leaving India partitioned between two governments. For all the mastodon trumpetings of old India hands, the remaining princely states would be cajoled or forced into one or the other. Even this date had to be brought forward. Confronted by violent disorders, which threatened to become uncontrollable, the last viceroy announced the British would go on 15 August 1947. The land, the army, the civil service, assets and government would be divided between Hindu and Moslem entities, and new borders were drawn up in indecent haste. In the course of this messy partition,[13] tens of millions found they had suddenly become religious minorities. In ragamuffin armies they criss-crossed the new, uncertain and unmarked borders. Unknown numbers were slaughtered; figures from 2–5 million have been suggested. Many felt betrayed by the abruptness of Britain's departure.[14]

On that 15 August, Prime Minister Nehru, that child of empire with his London connections, English style and Cambridge degree, welcomed independence in silvered words: 'Long years ago we made a tryst with destiny and now the time comes when we shall redeem our pledge, not wholly or in full measure but very substantially. At the stroke of the midnight hour, when the world sleeps, India will wake to life and freedom.' Less than six months later the apostle of non-violence, Gandhi, was assassinated by a Hindu fanatic. Nehru took sole charge of the new India and remained prime minister until his death in 1964. A decade later Nehru's daughter and successor, Indira Gandhi, strengthened the equation of Hinduism and Indianness, and of both with populist democracy. A separate Pakistan continued to live in fear of an Indian invasion.

As the empire had always been diverse, so decolonization, too, was handled differently in various places. In 1945 Malaya was no longer a model of political quiet and economic development. That October the British announced a new Malayan Union, merging the territories into one state. This offered a path to self-government, tried to establish some racial balance as between Malays, Chinese and Indians and was intended to promote both nation-building and economic development, especially through greater scope for Chinese business energies. But in 1946 the United Malays National Organization (UMNO) was formed and polarized the Union's affairs by race. Within a year the

Malays made the Union unworkable, triggering moves towards a federal constitution. But that, too, encountered difficulties. On one side were Malay radicals, partly inspired by the Indonesian revolution. On the other was the Malayan Communist Party (MCP). It had sprung from the wartime anti-Japanese resistance, led by communists and organized and trained by the British. It had strong support, especially among the Chinese, who suffered from shortages, inflation and obstacles to social mobility. As the Party's industrial strategies in Singapore were failing, faced by British support for non-communist groups, a Chinese communist insurgency began in June 1948.

Its leaders seem to have calculated that the British, after quitting India and Palestine, would not accept a long and costly involvement in Malaya. But by 1948 the Cold War was in full swing, Britain wanted to reassert itself, the MCP seemed a minor opponent and anyway the Malayan economy was important to Britain. However, suppressing the insurgency turned out to be hard. The rebels were confined to jungle areas, but had broad sympathy among urban Chinese, especially after the 1949 communist victory in China and Chinese victories in the Korean War. It took the British-led effort seven years to break guerrilla resistance, and for UMNO to conciliate general Chinese opinion on the path to independence. Only then could elections come and, in August 1957, the establishment of an independent Federation of Malaya and the departure of British troops. Six years later, with the addition of North Borneo, Sabah and Sarawak, Malaya became Malaysia.

In Indonesia, British forces at first took over from the surrendering Japanese. Pending the return of the Dutch, they had to deal with Indonesian nationalists, now in control of many areas. Java was short of food and in the post-surrender chaos the traditional notables, on whom the Dutch had relied, were undermined. The new Republic was weak, even after Sukarno proclaimed it in August 1945. The national movement itself was weakened by internal disputes, had difficulty mobilizing the peasantry and hoped for an amicable settlement with the Dutch. And indeed, in November 1946, Dutch and republicans agreed to form a federated Indonesia. But in mid-1947 the Dutch, with 150 000 soldiers, tried to draw a ring around the republican zone in Java. The action ended, partly because of Australian protests at the UN over a conflict so close to Australia's northern shores. Further military action followed in December 1948, when Sukarno and other leaders were captured. But the Dutch were stopped by the UN Security Council and it became clear they would leave Indonesia.

Indonesian nationalism received strong support from Australia, Ceylon, India, Iraq, Pakistan and Saudi Arabia. More importantly, the Americans, fearing the spread of communism and strongly committed to Western Europe's reconstruction, wanted Dutch resources spent there, not dissipated in the East Indies. By September 1948, when Sukarno put down a communist rebellion in his own ranks, Washington decided the republicans were acceptable. An August 1949 Indonesian-Netherlands conference at The Hague produced a United States of Indonesia, with Sukarno as President.

His governing style combined ancient ideas with new needs. Javanese political philosophy requires a polarity of good and evil and a continuing rhythm of change from times of chaos to times of peace under a just king. He used these traditional notions both to organize politics at home and to inflame foreign issues, as did other leaders of newly invented entities. By the 1950s Indonesia had parties and elections, but in very different fashion from that of normal democratic politics. Indonesia's central disputes had to do with such things as ideologues of revolution confronting Moslem defenders of faith, and claims on West Irian or the 'Confrontation' with Malaysia became ways of stimulating anti-colonial patriotism at home.

Apart from India, the sharpest conflicts in the region were in Indo-China. For the French, its continued association was vital. Given its roles as an 'associated state' in the French Union, and in plans to reposition France in the world, digesting its new revolutionary group became one of the Union's chief aims. Eliminating the communists was secondary; after all, in 1946 communists sat in the government in Paris itself. In this tussle the Indo-Chinese communists faced major difficulties. The Chinese nationalist army, still in northern Vietnam in 1945–6, had brought in a number of anti-communist Vietnamese politicians. The Vietminh tried to cope with these, and the French, while simultaneously trying to outmanoeuvre the Chinese generals in the North. Yet though the French had both foreign and local help, their plans had fatal weaknesses. They were ultimately unable to enlist broad popular support, instead of merely elites. Indeed, the Japanese, the French and, later, the Americans, all failed to develop a Westernized political system in the face of Vietnam's own political and cultural traditions. In the end, only the communists came to understand how to graft both nationalism and socialism onto those strong roots. In Vietnam the French Union, for all its lofty pretensions, remained an empty shell.

The writing was on the wall when Ho won solid support in the February 1946 elections. The French tried to contain the Vietminh with political coalitions. Although they now had 30 000 troops in Vietnam, at first both sides tried to avert war. But while Ho made gestures of cooperation, his colleague Vo Nguyen Giap prepared Vietminh forces for armed struggle. At the end of 1946 Franco-Vietminh arrangements broke down and, assuming that Ho was planning to attack, the French attacked the Vietminh first, opening the first Indo-Chinese war.

Initially, it was a struggle between roughly half the population supporting Ho against the other half allied with the French, whose regular forces at first dominated the towns and lines of communication. But although the French suffered from inadequate resources[15] and had little experience of the new-style insurgency warfare, the Vietminh had to do much more than wage guerrilla war or win victories in the field. They had to 'win hearts and minds'. So Ho's people waged a systematic campaign of terror, routinely assassinating dissenters or opposing villagers, taxing the peasants, conscripting young men. This had three aims. One was to organize support from young bureaucrats and intellectuals into a nation-wide movement. Another was to campaign against that half of the population which wanted pro-French solutions to the country's problems. The third was to provoke a French counter-terror to induce Vietnamese resentment and support for the Vietminh. Together with that, Vietnamese had to be persuaded that pro-French groups were mere puppets, and international opinion to be convinced that this was not a Vietnamese civil war but an anti-imperialist struggle for national liberation.

Initially, Ho had only limited support from his major patrons, in Moscow, for whom Southeast Asia was insignificant compared with Europe. The first turning point in his struggle therefore came in 1949, when Mao Zedong seized power in China, changed the balance of power in East Asia and the Pacific, and became the main regional counterfoil to America. China also provided Ho with a friendly hinterland, source of supply and active military advice. Indeed, in the final battle of the war, at Dien Bien Phu, the Vietminh had support from Chinese guns and gunners.

The indirect participation of China on one side and the USA, as France's ally, on the other made the struggle into an important part of the global Cold War. That gave its short-term outcome, the French withdrawal in 1954, an interim flavour. The settlement was produced by great-power intervention, a conference at Geneva demonstrating that even the Chinese and the Soviets had become suspicious of Vietminh ambitions. It was agreed to divide Vietnam into separate northern and southern states. Although Ho had gained a great deal, for the Vietminh nationalists partition was only half a victory. Almost one million Catholics fled from the North to the South, to escape communist rule. South Vietnam's need for aid to cope with this human flood embroiled the United States further, as did hardening convictions in Washington about containing communism.[16] In the meantime, the Vietminh launched a 'land reform' in the North which was also a peasant revolution. There was much killing – possibly some 100 000 died – and a much greater number still were interned in re-education camps.

The story of the next two decades is usually regarded as a liberation struggle: the French having been seen off, the Vietminh struggled not only for national unity but for liberation against the Americans. The truth was rather different. It was a struggle between nationalism, in its national communist and rigorously organized form, and much more old-fashioned kinds of Vietnamese social organization, represented by the South Vietnamese state. In other words, between the bourgeois and the fully nationalist roads to modern nation-state status. Nationalist enthusiasm won, as it had done almost everywhere for two centuries. By 1975 Vietnam was united under Hanoi's rule, its armies inflicting severe wounds not just on technically superior American forces but on the self-confidence of the American body politic.

Even unification was only part of the task facing a doubly victorious Hanoi. What the Vietminh captured in 1954 and later, in 1975, was still largely a pre-modern and pre-capitalist society. From the point of view of modern nation-state construction, the political institutions, the sense of nationhood, the capacity for mobilization, were well in place. But the war had taken a heavy human and material toll. Moreover, the new rulers' views about social and economic organization were quickly demonstrated to be entirely inadequate. For some time, rejection of foreign influence even extended to foreign business and capital. The government also had to cope with longer-term changes. Population movements and urbanization within Vietnam had been sharply accelerated by conflict. The city of Danang, for instance, which had some 60 000 inhabitants in 1957, had 150 000 a decade later and half a million by 1971. War and industrial development raised the population of Hanoi from under 200 000 in 1950 to 850 000 by the mid-1960s. And Saigon's population probably reached 2 million by 1970. These shifts contributed to the serious social and economic problems facing the newly united country.

A word should also be said about Japan. Never colonized, Japan became a *de facto* colony under allied occupation in 1945. Its dominant figure was the flamboyant American pro-consul, General Douglas

MacArthur, who behaved much like one of the former *shoguns*. He was colourful, shrewd, courageous and disinclined to listen to anyone, including his superiors in Washington. Under him, the occupiers had grand ambitions, rather like the old European liberal imperialists. His technocrats, children of President Franklin Roosevelt's New Deal, planned to remake Japan's society and economy along Western lines. That meant not only demilitarization but the breakup of the old industrial conglomerates.

More importantly for Japan's longer-term development, the Americans introduced a new constitution in May 1947. They reformed political life and imposed more democratic institutions. They legalized trade unions and organized elections. They reformed the school system, replacing the nationalistic texts of pre-war years; and wisely ended the occupation in April 1952. By then, fortuitously, the economic and industrial demands created by the Korean War had kick-started the Japanese economy and begun its trajectory to the 'miracle' of the 1960s.

Chinese affairs remained complicated. During the Second World War Washington was intent on propping up China, not only as part of the Allied war effort but as one of the 'Big Four' who would decide the post-war global balance. But it remained unclear which side in China's civil strife, and whose version of national reform, would prevail. The West naturally supported the nationalist government. So did Stalin, since it was battling the Japanese and keeping them away from Siberia. The Soviets even pressed Mao to help the common struggle against Japan by not fighting the nationalists. However, the communists not only fought the nationalists, they even cooperated with the Japanese to strengthen their own position.

Just before the war ended, the Soviets occupied Manchuria, but signed a treaty of friendship with the nationalists, recognizing them as the legitimate government of China and promising aid. Later, they agreed to Jiang Jieshi's requests that they should stay in Manchuria until the nationalists were strong enough there to prevent a communist takeover. However, the Soviets did turn over captured Japanese weapons to the communists before evacuating the province in 1946. Moscow was clearly playing the two Chinese sides off against one another to prevent the emergence of a single, effective political authority.

President Truman sent General George Marshall to China in 1946–7 to negotiate a reconciliation between the two sides and produce a coherent Chinese administration. Marshall, one of the major architects of victory in the Second World War, had served as Chairman of the

Joint Chiefs, and was destined for some of the highest offices of government. But his China efforts failed. The nationalist government had long been weakened by the loss of its coastal bases as well as by corruption and inefficiency. Mao Zedong's people, by contrast, had learned how to rally the peasantry. In 1949 China's long revolutionary travail, foreshadowed in the 1850s and begun in 1911, ended in victory for Mao's commitment to thorough-going, centralized national reform and restructuring.

In sum, European colonization in Asia came about for a great variety of reasons not to be compressed into any single neat theory. Neither for their arrival nor their rule nor their departure was there any one principal cause. Human affairs are not so tidy. Instead, it is a story of the variety and unpredictability of human nature, of brilliant eccentrics and a kind of haphazard inevitability, at least as much as of scientific categories or social forces. While there are common elements across regions and peoples, the precise mixture, and the timing, differ. Initially, the Europeans wanted to trade, not annex. Colonies could be started where land seemed unoccupied, or for religious reasons, or in self-defence. Once a foothold had been gained, expansion was quite often the result of accident.

In spite of the lure of wealth, and the riches acquired by a few, colonization was of very little profit for the colonizing states, let alone for the West in general. Spain and Portugal, the most dynamic countries of Europe in the fifteenth and sixteenth centuries, were undermined more than helped by their colonial riches. Britain prospered before it made its larger imperial conquests and apart, perhaps, from the protected trade of the second half of the eighteenth century, the empire was never responsible for more than a fraction of its wealth. Those countries which experienced the most dynamic economic 'miracles' after 1945, Germany, Japan, Italy, and the four Asian 'tigers', did not have colonies, or lost those they had had before their 'miracles' occurred. Holland, France and Belgium had rapid economic growth only after their colonial periods, not before. The richest countries of Europe, Switzerland and Sweden, never had colonies at all. The reason is obvious: colonies are expensive, and not only in money.

At the same time, although all colonizers proclaim their civilizing mission, for none was that more justified than for the West Europeans. Modern hygiene, medicines, birth control, rationalized production, science and modern education and administration, came from the West, not the less developed. What evolved were social systems embodying a massive cultural transfer from Europe, of laws, administrative norms, social assumptions, technologies and political outlook. New relationships emerged between power and consent, duty and liberty, and new ideas about the legitimate bases of government. Not least, it was the colonial governments which developed an urbanized, Western-educated, middle-class elite whose young men and women understood Western philosophies, sympathized with the intellectual radicalisms of the colonial metropoles and spearheaded the national revolutions. It was these ideas and people who were the precondition for the socio-political upheavals in India, Japan, Vietnam and elsewhere, which made decolonization not only possible but necessary.

For these societies, to construct an identity meant constructing a new history to give the nation a unique origin, deeply rooted in the Rights of Man, racially distinct, historically particular, territorially defined. In the eyes of the decolonized and their leaders, the whole tale of 'liberation' became a kind of secular bible story. It was a tale of rebirth, of righteous fulfilment, a morality tale about a march in tune with the laws of men and Gods. From an inherited ethnic separatism there grew not only national consciousness but mass politics, with each individual no longer a passive subject but an active participant. Dominant and unifying political definitions emerged, with individuals becoming, in principle if not always in practice, participants in creating a common will, with rights and duties to the whole, able to be mobilized in the pursuit of common ends. Operationally, it was based on the mass organization, imbued with a sense that freeing the nation from external rule was prior to freedom for the individual, and probably a condition for it. It was this which made the rejection of the foreign claims into a matter of practical politics. Neither in India nor in Japan, Indo-China, China or the Indonesian archipelago had pre-nation-state political concepts or organizational forms had the means to resist the European ascendancy. What was therefore critical in each case was the development, variously between 1860 and the 1930s, of an assertive political nationalism in imitation, and only then in rejection, of the dominant Western power.

There is a temptation to portray what happened as somehow always inevitable. While decolonization after 1945 was often difficult and traumatic, the tides of Europe's colonial history appear to have been set well before 1945. The political, educational and administrative conditions to establish sovereign modern states were by then in place, at least in the major colonies or – as in the case of Japan and to a degree in China – in regions strongly influenced by European expansion.

Opinions and attitudes had already shifted towards making decolonization necessary.

India is a striking example. Before the concluding decades of the nineteenth century the idea of 'India' scarcely existed as a basis for effective administration and governance, or for mass mobilization. It was the foundation of the Congress Party, the first Indian political grouping to be organized along lines akin to those of Europe, which heralded the start of effective resistance. Alongside that came the nationalist exploitation of an increasingly centralized governmental machinery created, in India as in Vietnam, by the colonial power, and in Japan by the nationalist reformers of the Meiji restoration. It may be that the absence of any such effective machinery in China before the advent of Mao Zedong was itself critical in delaying the national and nationalist triumph.

Not that principles of nationality and the nation-state were ever a guarantee of peace. Rather the opposite, whether they were employed to aggregate smaller groupings or to justify a process of division and secession, especially of and from empires. As Rousseau well understood, if there were no states, there would be no wars. But as Hobbes had pointed out even earlier, and as the turmoil of the seventeenth century made very clear, there would be no peace either.

In the ex-colonial world, this nation-state has been especially powerful in its socialist version. After 1945, links with the socialist opponents of the West were bound to be attractive for the 'emerging' states. But there was more. Whether in democratic socialist forms or, more commonly, some version of Marxism-Leninism, socialist communitarianism dovetailed more easily than individualism or parliamentary representation with the hierarchical and family-centred traditions of the Hindu or Confucian or Buddhist worlds. Not for nothing did many liberation movements, often influenced by Western socialism, adopt the terminology of 'comrade'. Nor was it accidental that the army often became the shield and protector of the revolution, as well as the nation; while military ideology remained redolent of an old-fashioned national patriotism.

By the decade of the 1960s, it all seemed a neat enough rounding off of five centuries of European expansion and world domination. But was it? What does it mean to suggest that the story is finished? What, indeed, does 'colonization' really mean? In what ways was the experience of the Europeans in Asia, or the Asian experience of Europe, special or unique? And did the end of formal colonization change the substance or merely the forms of relations between societies and states?

8
Concluding Ironies

'Colony' and 'colonization' have many meanings. Not all relate to human affairs: the word can mean a colony of bees or ants. Even in its narrower sense, colonization and decolonization, quasi-colonization and recolonization have occurred, in one form or another, since human societies began. The words can mean a group of humans set down in a void, like a colony in Antarctica or on the moon. Or there is colonization as settlement, meaning settlers becoming, over time, part of the local population, as with some invaders of China. Or it can mean the elimination or expulsion of the existing population: recently known as 'ethnic cleansing'. This, too, is ancient and common. One thinks of Cromwell, encouraging large-scale English migration into a thinly populated Ireland, to make it English, or the expulsion of millions of Germans from Eastern and Central Europe after 1945, and the attempts by Tutsis and Hutus in Central Africa to get rid of one another. More commonly, however, colonization, especially by Europeans in Asia, has meant imposing political rule over the people and territory said to be colonized.

In this sense, too, colonization is ancient and routine. The Romans colonized Gaul and Britain. The Normans colonized Sicily and England. The Mongols colonized parts of China. The Arabs colonized the Berber regions of North Africa. Indeed, Islam converted more than half of Asia by the threat of the sword. Russia occupied half of Asia and the eastern half of Europe. China has more recently colonized Xinjiang, not to mention Manchuria, Mongolia and Turkestan. Its colonization of Tibet since the invasion of 1950 led to the flight of the fourteenth Dalai Lama and some 100 000 Tibetans to India.[1] India, Burma and Indo-China were colonized by the Mongols and the Chinese long before the British and French came along. Korea was ruled by China, then by Japan. The Dutch struggle for independence at the end of the sixteenth century was one instance of decolonization, as was the American War of Independence. It is form rather than substance that tended to change in the age of the nation-state.

In its contemporary and largely pejorative meaning, however, 'colonialism' is a complex and haphazard product of the liberal European nationalism and the nation-state construction of the eighteenth and nineteenth centuries. It is they which consolidated the notion that humanity is naturally divided into entities called 'nations'; that these are separated from one another by some amalgam of territory, ethnicity, culture and religion; that – most importantly – each of these nations has a natural right to self-determination and self-government; and that government of any one of them by members of another nation is inherently unjust and oppressive. None of these ideas have been universally held. Very different notions dominated China or India for most of their recorded history, or the mediaeval *respublica christiana* of Europe, or the Ottoman or Austro-Hungarian empires, or the Soviet Union or contemporary Russia or Nigeria.

It follows that the whole terminology of 'colonization' and 'decolonization' can be seriously misleading. As commonly used, it tries to isolate one period and one kind of relationship from a much longer history and a more complex web. It can obscure wide differences among societies, religions and political attitudes. It treats the social entities involved in inappropriately anthropomorphic terms. It presents each of them as either object or subject, as master or victim. And it obscures the lasting legacies which colonies and colonizers have alike derived from relations between them.

Issues of power confuse matters. The usual antonym to 'colony' or 'colonized' is 'independent' or 'sovereign'. These concepts deal with legal status and political power. Sovereignty is most easily determined over the issue whether a state can maintain itself. From 1954 to 1975 the supporters of South Vietnam argued that it was an independent state, and attacks upon it constituted external aggression. In 1975 it failed to sustain itself and arguments everywhere about its independent status abruptly ceased. National sovereignty, while permitting a measure of 'interdependence', is also by definition incompatible with acceptance of any overriding and rule-making external authority. In Europe itself, there have been many attempts to achieve unity. Some have tried by creating a political Leviathan, like the empires of Rome and Charlemagne, Charles V, Louis XIV, Napoleon, Hitler or currently, in the consolidation of the European Union. Others have sought unity under a universal moral law, like the *respublica christiana*, or the ideologies of the Rights of Man and the French Revolution, or the international socialism preached by post-1917 communism, or the ideology of Wilsonianism which fuelled the League of Nations and the United Nations.

In reality, of course, states are, and have always been, interdependent with others. Argument therefore swirls around ideas of comparative rather than absolute power. A state is sometimes said to lack independence or 'sovereignty' if it is economically or politically dependent upon others. Here, independence is defined by what the 1918–20 reformers of Europe termed 'viability': a state capable of being politically and economically self-sustaining. More recently, in an era when external economic relations have had increasing importance, debate has focused on comparative advantage in trade, and has produced endless discussions of 'neo-imperialism': a state of dependence on foreigners which belies a country's formal independence. Most of this has been unproductive. Economic and financial interdependence has burgeoned everywhere. A state's size, geography and resources are often critical factors in such exchanges. But while many mini-states, formally independent, are clearly too weak to be viable in any sense, it is culture that makes all the difference in economic development. Switzerland, Sweden and Singapore are small and resource-poor, yet rich. Everyone desires greater market and political certainty, ability to resist undesirable foreign competition, and greater clout for the home state. Competitive advantage therefore depends on many things, including the wisdom and abilities of the leadership. Yet the skills of first-generation nationalist revolutionaries may be a quite inadequate guide to their subsequent ability to govern. Men who make revolutions are usually very different from the men whom the revolution has made, and who have to deal with the new responsibilities of independence. And relations between states, developed or otherwise, give unsentimental primacy to state interests and to the balance of power.

So far as British, French and Dutch colonialism in Asia is concerned, history has treated all the participants, whether imperial statesmen, metropolitan liberals or colonial liberators, with consummate irony. The fundamental claim of 'liberation' was that it would bring greater freedom and democracy. But who or what was actually 'liberated' by decolonization? The idea that the achievement of political independence by 'India' or 'Vietnam' is a triumph of liberty echoes the anthropomorphic nineteenth-century European view of the state. It also begs questions about the relationship between individual freedom and state power which have preoccupied philosophers and politicians for millennia. In many 'new' countries individuals have enjoyed much less freedom than they did under colonial rule. Would individual Vietnamese or Burmese indeed have been worse off if French or British rule had continued for another two decades?[2] As for notions of equality, so often associated with ideas of liberty, they are seldom defined, and mostly concern a good which some group claims to have been denied. Yet it is clear enough that history, culture, language, even ethnicity and certainly geography contradict the ideology of generalized 'equality' and must continue to do so.

Everywhere, and not least in the West, the state has since 1945 become markedly more intrusive, bureaucratic, legalistic and commanding; a situation that stems from at least three somewhat contradictory developments. One is the need for closer state monitoring and control of an increasing variety of trans-border activities including, not least, population movements and a greater volume of economic activity. Indeed, multi-national corporate activities are often more clearly instruments of national policy than they once were. In the middle of the nineteenth century most governments cared little about what individual businesses got up to abroad. By the last quarter of the twentieth century, presidents and prime ministers routinely engaged themselves in promoting the foreign activities of domestic corporate interests. They actively helped their own aerospace or defence industries or investment banks to obtain larger shares of the global market. A second development is the appearance of novel technologies of command and communications, creating new possibilities for close regulation, divorced from ownership.[3] Public rhetoric about privatization, competition and freer markets has often merely disguised increasingly complex networks of regulation and supervision.

A third stems from increasing social, regional and religious volatilities at home, combined with steadily growing voter demands for services. In the West, and following the constraints of the Cold War, individual freedom has been increasingly defined as freedom of personal action; but combined with the absolute obligation of the modern state to safeguard individual as well as social welfare. Citizens in the advanced world now claim a 'right' to good health, housing and education, with large majorities assuming that the taxes to make that possible should be paid by someone else. But preventing state power from becoming arbitrary, and inconsiderate, conflicts with the need to strengthen it as a resource and first-aid kit. Moreover, the regulatory framework becomes increasingly important to the maintenance of the unity and cohesion which is a condition for the state's ability to provide detailed services. Importantly, this advance of the collectivist order after 1945 affected the international order also.

The 'democracy' which rested on national unity and parliamentary representation has also changed its shape as populism and bureaucracy brought important shifts in the nature of political representation and the legitimation of authority.[4] The electronic media, especially in the advanced countries, created the illusion of direct contact between voters and political leaders who could also use electronic means for instant polling. That has tended to replace 'consent of the people' by the acceptance of a semi-monarchical figure, whose position is sustained by the quasi-plebiscites of polling and periodic general elections. The leader's ability to govern – even to conduct undeclared wars as in the Falklands, Vietnam, Kosovo, the Gulf, not to mention wars in many parts of Southeast Asia or Africa – is further underpinned by a civil bureaucracy with huge regulatory powers and a well organized party machine. Many modern presidents or prime ministers could legitimately echo Louis XIV's '*L'État c'est moi*'. Over the last half century, versions of this mass populism have spread across most political systems. It has led, via a much diminished popular interest in the details of formal politics, to the erosion of many traditional constitutional checks and balances. These phenomena were already pronounced in the major European fascist systems which regarded themselves as socialist.[5] They spread throughout the socialist world centred on Moscow. Their *mores* now colour virtually all modern democratic systems. It was similarly emotional mass support for charismatic leaders that helped to make the old order untenable in many colonies.

In the West, all this has been accompanied by a politically powerful romantic revival. This emphasized the politics of feeling at the expense of politics of argument or persuasion. It was typified by the 'baby boomers' revolt, afflicting the Western world from the late 1960s, which often looked like a revolt against everything. It was itself strongly encouraged by an electronic media culture emphasizing emotion, sincerity, dedication, wholeheartedness and a celebration of 'doing what you think is right'. It was a revival of the belief, as Isaiah Berlin has put it, in the transcendent importance of the motive rather than the consequence.[6]

The very notion of loyalty to the state, even acceptance of its identity, has also weakened. The increasing force of globalized links of finance, information, production, marketing, transport and travel have given increasing power to the global elite networks. These groupings – which Peter Berger has called the Faculty Club and Davos cultures – developed loyalties and private rules extending well beyond nation-states and governments. They also created great numbers of sophisticated non-governmental organizations and non-state methods of achieving political aims.

Such groups tended to regard nationalism as recessive, reinforcing the post-1945 distaste for nationalist phenomena. They, and liberal internationalism generally, challenged older national loyalties in the name of an indistinct but powerful 'multi-culturalism'. This rested in part simply on easy trans-border travel, but also on traditional moral notions about the brotherhood of man, on a post-1945 loss of national and cultural self-confidence, as well as on the growing competition, in an era increasingly dominated by the importance of knowledge, to attract energetic, skilled and enterprising people from anywhere. Yet it was also bound to raise questions about 'who, now, are "the people"?' Are nationality and citizenship, drained of their older emotional meanings, becoming a mere administrative convenience?'

The reaction to these trends was to make nationalism, albeit in narrower forms, more powerful than ever. It was often smaller, more clearly defined and more familiar entities which became central foci of loyalty. Localities, regions, provinces, towns and especially ethnic groups became more assertive. They ranged from the peoples of Austria-Hungary,[7] or of the former Soviet Union, or from Scots and Irish in Britain, Basques in Spain, *Québequois* in Canada to native American or Aboriginal 'nations' in the USA or Australia. Ancient values of ethnicity proved enduring. 'The Patriotic animus,' said Thorstein Veblen in 1917, 'appears to be an enduring trait of human nature. It is archaic, not amenable to elimination ... and ... not ... to be mitigated by reflection, education, experience or selective breeding'.[8] Being biologically based, it has to do with basic group identification, even a sense of self.[9] For such groups the larger 'nation' of the state, which had once meant freedom, had itself become oppressive.

Attempts continued to resolve tensions between ethnicity, especially religion, and national self-determination. Between 1918 and 1939 self-determination meant arranging borders so as to enclose 'liberated' nations. From 1945 the opposite tactics dominated: peoples were moved to accord with borders. It happened with ancient German settlements throughout Eastern Europe, equally ancient Arab areas of Palestine, Cossacks in Russia as well as Moslems and Hindus in India, as well as Serbs, Croats and others in the Balkans. However, since there is no logical limit to fragmentation in the name of group liberation, self-determination tends to multiply the number of states, including those which, while independent, are too small to be viable. Other attempts involve 'multi-culturalism' within national borders. The trouble with this – where it is not simply a semantic placebo – is that truly peaceful coexistence usually requires that some distinctions be regarded as simply insignificant. The very focus on eliminating disputes, or ensuring fair allocations, between ethnic groups, actually mandates what it purports to remove: concentration on such distinctions.

Difficulties of these kinds also appeared in the ex-colonies. It is one of the major ironies of decolonization that the moment of self-conscious national unity, achieved in gaining independence, should often have been so brief. Nationalism had strengthened an acute sense of who was not 'us', and against whom or what one's group identity had to be asserted. Its decline was therefore accelerated by the weakening of the previously central ideology of anti-colonialism. Liberation itself deprived these societies of their single pre-eminent focus for resentment, with the result that domestic fissions became more prominent, contained only by a stress – even invention – of new foreign dangers. Unsurprisingly, the leaders of these new nations regularly talked about 'nation-building': with the clear implication that the nation had yet to be built.

The new states tended to maintain their cohesion, not only by renewed stress on nationalist principles but also by the use of force. The easy Western assumption that, as societies modernize, they become more secular, and that national unity produces stronger civil societies, proved unjustified. As the more comprehensive nationalism of liberation weakened, ordinary folk tended to return to older loyalties. Ethnic, communal, religious or caste separatism, violence and assassination remained endemic in many regions, from China's north-west to the Middle East.[10] In many parts of Asia, at marriage, colour and shading matter greatly. In India, social or caste divisions or princely rankings remain powerful.[11] In Vietnam, Saigon (or Ho Chih Minh City) has reasserted its commercial dominance. In China and India, provincial assertiveness has grown. Ethnic and religious loyalties in India have produced Hindu-Moslem clashes, battles against Sikhs, and the murder of Nehru's daughter and grandson. Minority groups have for years conducted armed struggle in the Philippines and Burma (Myanmar) and brought ethnic civil war to Sri Lanka. Even in China, though most major groups agree that 'I am Chinese', there has been ethnic and religious strife in Tibet and Xingiang as well as forcible repression of dissent in various places. And inter-provincial tensions have been contained, among other things, by official highlighting of dangers from Japan and in Taiwan, not to mention the carefully nurtured sense of victimhood *vis a vis* the West.

In Indonesia, unrest was for a long time kept in check by two presidents who, until the 1990s, reverted to the highly traditional Javanese role of a *'ratu adil'*, a just king, and, behind a spurious constitutionalism, used the army as the glue of the nation. The result was, unusually among the decolonized, some three decades of political stasis with modern national construction left somewhat incomplete.[12] But then ethnic and religious separatism reappeared, not least among Moslems.[13] At the time of writing East Timor has achieved independence and Aceh and other regions might follow.

Externally, too, liberation and decolonization have failed to bring the independent freedom of manoeuvre they once seemed to promise. Instead, the dependencies of the colonial era have given way to novel structural constraints in a reshaped concert of powers.

To begin with, the imperial countries, deprived of colonial responsibilities, were able, after 1945, to concentrate on their own economic and especially technical development, and to do so with startling success. The result has been that, with the exception of Japan, the production, wealth and technology gap between these ex-imperial powers and the USA on the one hand, and the ex-colonies on the other, grew dramatically. The richest and most advanced countries, which have reaped most benefit from technological innovation, knowledge-based activities or globalized information streams, are largely those that once ran colonial empires. And insofar as these technically more advanced countries depended on trade, it was overwhelmingly trade with one another and not with the ex-colonies.[14] Not only that, but decolonization ended the imperial powers' sense of direct responsibility for their possessions. For that reason, too, the relative power of the metropoles grew, not only in economic clout but in 'soft power'.

Three kinds of change followed: in the optimal scale for political and economic organization, and in an aggressive and revolutionary Western liberalism expressing itself both in dominant ideas and in practical interventionism. The conjunction between clout and scale of political and economic operation came to seem almost as compelling as it had a century earlier when France and Britain agonized about how to stay at the top table of international affairs. Now these advantages of economic and political scale produced a marked growth of regionalism. It is another of the ironies of the late twentieth century that at the very time when colonial demands for national independence became irresistible, the ex-imperial powers themselves began to yield more powers to joint and cooperative arrangements, partly in the interests of growing (joint) international influence. America's uniquely strong military, financial and technical position in the 1990s was supplemented by institutional links with Canada and Mexico. In Europe, much of the drive for unity clearly stems from a wish to construct a European superpower, perhaps even to rival the USA. Not surprisingly, newly independent countries in Africa, Southeast Asia and elsewhere have tried to follow the trend, inevitably affecting all questions about the function and locus of sovereignty, authority and political legitimacy.

Moreover, the ex-colonies have found themselves strongly influenced, not just by Western economic and political power, but by an aggressive and ideologically inflexible Western liberalism operating in the name of 'human rights', 'free markets' and 'democracy'. To be sure, for the first four decades after the Second World War the Cold War confrontation gave the ex-colonies a good deal of room for manoeuvre, for instance through the 'non-aligned' grouping. But the end of this Cold War left the USA as the sole superpower, dominant not just militarily but technologically, in wealth and cultural magnetism. At the same time Europe grew economically, technically and in confidence.

As that happened, the West began to insist on promoting its own 'values' and systems, perhaps most powerfully in the realm of ideas. Whether in politics, economics, social, or even in scientific arrangements there is, remarkably, no current challenger to the West as a source of ideas of potentially global interest. Still less as a source of plausible alternatives to the West's dominant 'values'. Asia has little resonance beyond its own borders.

The West has also, especially since 1989, used global interdependencies, and the growing network of governmental and non-governmental organizations, to stabilize international affairs in its own interests or the promotion of its values, going far beyond the encouragement of economic globalization, supported by mechanisms like the World Trade Organization and the International Monetary Fund. It has even, in recent years, largely freed humanitarian concerns or anti-crime campaigns from the constraints of national boundaries and sovereignties. It extends to the kidnapping of suspected drug traffickers or war criminals from Latin America or the Balkans respectively, and putting them before 'international courts' in whose establishment, structures and procedures the countries of which these persons are citizens have had no say. It even includes waging war – most easily 'virtual' war as in the Balkans – for 'humanitarian' ends with or within other sovereign states. Somalia, Ethiopia and Yugoslavia are cases in point. And many Non-Governmental Organizations, like Green groups, have become notoriously paternalist, even colonialist, in the countries where they operate. No obvious end to these trends seems in sight.[15]

It is true that much of this has had benign results. Wealth has been increased, security promoted, some nasty regimes constrained. German and Japanese democratization, and their economic 'miracles' owe much to Western, especially American, help. The West faced down a Soviet Union which was indeed an 'evil empire'. America has been critical to the successes of the IMF, and the rescue of Mexico, Brazil and South Korea from economic collapse. Western influence on the policies of every one of the ex-colonial countries has been very great.

In this new world East and Southeast Asia have made remarkable economic progress, at rates which, until the economic downturn of 1997–9, were historically unprecedented.[16] To be sure, some Asian leaders tried to attribute success to exceptional Asian structures, virtues and values, whether as a buttress for local customs and cultures, or a defence against self-serving Western views about Western economic and social practices. (This may have obscured the point that both the triumphs and more recent disasters of many Asian economies were similar in type and sequence to previous economic transformations elsewhere.) Yet the reality has been that the ex-colonies have relied critically on the ex-colonizers for markets, technology transfer, capital, investment and, not least, military protection. Japan relies almost entirely on American strategic protection and is economically probably much more dependent on the USA than it was under the much-resented 'unequal' treaties of the 1850s. China is also more dependent on US markets, Western technology and US financial cooperation than imperial China ever was on the British.[17] South Korea relies quite fundamentally on US protection, and markets while Indonesia's very cohesion depends on Western loans and political support. The European ex-colonizers, too, have found it easier to dictate economic terms, directly or through the IMF, to countries needing development aid and credits. Help from them has sometimes been of critical importance, as with British help to Malaysia or parts of the Middle East, or French aid in Africa. The USA has perhaps gone furthest in imposing its preferred standards on others. It has prevented its firms, when doing business in Latin America, Asia or Africa, from engaging in the habitual local bribery. Washington has even insisted that Japan should change its institutions, customs and monetary management to make trade 'fairer' in American eyes.

Three rather obvious conclusions can be drawn. One is that this new Western liberalism is startlingly reminiscent of many of the missionary and liberal imperialist efforts of the later nineteenth century. Another is that this new system is profoundly subversive of those principles of inviolable state borders and sovereign self-determination of states within which – and only within which – representative and constitutional democracy (as distinct from populist and plebiscitary practices) is actually possible.

A third is that whatever else the new system may have given the ex-colonies, it has not been the independent freedom of manoeuvre which they thought independence would bring. In other words, the leaders of ex-colonial 'new' nations, for all their protestations of superior sensitivity and virtue, have found themselves – as Machiavelli might have told them – operating much like others in a world of sovereign states. Events have once more underlined ancient lessons about the importance of power, the hollowness of moral postures insufficiently geared to reality, and the impermanence of all political patterns. In the early 1950s Pandit Nehru was much given to lecturing the West on moral standards, but soon found himself obeying the normal dictates of state power, whether in invading Goa or conducting wars against Pakistan or China. President Sukarno of Indonesia used 'Konfrontasi' against Malaysia to rally opinion at home. China has insisted on its historic victim status while overrunning Tibet and claiming the South China Sea. Nor have broader political and strategic problems disappeared. Problems of power of an entirely old-fashioned kind have lain behind conflicts in Cambodia and Laos, disputes between India and Pakistan, Indonesia and Malaysia, and between Vietnam and China; just as they did in the Korean, Vietnam and Gulf wars or in China's claims over the South China Sea, concerns about North Korea or the modalities of the US-Japanese alliance.

The argument of this book, then, is that nationalism in Europe created the social energies and organizations which made it possible for later colonialism to be more interventionist and commanding. It was equally essential in stimulating countervailing nationalist beliefs and structures in the colonies. That was only a part, albeit a very important one, of the larger process of modernization most of whose elements, no doubt fortunately, have nothing to do with politics or social structures, or even with industrial or economic power.

It seems reasonably clear that neither 'colonization' nor 'decolonization' can be given a clear definition in historical time. French colonization in Indo-China did not start with the arrival of the first French traders or missionaries any more than the first Dutchmen in Java created a colonial possession. And whether British colonialism in Malaya or Dutch colonialism in Indonesia can be said to have ended, other than formally, with the achievement of Malayan or Indonesian independence has been much debated. All kinds of relations between former colonies and colonizers have intensified, not diminished, since the colonies' formal independence. Whether in the case of Dutch relations with Indonesia, or British relations with India or Pakistan, or Western relations with China or even Japan, the links have grown far beyond trade, investment and financial dealings. They encompass education, legal ties, cultural exchanges and a host of other matters.

For such reasons, too, it is not possible to disentangle the legacies bequeathed by the colonizers to their former dependents from the colonial powers' own debts to their colonies. The colonies, for better or worse, were forced into social, educational, economic and industrial revolution. They acquired modern medicine and enhanced life expectancies. They absorbed and adapted European notions of law and administration. They acquired new educational and language opportunities for their young folk and were exposed to new beliefs. They were, in short, dragged into the modern world and forced to act independently within it.

The colonizers, for their part, learned lessons which may, in some ways, have been equally lasting, profound and valuable. At the latest by the end of the nineteenth century, imperialism and the empires exerted a profound influence, not only on the politics of the metropoles but on their literature, painting and cultures generally.[18] Britain, France and Holland have all been deeply affected by immigrant flows from their former colonies. Algerians in France, Javanese in Holland, Indians and Caribbeans in Britain, have greatly changed social customs and attitudes and even politics. It is no longer a matter of remark that persons with brown or black skins should sit in the French or Dutch parliaments or on the red benches of the House of Lords in London. Citizens of non-European background have risen to high positions in the law, in industry, in finance. Perhaps more to the point, the British, Dutch and French economies depend in some measure – possibly more than for most of the colonial period – on links of finance, trade and investment with former colonies.

But the matter goes much further. More Indians live in Britain and more British people in India, more Indonesians live in Holland and more Vietnamese and North Africans in France than was ever the case in the days of empire. Scientific and cultural influences have been profound. It is no coincidence that some of the most celebrated modern French writers should, like Albert Camus, have had a North African background; or that, by the 1990s, some of the most brilliant and innovative prose in English, should come from Indian writers like Salman Rushdie or Arundhati Roy; or that Zubin Mehta, Seiji Ozawa or Michiko Uchida should be in the front rank of Western musicians; or that sports in Europe – cricket, football, athletics – should often be dominated by athletes of non-European origin; or that India should have produced economists like Amartya Sen and Jagdish Baghwati; or that Asian foods are found in every West European supermarket; or that millions of Europeans drive Japanese or Korean-made cars.

Confronted with such a kaleidoscope, not to mention the restless search for novelty, the pendulum of historical interpretation continues to swing, turning villains into heroes and, more rarely, sages into mountebanks. Given the most prominent public and scholarly prejudices as the twenty-first century begins, debate about 'colonialism' seems sure to run and run.

Notes and References

Introduction

1. T.H. Marshall, *Class, Citizenship and Social Development* (Garden City, NY: Anchor Books, 1965), p. 72.

1 The Asian Order

1. They captured the last of the Abbasid caliphs and, to avoid offending heaven by shedding the blood of princes, put him in a sack to be trampled to death by horses. They also destroyed Mesopotamia's ancient irrigation systems with effects lasting to the present day.
2. Meaning 'divine wind'. The same word was used, almost seven centuries later, for the suicide flyers who tried to stem attacks on Japan in the closing months of the Second World War. They caused heavy losses to the US fleet.
3. The Serb military aristocracy quickly became a standard part of the Ottoman forces – quite contrary to later south Slav mythology.
4. Trade took time to develop, as the Mongols had destroyed the trading cities of Central Asia and slaughtered their inhabitants, except for useful artisans who were carted off to the Far East.
5. cf. Louis Levathes, *When China Ruled the Seas: The Treasure Fleet of the Dragon Throne 1403–33* (New York: Simon and Schuster, 1994).
6. Clearly, if China's 1980s and 1990s policies of one-child families succeeded, within a couple of generations Chinese children would have no brothers, sisters, aunts, uncles or cousins. The inherited structures of Chinese society would disintegrate.
7. Was that cultural imperialism? V.S. Naipaul has commented that:

   A convert's world view alters. His holy places are in Arab lands; his sacred language is Arabic. His idea of history alters. He rejects his own; he becomes, whether he likes it or not, a part of the Arab story. The convert has to turn away from everything that is his. The disturbance for societies is immense, and even after a thousand years can remain unresolved; the turning away has to be done again and again ...

   Beyond Belief: Islamic Excursions among the converted peoples (London: Little Brown, 1998).

8. cf. Clifford Geertz, *Islam Observed; religious development in Morocco and Indonesia* (Chicago: Chicago University Press, 1968).
9. It was a folk Islam that first spread in Java, Borneo, Sumatra and the Celebes. Scriptural Islam only came in the nineteenth century, with the

advent of steamships, pilgrimages to Mecca and the possibility of elite education in religious schools and seminaries in Cairo. In the meantime, many Moslem converts in Java practised their traditional mysticism while Chinese Christians continued with ancestor worship.

10. It is estimated that China's population was probably some 100–150 million in 1650, 200–250 million in 1750, over 300 by 1800, 400 by 1850 and 500–650 in 1950.

11. People could be moved around like cattle. They still are, as demonstrated in the 1990s removal of villagers to make way for the Three Gorges dam. In the orgy of Chinese ship-building of 1404–07 hundreds of carpenters, sailmakers, smiths and other artisans were simply ordered to move to the shipyards and dry-docks (which Europe did not have until several centuries later).

12. Joseph Buttinger, *A Dragon Defiant* (Newton Abbott: David and Charles, 1972), p. 31.

13. Ibid., p. 55.

14. Derived from *bushi* or military gentleman.

2 Explorers, Soldiers, Priests and Traders

1. The Black Death, in 1346–49, killed off a quarter to half of Europe's population.

2. In the twenty-first century Chinese and Italians could still debate which of them had invented spaghetti.

3. Some scholars say this is exaggerated: what Martel beat was not much more than a raiding party.

4. Paul Bairoch, *Economics and World History: Myths and Paradoxes* (Chicago: University of Chicago Press, 1993), pp. 101–10; Thomas McCraw (ed.), *Creating Modern Capitalism* (Cambridge, MA: Harvard University Press, 1997), p. 1.

5. Europe's peasants could not yet store winter fodder for cattle. Many peasants kept one male and one female of each species in their huts and slaughtered the rest in the autumn. A month or two later, even dried or salted meat had gone off and spices were needed to disguise the taste. Demand was naturally high. Proper refrigeration came much later. In the middle of the seventeenth century Francis Bacon experimented with it by stuffing a chicken with snow: he caught a cold doing it, and died. Refrigeration apart, pepper was used as a physic, ginger to aid digestion, and cloves to strengthen the liver, the heart and eyesight. Even more helpfully, in small quantities and with milk, cloves were thought to be an aphrodisiac.

6. cf. A report by James Pringle in *The Times*, 23 May 1998, p. 17, on a rare visit by Western reporters to the Xanadu site, which turns out to be in the Inner Mongolian grassland, some 170 miles from Beijing.

7. Long before the Europeans came to Africa there was a lively slave trade among local chiefs, as well as with Arabs, who ran their sugar industry by slave labour. African states and tribes went to war with each other often enough to have lots of prisoners to sell. (Classical Greece and Persia had similar habits with prisoners taken in war.) The Portuguese therefore had no difficulty buying slaves from West African or Arab traders. See, for

instance, Murray Gordon, *Slavery in the Arab World* (New York: New Amsterdam, 1989), esp. pp. 105–27. Also Hugh Thomas, *The Slave Trade; the History of the Atlantic Slave Trade* (New York: Simon and Schuster, 1997).

8. Even though Moorish commanders may have been more hindered than helped by some of their North African Berber mercenaries.

9. When its last Moorish ruler, Boabdil, withdrew from the city, he wept. His mother commented coldly: 'You weep like a woman for a city you could not defend like a man.'

10. Quoted in G.F. Hudson, *Europe and China* (London: Arnold, 1931), p. 201.

11. The Portuguese, whom the locals quaintly called 'white Bengalis', had ships and cannon, while the locals only had pikes and bows and arrows. Furthermore, though Malacca could call on 100 000 men, most of them were poorly paid Javanese with no love of the ruler.

12. Magellan reached Guam and the Philippines, where he died in an encounter with natives. Of his fleet, the *Vittoria* reached home in 1522, three years after setting out, with eighteen survivors out of the several hundred who had left home.

13. Named after the prince who would become King Philip II of Spain.

14. The title of Oscar Spate's splendid book *The Spanish Lake* (Minneapolis: University of Minnesota Press, 1979).

15. By the sixteenth century, Spain had agreed that Portugal should have the lands of the future Brazil.

16. Trading between Malacca, China and Japan was said to carry profits of up to 2000 per cent.

17. At first, Castile, like Portugal, looked west rather than south–North Africa looked difficult and unprofitable – while Aragon tended to go east into the Mediterranean. The westward thrust began by making money in the Canaries.

18. Fifty years later Portuguese carracks sailing to India might displace 500–1000 tons.

19. The classic account is by Bishop Bartolomé de las Casas, Bishop of Chiapa 1474–1566, *Brevísima relación de la destrucción de last Indias* (Brief Relation of the Destruction of the Indies) (1552) (Madrid: Anjana, 1983).

20. T. Todorov, *La Conquête de l'Amérique* (Paris: Seuil, 1982).

21. Quoted in Hubert Deschamps, *The French Union: history, institutions, economy, countries and peoples, social and political changes* (Paris: Berger-Levrault, 1956), p. 3.

22. Drake was a fairly typical figure. Probably a preacher's son, brought up in Plymouth by a family of freebooting traders, he became a slave trader and graduated into piracy. He became respectable only much later, as a naval commander in the Queen's service.

23. The equivalent September 2000 purchasing power would be some £103 millions. Time series on purchasing power parities made available by courtesy of the Bank of England, hereafter referred to as BoE tables.

24. Fernand Braudel quotes the historian Selaniki Mustafa Efendi, who reported in astonishment on the arrival of the second English ambassador to the Ottoman court, the Sublime Porte, in 1593: 'A ship as strange as this had never entered the port of Istanbul. It crossed 3700 miles of sea and carried 83 guns, besides other weapons. The outward form of the firearms was in

the shape of a swine.' *La Mediterranée et le monde méditerranéen à l'époque de Philippe II* (2 vols) (Paris: Armand Colin, 1986).

25. Queen Elizabeth's intelligence system was so good that the invasion plans were studied in London before the armada even sailed.

26. It was part of the dowry of Catherine of Braganza, whose marriage to Charles II consolidated an Anglo-Portuguese interest in opposing the Dutch.

27. G.H. Wilson, 'Trade, Society and the State', in H.J. Habakkuk and M. Postan (eds), *The Cambridge Economic History of Europe*, Vol. IV, *The Economy of Expanding Europe in the Sixteenth and Seventeenth Centuries*, E.E. Rich and C.H. Wilson (eds) (Cambridge: Cambridge University Press, 1967), p. 522.

28. With all its familiar risks. In the 1630s the Dutch tulip 'bubble' burst after the issuing of options very like some financial instruments of the 1990s.

29. C.R. Boxer, *The Dutch Seaborne Empire 1600–1800* (London: Hutchinson, 1965), p. 4.

30. He held office twice: from 1618–23 and from 1627 to his death in 1629.

31. A Moslem Malay group in the Southern Philippines.

32. Hugo de Groot (Grotius), *De jure belli ac pacis* (Paris: Apud W. Buon, 1625).

33. Named after the Dutch province of Zeeland.

34. One of them, the *Heemskirk*, also bequeathed her name to one of modern Tasmania's better red wines.

35. Education, too. The first major Dutch university, Leiden, was founded in 1575 and Utrecht followed in 1636.

36. An excellent discussion of the wall's history and meaning is in Arthur Waldron, *The Great Wall of China; From History to Myth* (Cambridge: Cambridge University Press, 1992).

37. Both the Russian and Chinese negotiators seem to have used Jesuits, who could do the interpreting.

38. The emperor's response to Macartney is quoted in Alain Peyrefitte, *The Collision of Two Civilisations* (London: HarperCollins, 1993).

39. Ieyasu handed over the shogunate to his son in 1605 but retained effective control until his death eleven years later.

40. The Dutch discovered some sixty local languages in the Moluccas alone.

3   Nationalism and Revolution in Europe

1. The earliest Hittite texts display notions of ethnic or cultural grouping. So does Mycenean Greek.

2. The chief early theoretician of the secular state was Machiavelli, followed by Jean Bodin and others.

3. The Council of Trent, which ended in 1563, condemned clerical abuses (against which Luther had railed), defined correct doctrine, and reformed the supervision of church affairs.

4. Followers of Cornelius Jansenius, Bishop of Ypres.

5. The phrase is Liah Greenfeld's in *Nationalism: Five roads to modernity* (Cambridge MA: Harvard University Press, 1992), p. 111.

6. That was not, *per se*, a new idea. In ancient times, kings had often served as well as ruled. And both *Magna Carta* in 1215 in England and the famous

oath of allegiance of the Aragonese *Cortes* of Ferdinand's day made respect for prior rights a condition of royal power.

7. Wilson, 'Trade, Society and the State', op. cit., p. 571.
8. The Journals of the House of Commons, Vol. 1, p. 243.
9. Christopher Hill and E. Dell, *The Good Old Cause 1640–1660* (New York: Augustus M. Kelley, 1969), p. 307, cited in Greenfeld, *Nationalism*, op. cit., p. 73.
10. In some German principalities, one person out of three died.
11. Cobbett, *Complete Collection of State Trials Vol. V (1640–1649)* (London: Longmans, 1828), Cols 990–1142.
12. S.R. Gardiner, *The Constitutional Documents of the Puritan Revolution 1625–1660* (3rd edn) (Oxford: Clarendon Press, 1906), p. 387.
13. D.L. Keir, *The Constitutional History of Modern Britain* (7th edn), (London: Adam and Charles Black, 1964), pp. 267 et seq.
14. As Blackstone, the greatest legal authority of eighteenth-century England, was to put it, regular forces should be seen: '... only as temporary excrescences bred out of the distemper of the State, and not as any part of the permanent and perpetual laws of the Kingdom.' (Commentary on the Laws of England, Book 1, Chapter 13 (4th edn London 1777, Vol. I), p. 412, cited in Michael Howard, *War in European History* (Oxford: Oxford University Press, 1976), p. 88.
15. In his two 'Treatises of Civil Government'.
16. J.L. Talmon, *The Origins of Totalitarian Democracy* (London: Secker and Warburg, 1952).
17. Greenfeld, *Nationalism*, op. cit., p. 176.
18. Hegel, *Vorlesungen über die Philosophie der Geschichte*, trans. J. Sibree (New York: P.F. Collier and Son, 1902).
19. *Dissertation pour être lues; la première sur le vieux mot Patrie;la seconde sur la nature du peuple* (La Haye, 1755).
20. A Vicar of Bray-like figure, best remembered for his account, in old age, of what he had done during his long life since before the 1789 revolution: '*j'ai survécu*' (I survived).
21. *Qu'est ce que le Tiers Etat?* (Paris, 1788), p. 67.
22. Isaiah Berlin, *The Roots of Romanticism*, ed. Henry Hardy (Princeton: Princeton University Press, 1999).
23. Quoted in Lord Acton, *Lectures on Modern History* (London: Collins, 1960), p. 311.
24. In Paris, the Duc de Choiseul remarked as early as 1765 that London's conquest of Canada would lead to friction with the Americas and eventual loss of the colonies.
25. Grenville's Stamp Act of 1765 was introduced largely because the North American colonies paid only some £100 000 per annum in taxes while Britain's population, three or four times as large, paid a hundred times as much. But even that Stamp Act would only have raised one sixth of the annual cost of £350 000 (2000 = £25 million, BoE) needed to keep British land forces in North America to guard against the French and the Indians. Nor were the Americans were any keener to pay taxes to continental congresses than to the British, or than they were to be two centuries later under Presidents Reagan, Bush and Clinton. George Washington's army

was financed by printing money, through inflation, and hoping for revenue later.

26. J.H. Plumb, *England in the Eighteenth Century* (London: Penguin, 1990), pp. 124–5.

27. *Wealth of Nations*, Book IV, Ch 7 (2 vols, London, 1776) new rev. edn, ed. J.S. Nicholson (London: Nelson, 1884).

28. *North Briton*, No. 45, 1763.

29. Edmund Burke, *Thoughts on the Cause of the Present Discontents* ed. W. Murison (Cambridge: Cambridge University Press, 1913), p. 67.

30. Doniol Henry, *Histoire de la participation de la France à l'établissement des États-Unis d'Amérique. Correspondence diplomatique et documents* (5 vols) (Paris: 1885–9), quoted in Piers Mackesy, *The War for America 1775–1783* (Lincoln: University of Nebraska Press, 1993), p. 28. Mackesy's is by far the best assessment of the war, and of British policies, from a British perspective.

31. His fervour went beyond politics. He fathered an illegitimate child by the daughter of a surgeon from Blois.

32. Jacques Godechot (ed.), *Les Constitutions de la France, depuis 1789* (Paris: Garnier-Flammarion, 1970), quoted in Greenfeld, *Nationalism*, op. cit., p. 172.

33. Jürgen Habermas, *Between Facts and Norms; Contributions to a Discourse Theory of Law and Democracy*, trans. R.E. Williams (Cambridge: Polity, 1996), pp. 492, 495.

34. The period is fascinating in its sheer confusions. The Jacobins displayed a quasi-liturgical devotion to the 'Goddess of Reason' and to social purification; but Paris was also swarming with prophets, seers and mystics of both sexes and none. For instance Catherine Théot, Robespierre's sister-in-law, the 'Mother of God', held religious services and dispensed 'Seven Gifts of the Holy Ghost'.

35. Montesquieu (1689–1755) in his *Esprit des Lois* (The Spirit of Laws).

36. Isaiah Berlin, *The Sense of Reality; Studies in Ideas and their History*, ed. Henry Hardy (London: Chatto and Windus, 1996), p. 19.

37. When Napoleon Bonaparte crowned himself Emperor in 1804 Beethoven, in disgust, decided to name it the 'Eroica' instead.

38. David Landes, *The Wealth and Poverty of Nations* (London: Little Brown, 1998), p. 137.

39. cf. Zeev Sternhell, *The Founding Myths of Israel: Nationalism, Socialism and the Making of the Jewish State* (Princeton: Princeton University Press, 1997).

40. Soetan Sjahrir, *Out of Exile: based upon letters*, trans. with an introduction by Charles Wolf Jr (New York: John Day, 1949), p. 207.

41. Howard G. Brown, *War, Revolution and the Bureaucratic State; Politics and Army Administration in France 1791–1799* (Oxford: Clarendon Press, 1995), pp. 9, 266.

42. The role of war has nowhere been more elegantly discussed than in Howard's brief but magisterial *War in European History*, op. cit.

43. W.H. McNeill, *The Age of Gunpowder Empires 1450–1800 (Essays on Global and Comparative History)* (Washington DC: American Historical Association, 1989), Chapter 4, esp. p. 23.

44. Tom Pocock, *Battle for Empire: The very first World War* (London: Michael O'Mara, 1998).

45. Howard, *War in European History*, op. cit., p. 80.

46. G.R. Elton has written of '... the change from a civil service recruited from the King's personal servants to one staffed by professional careerists outside the household ...', *The Tudor Revolution in Government* (Cambridge: Cambridge University Press, 1959), p. 423.

47. G.E. Aylmer, *The State's Servants; the Civil Service of the English Republic 1649–60* (London: Routledge and Kegan Paul, 1973), pp. 341, 321. The 2000 equivalent is £107.3–121.6 million (BoE tables).

48. Wilson, 'Trade, Society and the State', op. cit., p. 522.

49. *'Depuis Louis XV surtout, le traditionalisme des formes masque l'émergence d'un pouvoir administratif ... L'Administration s'affirme comme une puissance virtuellement autonome.'* François Burdeau, *Histoire de l'administration française; du 18e au 20e siècle* (Paris: Montchrestien, 1989), p. 28.

50. Henry Parris dates the emergence of a permanent civil service at around 1780. What existed before was 'not permanent, it was not civil, and it was not a service'. cf. his 'The Origins of the Permanent Civil Service 1780–1830', *Public Administration*, Vol. 46, 1968, pp. 143–66.

51. Clive Church, *Revolution and Red Tape: The French Ministerial Bureaucracy 1770–1850* (Oxford: Oxford University Press, 1981); and Brown, *War, Revolution and the Bureaucratic State*, op. cit.

52. Burke, *Thoughts on the prospect of a Regicide Peace* (London: J. Owen, 1796).

53. cf. Wantje Fritschy, 'Taxation in Britain, France and The Netherlands in the Eighteenth Century', in Marjolein t'Hart, Joost Jonker and Jan Luiten van Zanden, *A Financial History of the Netherlands* (Cambridge: Cambridge University Press, 1997), Chapter 3, p. 59.

54. There was, of course, no income tax. Around 1760, land tax was some 60 per cent of direct taxes but only some 11 per cent of total revenue. cf. P.K. O'Brien, 'The Political Economy of British Taxation 1660–1815', *Economic History Review*, 41, 1988, pp. 10–11 and table 5.

55. All bracketed figures in this passage are from the BoE tables.

56. O'Brien, 'Political Economy of Taxation', op. cit, pp. 1–32. See also P. Mathias and P. O'Brien, 'Taxation in Britain and France 1715–1810; A comparison of the social and economic incidence of taxes collected for central governments', *Journal of European Economic History*, 5, 1976, pp. 601–50.

57. Peter Botticelli, 'British Capitalism and the Three Industrial Revolutions', in McCraw (ed.), *Creating Modern Capitalism*, op. cit, p. 55.

58. Peter Mathias, *The First Industrial Nation: an economic history of Britain 1700–1914* (London: Methuen, 1969), p. 39, table III.

59. Charles Wilson, *Queen Elizabeth and the Revolt of the Netherlands* (London: Macmillan, 1970), p. 573.

60. Botticelli, 'British Capitalism and the Three Industrial Revolutions', op. cit, p. 12.

61. But 'capitalism' did not become generally used until around 1850, and then as an antonym for 'socialism'.

62. Quoted in Plumb, *England in the Eighteenth Century*, op. cit., p. 114.

63. Mathias, *The First Industrial Nation*, op. cit., p. 94.

64. The earlier figures are from Karl F. Helleiner, 'The Population of Europe from the Black Death to the End of the Vital Revolution', in Habakkuk and Postan (eds), *Cambridge Economic History of Europe*, Vol. VI, *The Industrial*

Revolutions and After, I, op. cit., Chapter 1, p. 67. The later figures are from D.V. Glass and E. Grebnik, 'World Population 1800–1950', ibid., p. 61.

65. The romance of South America has cast its spell on the minds of Englishmen since the days of the buccaneers. A South Sea Company was floated in London, to offer a huge reduction of Britain's public debt in exchange for a monopoly of Spanish trade. The shares of the company multiplied by eight, frenzy led to crash, and a lot of people lost their shirts.

66. Plumb, *England in the Eighteenth Century*, op. cit., p. 77.

67. Joseph Schumpeter, *Capitalism, Socialism and Democracy* (10th impression) (London: Unwin University Books, 1965), p. 79.

68. David S. Landes, 'Technological Change and Development in Western Europe 1750–1914', in Habakkuk and Postan (eds), *Cambridge Economic History of Europe*, Vol. IV, *The Industrial Revolution and After*, op. cit., p. 275.

69. Mathias, *The First Industrial Nation*, op. cit., p. 121.

70. As early as the 1720s mathematicians had begun to devise tables of life expectancies which became an essential aid to insurance.

71. Nick Crafts, 'The Industrial Revolution', in Roderick Floud and Donald McCloskey (eds), *The Economic History of Britain since 1700* (2nd edn) (Cambridge: Cambridge University Press, 1994), Vol. 1, p. 47. Peter Mathias and John A. Davis give slightly different growth figures for England and Wales: 1710–40: 0.2 per cent; 1740–80: 1 per cent; 1780–1800: 2 per cent; 1800–31: 3.06 per cent. cf. Mathias and Davis (eds), *The First Industrial Revolution* (Oxford: Blackwell, 1989), Chapter 1, p. 7.

72. It went up even more quickly elsewhere: by fifteen in Germany, eighteen in the USA and twenty-five in Japan. Angus Maddison, *Dynamic Forces in Capitalist Development* (New York: Oxford University Press, 1991), pp. 6–7.

73. P.C. Emmer, *The Economic Impact of Dutch Expansion Overseas 1570–1870* (Revista de Historia Economica, Madrid: Centro de Estudios Constitucionales, 1999), pp. 22–4.

74. G. Ellis, *History of the Late Revolution in the Dutch Republic* (London: J. Edwards, 1789), p. 66.

75. A brilliant and detailed account of this period can be found in Simon Schama, *Patriots and Liberators; Revolution in the Netherlands 1780–1813* (New York: Alfred Knopf, 1977).

4   From Trade to Empire

1. Thomas Babington Macaulay, 'Frederic the Great', *The Edinburgh Review*, April 1842 (a review essay on Thomas Campbell (ed.), *Frederic the Great and his Times* [2 vols], London, 1842).

2. In this passage, figures in brackets are the 2000 equivalents, taken from the BoE tables.

3. Moderate or not, contentment eluded him. He died aged forty-nine, whether by his own hand or his wife's is not clear.

4. Since travel to and from London took nine months, local administration was, in practice, left to the governors of the Calcutta, Madras and Bombay presidencies.

5. Quoted in Rajat Kanta Ray, 'Indian Society and the Establishment of British Supremacy', in P.J. Marshall and Alaine Low (eds), *The Oxford History of the British Empire*, Vol. II, *The Eighteenth Century* (Oxford: Oxford University Press, 1998), p. 508.

6. P.J. Marshall, 'The British in Asia: Trade to Dominion 1700–1765', in Marshall and Low (eds), *The Oxford History of the British Empire*, Vol. II, *The Eighteenth Century*, op. cit., Chapter 22, p. 504.

7. It was ended by Lord Mansfield's judgment in *Somersett's case*, about a West Indian slave kept on a ship in the Thames while his master was in London. Mansfield famously observed that slavery was so odious that only positive law might make it legal: 'the air in England is too pure for any slave to breathe; let the black go free.' Some 10 000 slaves held in England were released.

8. Not that the colonists objected to all restraints on trade. The 1774 Declaration of Rights by the First American Continental Congress said that '... we cheerfully consent to the operation of such Acts of the British Parliament, as are *bona fide*, restrained to the regulation of our external commerce, for the purpose of securing the commercial advantages of the whole empire to the mother country ...'.

9. A sect whose members strangled unsuspecting travellers in the name of religion. Hence the modern word 'thug'.

10. The Indian custom of widows burning themselves to death on their husband's funeral pyre. Not all widows went willingly. When the British banned the practice, some Indians appealed to Sir Charles Napier, by then the governor of Sind, not to ban this old and venerated custom. Napier replied that Britain had an old and venerated custom of hanging people who burned widows alive, and he was quite committed to enforcing it.

11. Which is said, perhaps apocryphally, to have produced one of the more famous puns of British imperial history. The British commander, that same choleric Sir Charles Napier, clearly had a decent classical education. On occupying Sind, he reported back with a one-word telegram, in Latin: 'Peccavi' (I have sinned).

12. In 1819, for example, Rammohan Roy founded a group to restore Hindu monotheism.

13. Giuseppe Verdi's opera *Aida* was composed for the opening festivities.

14. J.C. Van Leur, *Indonesian Trade and Society* (The Hague: Van Hoeve, 1967), p. 169. See also John Smail, 'On the Possibility of an Autonomous History of Modern South-east Asia', *Journal of Southeast Asian History*, Vol. 2, 1961, p. 92; and J.D. Legge, *Indonesia* (New Jersey: Prentice-Hall, 1964). As noted, in Indonesia and elsewhere, Islam adapted to pre-existing beliefs and incorporated some of the old animism. One interpretation of modern Islamic fundamentalism is as rage at this historical process of dilution and adaptation.

15. Quoted in George Kahin, *Nationalism and Revolution in Indonesia* (Ithaca: Cornell University Press, 1970), p. 8.

16. B.H.M. Vlekke, *The Story of the Dutch East Indies* (Cambridge, MA: Harvard University Press, 1946), p. 178.

17. J.S. Furnivall, *Netherlands India; A Study of Plural Economy* (Cambridge: Cambridge University Press, 1939), p. 134. D.K. Fieldhouse gives a figure of 18 million per annum around the middle of the century, *The Colonial*

Empires; a comparative survey from the eighteenth century (2nd edn) (London: Macmillan, 1982), p. 333.

18. A.R.J. Turgot, *Oeuvres*, Vol. V (1923), quoted in Mackesy, *The War for America*, op. cit., p. 103.

19. Quoted in Robert Aldrich, *The French Presence in the South Pacific 1842–1940* (London: Macmillan, 1990), p. 2.

20. The letter flatly refusing British requests for trade seems to have been written three days before Macartney even set foot on Chinese soil.

21. Teng Ssu-yu and John K. Fairbank, *China's Response to the West 1839–1923* (Cambridge, MA: Harvard University Press, 1954), p. 19. See also Michael Loewe, *Imperial China: the historical background* (London: Allen and Unwin, 1966), pp. 213–14.

22. For the text, see 'Treaty between China and Great Britain signed at Nanking 29 August 1842', in *The Consolidated Treaty Series*, Clive Parry (ed.), Vol. 93 (1842) (Dobbs Ferry, New York: Oceana Publications, 1969), pp. 465–74.

23. Visitors to the modern PRC have often noted that students express fierce resentment of these ancient 'crimes' by Western states. The hordes of Chinese opium dealers have been conveniently forgotten; and statues put up to Commissioner Lin.

24. Archery and swordsmanship were stressed, but for character-building rather than for any military value. It was rather like the nineteenth-century German student custom of testing character by sabre duels.

25. Reading and writing naturally meant mastering ideographs, not Arabic script.

5   Imperial Apotheosis

1. J.A. Williamson, *Sir John Hawkins, the Time and the Man* (Oxford: Clarendon Press, 1927), p. 451; Charles Wilson, *Queen Elizabeth and the Revolt of the Netherlands* (London: Macmillan, 1970), both quoted in Michael Howard, *The Causes of Wars* (London: Unwin, 1983), p. 193.

2. Quoted in K. Bourne, *The Foreign Policy of Victorian England 1830–1902* (Oxford: Clarendon Press, 1970), p. 201.

3. That included repeal of the Corn Laws (to cope with famine in Ireland) and, in 1849, of the old Navigation Acts which had caused so much trouble with the Dutch.

4. Speech of 9 February 1871 in the House of Commons.

5. J.R. Seeley, *The Expansion of England* (2nd edn) (London: Macmillan, 1920), p. 62.

6. War aims statement of 9 September 1914. cf. Fritz Fischer, *Griff nach der Weltmacht: Die Kriegspolitik des kaiserlichen Deutschland 1914–1918* (Düsseldorf: Droste, 1961), pp. 107–12.

7. Jules Ferry, *Le Tonkin et la mère Patrie* (12th edn) (Paris, 1890). Foreword.

8. cf. George Watson, *The Lost Literature of Socialism* (Cambridge: Lutterworth Press, 1998), esp. Chapter 8.

9. Michael Howard, *The Franco-Prussian War* (New York: Collier Books, 1969), p. 455.

10. Kevin O'Rourke and Jeffrey Williamson, *Globalization and History: The Evolution of a Nineteenth-Century Atlantic Economy* (Cambridge, MA: MIT Press, 1999).

11. D.K. Fieldhouse, 'The Metropolitan Economics of Empire', in Judith M. Brown and Wm Roger Louis (eds), *The Oxford History of the British Empire*, Vol. IV, *The Twentieth Century*, (Oxford: Oxford University Press, 1999), pp. 98, 111.

12. British investment flows overseas increased between 1900 and 1914, reaching 7–8 per cent of GDP, but interest in new territories fell away. Fieldhouse has estimated that by 1914 the nominal value of accumulated British capital at home and overseas was some £5.783 billion (£275.8 billion), of which 42.6 per cent was in foreign countries, 31.6 per cent at home and 19.8 per cent in the empire. And of that in the empire, some nine tenths had gone to the Dominions which had fiscal and political autonomy. Fieldhouse, ibid., p. 96. Also, average rates of return on capital just before the war seem to have been 3.1 per cent in Britain, 3.5 per cent in the empire and 3.7 per cent in foreign countries. O'Rourke and Williamson, *Globalization and History* op. cit., suggest similar aggregate capital export figures.

13. Fieldhouse, 'The Metropolitan Economics of Empire', op. cit., p. 100. Measured in dollars, investments in Asia and Africa were some $2 650 million, compared with $6 350 million in the white Dominions and $9 085 million in the rest of the non-Empire world, half of that in the USA. France had invested some $1 200 million in Asia and Africa, and $8 130 million elsewhere, over a quarter of that in Russia. G. Barraclough (ed.), *The Times Atlas of World History* (London: Times Books, 1978).

14. Barraclough, ibid.

15. So, fortunately, were the activities in the Congo of that ruthless royal scoundrel, King Leopold of Belgium.

16. Robinson and Gallagher have, however, put forward the now well-known thesis which puts special importance upon 'informal imperialism', where direct political dominance is unnecessary.

17. Denis Judd, *Balfour and the British Empire* (London: Macmillan, 1968), p. 224.

18. Carlton J.H. Hayes, 'New Imperialism – New Nationalism', in Martin Wolfe (ed.), *The Economic Causes of Imperialism* (New York: Wiley, 1972), p. 69.

19. In 1862 Napoleon III sent 30 000 troops to Mexico and set up a puppet government under the amiable, courageous but not very effective Austrian Archduke Maximilian. By 1865 the French evacuated, the Mexican leader Benito Juarez, moved in, and Maximilian was shot.

20. G. Clark, *The Balance Sheets of Imperialism* (Washington DC: Carnegie Endowment for International Peace, 1936), pp. 5–6.

21. The German historian Erich Marcks, *Die imperialistische Idee in der Gegenwart* (1903), in E. Marcks *Männer und Zeiten* (2 vols) (Leipzig, 1911), p. 271.

22. As when Kaiser William II of Germany, farewelling troops about to leave for China to join in suppressing the Boxer rebellion, told them to kill all their prisoners.

23. A.P. Thornton, *The Imperial Idea and its Enemies: a study in British power* (London: Macmillan, 1959), p. 76.

24. Speech of 28 July 1885, quoted in Henri Brunschwig, *French Colonialism 1871–1914: myths and realities* (London: Pall Mall Press, 1966), p. 78.

25. A.P. Thornton, *The Imperial Idea and its Enemies*, op. cit., p. 72.

26. Chasseloup-Laubat, Minister of the Navy and the Colonies 1860–7.

27. See, for instance, the condemnation of Rudyard Kipling's fine poem 'The White Man's Burden' as 'racist', which says nothing about Kipling, but

much about the confusion of Western racial anxieties in the late twentieth century and early twenty-first.

28. In 1907 the Dacca and Chittagong divisions of Bengal contained some 17.5 million people. They were governed by just twenty-one British civil servants and twelve British police officers. J. Holland Rose et al. (genl eds), *Cambridge History of the British Empire*, Vol. V, *The Indian Empire 1858–1918*, H.H. Dodwell (ed.), (Cambridge: Cambridge University Press, 1932), p. 252.
29. Charles W. Dilke and Spenser Wilkinson, *Imperial Defence* (London: Macmillan, 1892), pp. 101–3.
30. cf. Sir Keith Hancock, *Smuts Vol. 1: The Sanguine Years 1870–1919* (Cambridge: Cambridge University Press, 1962), p. 108.
31. Quoted in E. Stokes, *The English Utilitarians and India* Oxford: Clarendon Press, 1959) pp. 45–6.
32. Quoted in Rupert Emerson, *From Empire to Nation* (Boston: Beacon Press, 1962), p. 77.
33. Two-thirds of them went to the USA.
34. cf. W.K. Hancock, *Survey of British Commonwealth Affairs*, Vol. II, *Problems of Economic Policy 1918–1939*, (London: Oxford University Press, 1940), p. 128.
35. Maurice Bruce, *The Shaping of the Modern World 1870–1939*, (London: Hutchinson, 1958), p. 431.
36. Inventions can have unforeseen results. News of the 1857 Indian Mutiny set off a currency panic in New York.
37. Edwin Arnold, quoted in Trevor O. Lloyd, *The British Empire 1558–1983* (New York: Oxford University Press, 1984), p. 177.
38. Largely composed of minority groups.
39. *Letters and Journals of James, Eighth Earl of Elgin* (ed. T. Walrond) (London: John Murray, 1872), pp. 213, 232.
40. Letter of 25 November 1861 to Captain Butler, Guernsey, quoted in Peyrefitte, *The Collision of Two Civilisations*, op. cit, p. 530.
41. Denis Twitchett and John K. Fairbank (genl eds), *The Cambridge History of China*, Vol. XIII, John K. Fairbank and Albert Feuerwerker (eds), *Republican China 1912–1949* (Cambridge: Cambridge University Press, 1986).
42. Mahan's *The Influence of Sea Power upon History 1660–1783* appeared in 1890 and his plea for US naval power in the *Atlantic Monthly* in December of the same year.
43. cf. Paul Deschanel, *Les intérêts français dans l'Océan Pacifique* (Paris: Nancy, 1888).
44. *New Cambridge Modern History*, Vol. XI, F. Hinsley (ed.), *Material Progress and World-wide Problems 1870–1898* (Cambridge: Cambridge University Press, 1962), p. 639.
45. A.J.P. Taylor, *The Struggle for Mastery in Europe 1848–1918* (Oxford: Clarendon Press, 1954), Chapter 1.
46. Michael Howard, *The Causes of Wars* (London: Unwin, 1983), pp. 16–17.
47. This was, of course, manhood suffrage. Votes for women came later.
48. The best-known early exploration of some of these phenomena is probably J. Ortega Y Gasset, *The Revolt of the Masses* (*La Rebelión de las Masas*, Madrid, 1930) (London: Allen & Unwin, 1932).
49. Which followed a failed government campaign in 1878 to destroy the growing social democratic movement.

50. Figures in brackets are, once again, the 2000 equivalents as from the BoE tables.
51. Mathias, *The First Industrial Nation*, op. cit., Appendix Tables 12–13, pp. 428–9.
52. Various sources naturally differ. One authority says central ministry staff figures rose in France from 175 000 in 1866 to over one million in 1947; and in Britain from 16 000 in 1780 to 54 000 in 1870. Another says central government staffs increased in France from 75 000 in 1866 to 799 000 in 1975; in Holland from 12 746 in 1877 to 146 940 in 1975; and in Britain from 40 300 in 1851 to 476 700 in 1968. cf. Peter Flora (et al.), *State, Economy and Society in Western Europe 1815–1975: A data handbook*, Vol. 1, *The Growth of Mass Democracies and Welfare States* (London: Macmillan, 1983).
53. There were various side effects. In 1850 there were already 755 companies listed on the London stock exchange; and in 1881 Britain had 1470 accountants while by 1981 there were 141 913. cf. Derek Matthews, Malcolm Anderson and John Richard Edwards, *The Priesthood of Industry – The Rise of the Professional Accountant in British Management* (London: Oxford University Press, 1997).
54. *The Communist Manifesto* (ed. Frederic L. Bender) (New York: Norton, 1988), p. 59. It is interesting to consider this passage in the light of moves towards European unification in the late twentieth century and early twenty-first.
55. *Communist Manifesto*, ibid., p. 57.
56. Joseph Schumpeter, *Capitalism, Socialism and Democracy*, op. cit.
57. The title of a pamphlet by the American journalist W.T. Stead.
58. The first note was dated 6 September 1899, the second 3 July 1900. They called for 'equal and impartial trade' with China and its maintenance as a 'territorial and administrative entity'. *Foreign Relations of the United States 1901*, Appendix (Washington, DC: USGPO, 1902), p. 12.
59. He was a true prophet. 'As long as we rule India,' he wrote in 1901, 'we are the greatest power in the world. If we lose it we shall drop straight away to a third rate power.' Seven years later he repeated that if Britain lost India 'Your ports and your coaling stations, your fortresses and dockyards, your Crown Colonies and protectorates will go too.' (1901: cf. David Dilks, *Curzon in India*, Vol. 1 [London: Rupert Hart-Davis, 1969], p. 113; 1908: quoted in Thornton, *The Imperial Idea and its Enemies*, op. cit, p. 145.) See also Max Beloff, *Imperial Sunset*, Vol. I, *Britain's Liberal Empire 1897–1921* (London: Methuen, 1969), p. 37. By the 1990s Britain's push to join the inner circle of the European Union largely rested on a quite similar wish to take a lead in a political entity of global importance.
60. Charles W. Dilke and Spenser Wilkinson, *Imperial Defence*, op. cit., p. 97.
61. Aaron L. Friedberg, *The Weary Titan: Britain and the Experience of Relative Decline 1895–1905* (Princeton: Princeton University Press, 1988), Chapter 5. During the Napoleonic wars, the British Army had, at most, something under 240 000 men. By the time of the Crimean War of 1856, it was only about 10 000 more. cf. Friedberg, ibid., p. 212, fn. 4.
62. Ronald Robinson and John Gallagher, *Africa and the Victorians: The official mind of imperialism* (London: Macmillan 1961), p. 462.
63. Quoted in Michael Howard, 'Empires, Nations and Wars', in Michael Howard, *The Lessons of History* (Oxford: Oxford University Press, 1993), p. 22.

64. Howard, *The Continental Commitment* (London: Temple Smith, 1972), p. 10.
65. Quoted in J. Romein, *The Asian Century. A history of modern nationalism in Asia* (London: Allen & Unwin, 1962), pp. 12–13.
66. Quoted in A.B. Keith (ed.), *Selected Speeches and Documents on British Colonial Policy 1763–1917*, Vol. II (Oxford: Blackwell, 1953), p. 353.
67. Much of this was suspect among respectable folk. Clearly, socialism meant beards, free love and not too much soap. See Alan Ryan, *New York Review*, 24 September 1998, p. 50.
68. The word comes from the *hashishiyun*, a Moslem murder cult of the time of the crusades.
69. Even much later, in 1935, Stalin found he had to play down class struggle in favour of united front tactics. He fought the Second World War with forthright appeals to the traditional national symbols of Mother Russia.

6   Imitation and Rejection

1. '... the basic social, economic and religious factors which determined the structure of Asian society remained unchanged until the 19th and in many instances until the 20th century ...' Boxer, *Seaborne Empire*, op. cit., p. 194.
2. Ernest Renan 'Qu'est ce qu'une nation?', in *Oeuvres complètes de Ernest Renan*, Vol. 1 (1882) (Paris: Calmann-Levy, 1947), pp. 887–906. For a general discussion, see my *Sovereignty through Interdependence* (London: Kluwer, 1997).
3. Ernest Gellner, *Thought and Change* (London: Weidenfeld and Nicolson, 1964), p. 168.
4. Though the *Academie Française* was given protective powers over the French language in 1635, and published its first dictionary in 1694, Maximilien-Paul-Emile Littré's *Dictionnaire de la language française* was only begun in 1844 and published in 1863–73. In London, though Samuel Johnson's dictionary was published in 1755, the first *Oxford English Dictionary* only began to come out in 1879.
5. Sunanda K. Datta-Ray, 'What's in a Name? The Politics of Defining Nationality in Asia', *International Herald Tribune*, 18 February 1999, p. 9.
6. There has been debate ever since about the precise meaning and implications of Wilson's often delphic utterances. His Secretary of State, Robert Lansing, saw the destabilizing implications of 'self-determination' at once. On 30 December 1918 he commented to his diary: 'The phrase is simply loaded with dynamite. It will raise hopes which can never be realized ... What a calamity that the phrase was ever uttered! What misery it will cause! ...' Lansing Papers, Library of Congress, quoted in Daniel Patrick Moynihan, *Pandaemonium; Ethnicity in International Politics* (New York: Oxford University Press, 1993), p. 83. See also David Fromkin, *The Way of the World: From the Dawn of Civilizations to the Eve of the Twenty-First Century* (New York: Knopf, 1999).
7. The reasoning was very similar to that behind Britain's resistance to Allied proposals, during the Second World War, for the dismemberment of Germany. In the 1943–4 discussions on post-war planning, the British sensibly maintained that dismemberment would be a heaven-sent issue for any future German nationalist.

8. On the maintenance of this uneasy balance, see Howard, *The Continental Commitment*, passim.

9. Whether in India or Vietnam or Indonesia, these processes had intriguing echoes of the ideas that Peter the Great brought to Russia from France and Germany. In each case, a gulf yawned between small but modern, educated groups, and the mass of people living in traditional ways.

10. In the early 1960s Jawaharlal Nehru, then Prime Minister, remarked only half in jest to the US Ambassador, John Kenneth Galbraith, that he was the last Englishman to rule India. Quoted in Dennis Kux, *India and the United States: The Estranged Democracies, 1941–91* (Washington DC: National Defense University Press, 1992). And Lee Kuan Yew of Singapore – educated at an English School, The London School of Economics and Cambridge – once observed that he was an 'Anglified Chinaman'.

11. Most intolerable of all, perhaps, was that many of the *evolués* actually enjoyed Westernization.

12. D.K. Fieldhouse, *The Colonial Empires; A Comparative Survey from the Eighteenth Century* (London: Weidenfeld and Nicolson, 1966), p. 400.

13. R. Tagore, *Towards Universal Man* (London: Asia Publishing House, 1961), pp. 117,123.

14. Which was by no means universally popular in Europe. In France and England many people thought of Wilson as J.P. Morgan had once done of Theodore Roosevelt going on safari: 'I hope that the first lion he meets will do his duty.'

15. The 1918 influenza epidemic killed some 25 million, or three times as many as the First World War. See Roy Porter, *The Greatest Benefit to Mankind* (London: Fontana Press, 1999), pp. 483–4.

16. *International Affairs*, Vol. 1951, p. 200. This generally held view strongly encouraged immigration, at first from Europe. In 1945 Australia's population was around 7 million. In 1999, by then with Asian as well as European immigration, it was around 19 million.

17. In December 1941, when Roosevelt and Churchill drafted the Declaration of the United Nations, stating war aims for all the Allies, the British War Cabinet wanted to avoid including India 'as a separate sovereign power'. Churchill, *The Second World War*, Vol. III (London: Cassell, 1950), p. 590.

18. Which sounds much like the Thai, Taiwanese and Korean reformers after 1950, as well as Chinese ones after 1978.

19. Here, too, the resulting political problems were much the same as those of China at the start of the 1980s.

20. W.D. Borrie, *Population Trends and Policies* (Sydney: Australasian Publishing, 1948), p. 236.

21. Sunil Khilnani, *The Idea of India* (London: Penguin, 1998), p. 2.

22. Including such items as pension payments for civil servants and soldiers, maintaining the India Office in London and meeting the interest payments on loans.

23. R.C. Dutt, *England and India 1785–1885: a record of progress during a hundred years* (London: Chatto and Windus, 1897), p. 45.

24. The biography of his wife is instructive. See Arun Gandhi, *Daughters of Midnight; the child bride of Gandhi* (London: Blake, 1998).

25. The British, not yet educated to political correctness, referred to them as 'Father, son and holy ghost'.
26. Beloff, *Imperial Sunset*, Vol. I, op. cit., p. 9.
27. It seems that officials in Delhi, acting with bureaucratic blindness, looked up the legal precedents from 1914 and took as model what had then been done in the case of Canada. It was quite understood that India would soon become a self-governing Dominion, but the lawyers concentrated on the fact that it had not yet done so. So the whole process of a quiet and steady move away from imperialism in India came unstuck. I am indebted for this observation to Sir Robert Wade-Gery.
28. Senior Indians were quite willing to accept that the Germans and Italians had to be stopped, but they were not going to be arbitrarily told by the British what to do.
29. B.R. Tomlinson, *The Political Economy of the Raj 1914–47: The Economics of Decolonization in India* (London: Macmillan, 1979), pp. 92–100.
30. David E.F. Henley, *Nationalism and Regionalism in a Colonial Context* (Leiden: KITLV Press, 1996), p. 1.
31. Kahin, *Nationalism and Revolution in Indonesia*, op. cit., p. 33.
32. There was, however, much resentment when the Dutch said agricultural problems might have scientific explanations rather than the will of Allah.
33. In Holland itself, before 1930 only the communists advocated full independence for Indonesia.
34. Anthony Reid, 'The revolution in regional perspective', cited in Henley, *Nationalism and Regionalism in a Colonial Context*, op. cit, p. 3.
35. Sjahrir, 'Out of Exile', ibid.
36. The rump government of unoccupied wartime France.
37. Quoted in Chester Cooper, *The Lost Crusade* (New York: Dodd Mead, 1970), p. 22.
38. E.R. Hughes quotes from a copy published, despite the ban, in 1897 in Sichuan. See *The Invasion of China by the Western World* (London: Adam and Charles Black, 1937), p. 108.
39. The force, under German command, entered the forbidden city on 28 August 1900 in the following order of march: 800 Russians, 800 Japanese, 400 British, 400 Americans, 400 French, 250 Germans, 60 Austrians and 60 Italians.

7   Decolonization as Aftermath

1. The French, the Dutch and others even raised troops to fight with Germany. Dutchmen manned a number of SS units and 10 000 of them fell. Gerald Newton, *The Netherlands* (London: Ernest Benn, 1978), p. 142.
2. J.A. Hobson, *Confessions of an Economic Heretic* (1938) (ed. M. Freeden) (Brighton: Harvester Press, 1978), p. 152.
3. Khilnani, *The Idea of India*, op. cit., p. 1.
4. In its modern meaning – as distinct from the usage 'Commonwealth of Massachusetts' – the term may have been first used around 1915.
5. Western public opinion seemed convinced that state agencies always try to maximize social welfare, whereas private effort is invariably selfish. Only recently have public sector motives been formally questioned, for instance

in Andrei Shleifer and Robert Vishny, *The Grabbing Hand: Government Pathologies and their Cures* (Cambridge MA: Harvard University Press, 1999).
6. Peter Flora and Arnold J. Heidenheimer (eds), *The Development of Welfare States in Europe and America* (New Brunswick: Transaction Publishers, 1982), p. 23.
7. Figures from Flora and Heidenheimer, ibid., table 9.1, p. 310; table 9.5, p. 319; table 9.10, p. 338; table 9.11, p. 339.
8. Macaulay, 'Frederic the Great', op. cit. p. 506. He was commenting on the Mogul empire.
9. He once remarked that he chased women 'to get rid of the burden of my ugliness'. Sartre, *War Diaries: Notebooks from a phoney war, November 1939 – March 1940*, trans. Quintin Hoare (London: Verso, 1964), p. 281.
10. Habermas, *Between Facts and Norms*, op. cit., p. 505.
11. Literally 'Law of blood'. German nationality was acquired by descent.
12. Habermas, *Between Facts and Norms*, op. cit., p. 505.
13. For instance, major non-Moslem sites were allocated to Pakistan and some of the sub-continent's finest Islamic buildings to India.
14. Not only in India. A year later, when Palestine was partitioned, Arabs remarked bitterly of the British that 'It is better to be their enemy than their friend. If you are an enemy, they will try to buy you. If you are a friend, they will surely sell you.'
15. By 1950 fully one quarter of all French officers and four out of ten non-commissioned officers were serving in Indo-China. It was not enough.
16. A global strategy of 'Containment' of communism stemmed from the advice that a senior diplomat, George Kennan, had given the US government in 1946. See Mr X, 'The Sources of Soviet Conduct', *Foreign Affairs*, July 1947.

8 Concluding Ironies

1. Many Tibetans, especially the aristocracy, originally saw the Chinese as modernizers and allies against religious conservatism. However, Chinese-style 'modernization' did much to destroy Tibet's religion, way of life, economy and language.
2. Of the British empire it has been said that it 'was, perhaps, the worst empire in the history of the world, except for all the others'. Felipe Fernandez-Armesto, *The Times*, 25 June 1998, p. 43.
3. Periods of 'privatization' and 'deregulation' in the USA and UK have rarely been what they seemed. Under privatization without adequate commercialization 'Politicians continue to use their control of regulated firms to pursue political objectives, but it is now less costly for them to do so.' Shleifer and Vishny, *The Grabbing Hand*, op. cit., p. 171. On regulation generally, see also my *Sovereignty through Interdependence*, op. cit., esp. Chapter 6.
4. The creation of European Monetary Union ('euroland') was a historic shift in political as well as economic relations among its eleven founder members. Yet, remarkably, not one of the eleven thought it necessary to put the decision to a popular vote; and nowhere does that omission seem to have created much resentment.

5. The early Hitler modelled his organizational ideas largely on Leninist precedents, and a favourite Nazi accusation against Roosevelt and Churchill was that they were 'plutocrats'. Only hours before committing suicide in 1945, Hitler and Göbbels once again agreed that they remained true socialists (as distinct from social democrats) to the end.

6. Berlin, *The Roots of Romanticism*, op. cit., p. 9.

7. In 1914 Austro-Hungarian mobilization orders were sent out in fifteen languages. Paul Kennedy, *The Rise and Fall of the Great Powers* (New York: Vintage Books, 1989), p. 216.

8. Thorstein Veblen, *An Inquiry into the Nature of Peace and the Terms of its Perpetuation* (1917) (New York: Kelley, 1964), p. 41.

9. The literature is large. For instance Harold Isaacs, *Basic Group Identity: The Idols of the Tribe* (New York: Harper and Row, 1975); Donald Horowitz, *Ethnic Groups in Conflict* (Berkeley: University of California Press, 1985).

10. The assassinations of Mahatma Gandhi, Indira Gandhi, Rajiv Gandhi or, in Israel, of Prime Minister Rabin, are cases in point. So are the killings of Sikhs in India, Hindus in Pakistan, Chinese in Indonesia and so on. On the religious nationalism behind the murder of Rabin, see Michael Karpin and Ina Friedman, *Murder in the Name of God* (London: Granta Books, 1999). One scholar has argued that by the mid-1980s about half of the world's independent countries had ethnically based difficulties. cf. Walker Connor (ed.), *Mexican Americans in Contemporary Perspective* (Washington DC: Urban Institute, 1985), p. 2.

11. In some Indian private schools, British structures also persist. Pupils are organized into different houses, denoted by different-coloured turbans.

12. The title of Adam Schwarz's book says it well: *A Nation in Waiting* (London: Allen and Unwin, 1994).

13. By the later 1990s Moslems numbered 175 out of Indonesia's 202 million people. Many of them felt that in 1949 President Sukarno had cheated them politically by teaming up with the communists; and they had been cheated again in the coups of the mid-60s which brought Suharto to power.

14. By the beginning of the twenty-first century only some 20 per cent of the GDP of the OECD countries depended on trade – about the same percentage as in 1900. See Robert Wade, 'Globalization and its Limits: Reports of the death of the National Economy are greatly exaggerated', in Suzanne Berger and Ronald Dore (eds), *National Diversity and Global Capitalism* (Ithaca, NY: Cornell University Press, 1996), p. 62; Linda Weiss, *The Myth of the Powerless State* (Cambridge: Polity, 1998), table 6-1.

15. It might be argued that the West, under American leadership, has moved from an international order of a Wilsonian community of self-determining nation-states to one reminiscent of imperial China, with an orderly grouping of 'tributaries' around a single centre of power and civilization.

16. See, for instance, The World Bank, *East Asian Miracle; Economic Growth and Public Policy* (New York: Oxford University Press, 1993).

17. China's payments surplus, and the stability of China's currency, depend greatly on the USA. In 1997, for instance, China's exports to the USA were $62.6 billion and her imports only $12.9 billion.

18. For instance Jonathan Schneer, *London 1900: The Imperial Metropolis* (London; Yale, 2000).

Bibliography

Acton, Lord, *Lectures on Modern History*, London, Collins, 1960.

Aldrich, Robert, *The French Presence in the South Pacific, 1842–1940*, London, Macmillan, 1990.

Anderson, Benedict, *Java in Time of Revolution*, Ithaca, NY, Cornell University Press, 1972.

Anderson, Benedict, *Imagined Communities: Reflections on the origin and spread of nationalism*, London, Verso, 1983.

Anderson, Benedict, *Language and Power: Exploring Political Cultures in Indonesia*, Ithaca, NY, Cornell University Press, 1990.

Aylmer, G.E., *The State's Servants: the Civil Service of the English Republic 1649–60*, London, Routledge and Kegan Paul, 1973.

Bain, Chester A., *Vietnam: The roots of conflict*, Englewood Cliffs, Prentice Hall, 1967.

Bairoch, Paul, *Economics and World History: Myths and Paradoxes*, Chicago, University of Chicago Press, 1993.

Banga, Indu (ed.), *Five Punjabi Centuries: Policy, Economy, Society and Culture 1500–1990*, New Delhi, Manohar, 1997.

Bank of England: Comparative Tables of Pound Values.

Barnouw, A.J., *The Making of Modern Holland*, London, Allen and Unwin, 1948.

Barraclough, G. (ed.), *The Times Atlas of World History*, London, Times Books, 1978.

Bauer, Otto, *Die Nationalitätenfrage und die Sozialdemokratie* (2nd edn), Vienna, Verlag der Wiener Volksbuchhandlung, 1924.

Baumgart, Winfried, *Imperialism: The Idea and Reality of British and French Colonial Expansion 1880–1914*, Oxford, Oxford University Press, 1982.

Beloff, Max, *Imperial Sunset*, Vol. I, *Britain's Liberal Empire 1897–1921*, London, Methuen, 1969.

Beloff, Max, *Imperial Sunset*, Vol. II, *The Dream of Commonwealth*, London, Macmillan, 1989.

Berlin, Isaiah, *The Sense of Reality; Studies in Ideas and their History* (ed. Henry Hardy), London, Chatto and Windus, 1996.

Berlin, Isaiah, *The Roots of Romanticism* (ed. Henry Hardy), Princeton, Princeton University Press, 1999.

Besançon, Xavier, *Les services publics en France du Moyen Age à la Révolution*, Paris, Presses de l'École national des ponts et chaussées, 1995.

Bingham, Woodbridge, Conroy, Hilary and Iklé, Frank W., *A History of Asia Vol 1: Formation of Civilizations, from Antiquity to 1600*, Boston, Allyn and Bacon, 1964.

Booth, Martin, *Opium: A History*, London, St Martin's Press, 1998.

Borrie, W.D., *Population Trends and Policies*, Sydney, Australasian Publishing, 1948.

Bose, Sugata and Jalal, Ayesha, *Modern South Asia: History, Culture, Political Economy*, Delhi, Oxford University Press, 1997.

Botticelli, Peter, 'British Capitalism and the Three Industrial Revolutions', in Thomas McCraw (ed.), *Creating Modern Capitalism*, op. cit.

Bourchier, David and Legge, John (eds), *Democracy in Indonesia: 1950s and 1990s*, Melbourne, Monash University, 1994.

Bourne, K., *The Foreign Policy of Victorian England 1830–1902*, Oxford, Clarendon Press, 1970.

Boxer, C.R., *The Dutch Seaborne Empire 1600–1800*, London, Hutchinson, 1965.

Braudel, Fernand, *Expansion and Reaction: essays on European expansion in Asia and Africa* (ed. H.L. Wesseling), Leiden, Leiden University Press, 1978.

Braudel, Fernand, *La Méditerranée et le monde méditerranéen à l'époque de Philippe II*, Paris, Armand Colin, 1986.

Braudel, Fernand, *A History of Civilizations*, New York/London, Penguin Books, 1993.

Brown, Howard G., *War, Revolution and the Bureaucratic State: Politics and Army Administration in France 1791–1799*, Oxford, Clarendon Press, 1995.

Bruce, Maurice, *The Shaping of the Modern World 1870–1939*, Vol. 1, London, Hutchinson, 1958.

Brunschwig, Henri, *French Colonialism 1871–1914: myths and realities*, London, Pall Mall Press, 1966.

Bull, Hedley, *The Anarchical Society*, London, Macmillan, 1977.

Burdeau, François, *Histoire de l'administration française du 18e au 20e siècle*, Paris, Montchrestien, 1989.

Burke, Edmund, *Thoughts on the Prospect of a Regicide Peace*, London, J. Owen, 1796.

Burke, Edmund, *Thoughts on the Cause of the Present Discontents* (ed. W. Murison), Cambridge, Cambridge University Press, 1913.

Buttinger, Joseph, *A Dragon Defiant*, Newton Abbot, David and Charles, 1972.

Cambridge Economic History of Europe (eds H.J. Habakkuk and M. Postan) – Vol. VI, *The Industrial Revolutions and After; incomes, population and technological change*, I and II (eds E.E. Rich and C.H. Wilson), Cambridge, Cambridge University Press, 1965–6. – Vol. IV, *The Economy of Expanding Europe in the Sixteenth and Seventeenth Centuries* (eds E.E. Rich and C.H. Wilson), Cambridge, Cambridge University Press, 1967.

Cambridge History of the British Empire (genl eds J. Holland Rose et al.), Vol. V, *The Indian Empire 1858–1918* (ed. H.H. Dodwell), Cambridge, Cambridge University Press, 1932.

Cambridge History of China (genl eds Denis Twitchett and John K. Fairbank) Vol. XIII, *Republican China 1912–1949* (eds John K. Fairbank and Albert Feuerwerker), Cambridge, Cambridge University Press, 1986.

Church, Clive, *Revolution and Red Tape: The French Ministerial Bureaucracy 1770–1850*, Oxford, Oxford University Press, 1981.

Churchill, W.S., *The Second World War*, Vol. III, London, Cassell, 1950.

Cipolla, Carlo M., *Guns, Sails and Empires: Technological Innovation and the Early Phases of European Expansion 1400–1700*, New York, Pantheon, 1965.

Cipolla, Carlo M. (ed.), *The Economic Decline of Empires*, London, Methuen, 1970.

Clark, Grover, *The Balance Sheets of Imperialism*, Washington DC, Carnegie Endowment for International Peace, 1936.

Cobbett, William, *Complete Collection of State Trials Vol. V (1640–1649)*, London, Longmans, 1828, cols 990–1142.

Colley, Linda, 'Whose Nation? Class and national consciousness in Britain 1750–1830', *Past and Present*, No. 113, 1986, pp. 96–117.

Commission Internationale d'Histoire des Mouvements Sociaux et Structures Sociales, *Mouvements nationaux d'indépendence et classes populaires aux XIXe et XXe siècles en Occident et en Orient*, 2 vols, Paris, 1971.

Communist Manifesto (ed. Frederic L. Bender), New York, Norton, 1988.

Cooke, James J., *New French Imperialism 1880–1910: The Third Republic and Colonial Expansion*, Newton Abbot, David and Charles, 1973.

Cooper, Chester, *The Lost Crusade*, New York, Dodd Mead, 1970.

Crafts, Nick, 'The Industrial Revolution', in Floud and McCloskey (eds), *The Economic History of Britain since 1700*, op. cit.

de Groot, Hugo (Grotius), *De jure belli ac pacis*, Paris, Apud W. Buon, 1625.

De Klerck, E.S., *History of the Netherlands East Indies*, Vol. 1, Rotterdam, W.L. & J. Brusse, 1938.

de las Casas, Bartolomé, *Brevísima relación de la destrucción de las Indias* (Brief Relation of the Destruction of the Indies) (1552), Madrid, Anjana, 1983.

Deschamps, Hubert, *The French Union: history, institutions, economy, countries and peoples, social and political changes*, Paris, Berger-Levrault, 1956.

Deschanel, Paul, *Les intérêts français dans l'Océan Pacifique*, Paris, Nancy, 1888.

de Vries, Jan, *European Urbanization 1500–1800*, Cambridge, MA, Harvard University Press, 1984.

Dilke, Charles, *Greater Britain*, 2 vols, London, Macmillan, 1868.

Dilke, Charles W. and Wilkinson, Spenser, *Imperial Defence*, London, Macmillan, 1892.

Dilks, David, *Curzon in India*, Vol. 1, London, Rupert Hart-Davis, 1969.

Doniol, Henry, *Histoire de la participation de la France à l'établissement des États-Unis d'Amérique. Correspondence diplomatique et documents*, 5 vols, Paris, 1885–9.

Duiker, William J., *The Rise of Nationalism in Vietnam 1900–1940*, Ithaca, NY, Cornell University Press, 1976.

Duiker, William J., *Vietnam: Nation in Revolution*, Boulder, Westview, 1983.

Dunmore, John, *Visions and Realties: France in the Pacific 1695–1995*, New Zealand, Heritage Press, 1997.

Dutt, R.C., *England and India 1785–1885: a record of progress during a hundred years*, London, Chatto and Windus, 1897.

Edmundson, George, *History of Holland*, Cambridge, Cambridge University Press, 1922.

Elgin, Earl of, *Letters and Journals of James, Eighth Earl of Elgin* (ed. Theodore Walrond), London, John Murray, 1872.

Ellis, G., *History of the Late Revolution in the Dutch Republic*, London, J. Edwards, 1789.

Elton, G.R., *The Tudor Revolution in Government: administrative changes in the reign of Henry VIII*, Cambridge, Cambridge University Press, 1953.

Emerson, Rupert, *From Empire to Nation*, Boston: Beacon Press, 1962.

Emmer, P.C., *The Economic Impact of the Dutch Expansion Overseas 1570–1870*, Madrid, Centro de Estudios Constitucionales, Revista de Historia Economica, [1999].

Emmer, P.C., and Mörner, M. (eds), *European expansion and migration: essays on the intercontinental migration from Africa, Asia and Europe*, New York, Berg, [1992].

Evans, Eric J., *The Forging of the Modern State: early industrial Britain, 1783–1870*, London, Longman, 1983.

Feis, Herbert, *Europe: The World's Banker 1870–1914*, New York, Kelley for the Council on Foreign Relations, 1964.

Ferry, Jules (ed.), *Le Tonkin et la mère-Patrie* (12th edn), Paris, 1890.

Fieldhouse, D.K., *The Colonial Empires; A Comparative Survey from the Eighteenth century*, London, Weidenfeld and Nicolson, 1966; 2nd edn, Macmillan, 1982.

Fischer, Fritz, *Griff nach der Weltmacht: Die Kriegspolitik des kaiserlichen Deutschland 1914–1918*, Düsseldorf, Droste, 1961.

Flora, Peter and Heidenheimer, Arnold J. (eds), *The Development of Welfare States in Europe and America*, New Brunswick, Transaction Publishers, 1982.

Flora, Peter (et al.), *State, Economy and Society in Western Europe 1815–1975; A data handbook*, 2 vols, London, Macmillan, 1983.

Floud, Roderick and McCloskey, Donald (eds), *The Economic History of Britain since 1700* (2nd edn), Cambridge, Cambridge University Press, 1994.

Foreign Relations of the United States 1901, Washington, USGPO, 1902.

Friedberg, Aaron L., *The Weary Titan: Britain and the Experience of Relative Decline 1895–1905*, Princeton, Princeton University Press, 1988.

Fritschy, Wantje, 'Taxation in Britain, France and The Netherlands in the Eighteenth Century', in Marjolein 't Hart, Joost Jonker and Jan Luiten van Zanden, *A Financial History of the Netherlands*, op. cit.

Fromkin, David, *The Way of the World: From the Dawn of Civilizations to the Eve of the Twenty-First Century*, New York, Knopf, 1999.

Furnivall, J.S., *Netherlands India; A Study of Plural Economy*, Cambridge, Cambridge University Press, 1939.

Gallagher, John and Robinson, Ronald, *The Imperialism of Free Trade: The Economic History Review* (2nd series), No 6, 1953, pp. 1–15.

Gallagher, John, *The Decline, Revival and Fall of the British Empire*, Cambridge, Cambridge University Press, 1982.

Gandhi, Arun, *Daughters of Midnight: the child bride of Gandhi*, London, Blake, 1998.

Gardiner, S.R., *The Constitutional Documents of the Puritan Revolution 1625–1660* (3rd edn), Oxford, Clarendon Press, 1906.

Gasset, J. Ortega y, *The Revolt of the Masses* (*Rebelión de las Masas*, Madrid 1930) London, Allen and Unwin, 1932.

Geertz, Clifford, *Islam Observed: religious development in Morocco and Indonesia*, Chicago, Chicago University Press, 1968.

Gelber, Harry, *Sovereignty through Interdependence*, London, Kluwer, 1997.

Gellner, Ernest, *Thought and Change*, London, Weidenfeld and Nicolson, 1964.

Glass, D.V. and Grebenik, E., 'World Population 1800–1950', in *Cambridge Economic History of Europe* (eds Habakkuk and Postan), Vol. VI, *The Industrial Revolutions and After*, II, op. cit., Chapter II.

Godeschot, Jacques (ed.), *Les Constitutions de la France depuis 1789*, Paris, Garnier-Flammarion, 1970.

Gordon, Murray, *Slavery in the Arab World*, New York, New Amsterdam, 1989.

Grant, Bruce, *Indonesia*, Harmondsworth, Penguin Books, 1967.

Greenfeld, Liah, *Nationalism: Five roads to modernity*, Cambridge, MA, Harvard University Press, 1992.

Grewal, J.S., *The Sikhs of the Punjab*, Cambridge, Cambridge University Press, 1990.

Habermas, Jürgen, *Between Facts and Norms; Contributions to a Discourse Theory of Law and Democracy*, trans. R.E. Wiliams, Cambridge, Polity, 1996.

Hall, A. Rupert, 'Scientific Method and the Progress of Techniques', in *Cambridge Economic History of Europe* (eds Habakkuk and Postan), Vol. VI, *The Industrial Revolutions and After*, I, op. cit., Chapter II.

Hall, John A., *Powers and Liberties: Causes and Consequences of the Rise of the West*, London, Penguin, 1986.

Hancock, W.K., *Survey of British Commonwealth Affairs*, Vol. II, *Problems of economic policy 1918–1939*, London, Oxford University Press, 1940.

Hancock, Sir W. Keith, *Smuts, Vol. 1: The Sanguine Years 1870–1919*, Cambridge, Cambridge University Press, 1962.

Harvey, Robert, *Clive: The Life and Death of a British Emperor*, London, Hodder and Staughton, 1998.

Hayes, Carleton J.H., *A Generation of Materialism 1871–1900*, New York, Harper and Row, 1941.

Hayes, Carleton J.H., *The Historical Evolution of Modern Nationalism*, New York, Macmillan, 1948.

Headrick, Daniel, *The Tools of Empire: technology and European imperialism in the nineteenth century*, New York, Oxford University Press, 1981.

Hegel, G.W.F., *Sämtliche Werke*, Vol. XI, *Vorlesungen über die Philosophie der Geschichte*, trans J. Sibree, New York, P.F. Collier and Son, 1902.

Helleiner, Karl F., 'The Population of Europe from the Black Death to the End of the Vital Revolution', in *Cambridge Economic History of Europe* (eds Habakkuk and Postan), Vol. VI, *The Industrial Revolutions and After*, I, op. cit., Chapter I.

Henley, David E.F., *Nationalism and Regionalism in a Colonial Context*, Leiden, KITLV Press, 1996.

Henley, David, 'Ethnographic integration and exclusion in anti-colonial nationalism; Indonesia and Indochina', *Comparative Studies in Society and History*, 37, pp. 286–324.

Herz, Martin, *A Short History of Cambodia, from the Days of Angkor to the Present*, London, Atlantic, 1958.

Hibbert, Christopher, *The Great Mutiny: India 1857*, London, Allen Lane, 1978.

Hibbert, Christopher, *George III: A Personal History*, London, Viking, 1998.

Hill, Christopher and Dell, E., *The Good Old Cause 1640–1660*, New York, Augustus M. Kelley, 1969.

Hobsbawm, E.J., *Nations and Nationalism since 1780*, Cambridge, Cambridge University Press, 1990.

Hobson, J.A., *Imperialism: A Study*, London, James Nisbet and Co., 1902.

Hobson, J.A., *Confessions of an Economic Heretic* (1938) (ed. M. Freeden), Brighton, Harvester Press, 1978.

Holland, R.F., *European Decolonization 1918–1981: An Introductory Survey*, London, Macmillan, 1985.

Horowitz, Donald, *Ethnic Groups in Conflict*, Berkeley, University of California Press, 1985.

Howard, Michael, *The Franco-Prussian War*, New York, Collier Books, 1969.

Howard, Michael, *The Continental Commitment*, London, Temple Smith, 1972.
Howard, Michael, *War in European History*, Oxford, Oxford University Press, 1976.
Howard, Michael, *War and the Liberal Conscience*, London, Temple Smith, 1978.
Howard, Michael, *The Causes of Wars*, London, Unwin, 1983.
Howard, Michael, *The Lessons of History*, Oxford, Oxford University Press, 1993.
Hudson, G.F., *Europe and China*, London, Arnold, 1931.
Hughes, E.R., *The Invasion of China by the Western World*, London, Adam and Charles Black, 1937.
Isaacs, Harold, *Basic Group Identity: The Idols of the Tribe*, New York, Harper and Row, 1975.
Jebb, Richard, *Studies in Colonial Nationalism*, London, Edward Arnold, 1905.
Jones, Eric L., and Mingay G.E. (eds), *Land, Labour and Population of the Industrial Revolution*, London, 1987.
Jones E.L. and Mingay G.E., *The European Miracle: Environments, Economics and Geopolitics in the History of Europe and Asia* (2nd edn), Cambridge, Cambridge University Press, 1987.
Judd, Denis, *Balfour and the British Empire*, London, Macmillan, 1968.
Kahin, George McT., *Nationalism and Revolution in Indonesia*, Ithaca and London, Cornell University Press, 1970.
Karpin, Michael and Friedman, Ina, *Murder in the Name of God*, London, Granta Books, 1999.
Keir, D.L., *The Constitutional History of Modern Britain* (7th edn), London, Adam and Charles Black, 1964.
Keith, A.B. (ed.), *Selected Speeches and Documents on British Colonial Policy 1763–1917*, Oxford, Blackwell, 1953.
Kelsey, Harry, *Sir Francis Drake: The Queen's Pirate*, New Haven, Yale University Press, 1998.
Kennan, George (Mr X), 'The Sources of Soviet Conduct', *Foreign Affairs*, July 1947.
Kennedy, Paul, 'Mahan versus Mackinder: Two Interpretations of British Seapower', in Paul Kennedy, *Strategy and Diplomacy 1870–1945*, London, Allen and Unwin, 1983.
Kennedy, Paul, *The Rise and Fall of the Great Powers*, New York, Vintage Books, 1989.
Khilnani, Sunil, *The Idea of India*, London, Penguin, 1998.
Kindleberger, C.P., *A Financial History of Western Europe*, London, Allen and Unwin, 1984.
Kohn, Hans, *A History of Nationalism in the East*, London, G. Routledge and Sons, 1929.
Kohn, Hans, *Nationalism and Imperialism in the Hither East*, London, G. Routledge and Sons, 1932.
Kubicek, Robert V., *The Administration of Imperialism: Joseph Chamberlain at the Colonial Office*, Durham NC, Duke University Press, 1969.
Kux, Dennis, *India and the United States: The Estranged Democracies 1941–91*, Washington DC, National Defense University Press, 1992.
Landes, David, 'Technological Change and Development in Western Europe 1750–1914', in *Cambridge Economic History of Europe* (eds Habakkuk and Postan), Vol. VI, *The Industrial Revolutions and After*, I, op. cit. Chapter V.

Landes, David, *The Unbound Prometheus*, London, Cambridge University Press, 1969.

Landes, David, *Revolution in Time*, Cambridge, MA, Harvard University Press, 1983.

Landes, David, *The Wealth and Poverty of Nations*, London, Little, Brown, 1998.

Langlois, John D. (ed.), *China under Mongol Rule*, Princeton, Princeton University Press, 1981.

Legge, John, *Indonesia*, New Jersey, Prentice Hall, 1964.

Levathes, Louis, *When China Ruled the Seas: The Treasure Fleet of the Dragon Throne 1403–33*, New York, Simon and Schuster, 1994.

Lloyd, Trevor O., *The British Empire 1558–1983*, New York, Oxford University Press, 1984.

Loewe, Michael, *Imperial China: the historical background*, London, Allen and Unwin, 1966.

Low, D.A. (ed.), *The Indian National Congress; Centenary Hindsights*, Delhi, Oxford University Press, 1988.

Low, D.A., *Britain and Indian Nationalism*, Cambridge, Cambridge University Press, 1997.

Macaulay, Thomas Babington, 'Frederic the Great', *The Edinburgh Review*, April 1842.

Macdonagh, Oliver, *A Pattern of Government Growth 1800–1860*, London, MacGibbon and Kee 1961.

Mackesy, Piers, *The War for America 1775–1783*, Lincoln, University of Nebraska Press, 1993.

Maddison, Angus, *Dynamic Forces in Capitalist Development*, New York, Oxford University Press, 1991.

Mahan, Alfred Thayer, *The Influence of Seapower upon History 1660–1783*, London and Cambridge, MA, Sampson Low and Co., 1890.

Majumdar, Ramesh Chandra, *The Sepoy Mutiny and the Revolt of 1857*, Calcutta, Firma K.L. Mukhdopadhyay, 1963.

Manning, Catherine, *Fortunes à Faire; The French in Asian Trade, 1719–48*, Aldershot, Hants, Variorum, 1996.

Marcks, Erich, *Männer und Zeiten. Antsätze und Reden zur neueren Geschichte* (2 vols) Leipzig, 1911.

Marshall, T.H., *Class, Citizenship and Social Development*, Garden City, NY, Anchor Books, 1965.

Mathias, Peter, *The First Industrial Nation: an economic history of Britain 1700–1914*, London, Methuen, 1969.

Mathias, Peter and O'Brien, P., 'Taxation in Britain and France 1715–1810: A comparison of the social and economic incidence of taxes collected for central governments', *Journal of European Economic History*, 5, 1976, pp. 601–50.

Mathias, Peter and Davis, John (eds), *The First Industrial Revolution*, Oxford, Blackwell, 1989.

Matthews, Derek, Anderson, Malcolm and Edwards, John Richard, *The Priesthood of Industry – The Rise of the Professional Accountant in British Management*, London, Oxford University Press, 1997.

Mayer, A.J., *The Political Origins of the New Diplomacy 1917–1918*, New Haven, Yale University Press, 1959.

McCraw, Thomas K. (ed.), *Creating Modern Capitalism*, Cambridge MA, Harvard University Press, 1997.

McKay, Elaine (ed.), *Studies in Indonesian History*, Melbourne, Pitman Publishing, 1976.

McNeill, W.H., *The Rise of the West: A History of the Human Community*, Chicago, Chicago University Press, 1963.

McNeill, W.H., *The Pursuit of Power; Technology, Armed Force and Society since AD 1000*, Oxford, Blackwell, 1983.

McNeill, W.H., *The Age of Gunpowder Empires 1450–1800 (Essays on Global and Comparative History)*, Washington DC, American Historical Association, 1989.

Miller, J.D.B., *Australian Government and Politics* (2nd edn), London, Duckworth, 1959.

Montesquieu, Charles Secondat, Baron de, *Esprit des Lois*, Books I–V (ed. E. Zévort), Paris, 1887.

Morley, John, *Diderot and the Encyclopaedists*, London, Macmillan, 1923.

Moynihan, Daniel Patrick, *Pandaemonium: Ethnicity in International Politics*, New York, Oxford University Press, 1993.

Naipaul, V.S., *Beyond Belief: Islamic Excursions among the converted peoples*, London, Little Brown, 1998.

New Cambridge Modern History, Vol. XI, F.H. Hinsley (ed.) *Material Progress and World-wide Problems 1870–1898*, Cambridge, University Press, 1962.

Newton, Gerald, *The Netherlands*, London, Ernest Benn, 1978.

O'Brien, P.K., 'The Political Economy of British Taxation 1660–1815', *Economic History Review*, 41, 1988, pp. 1–32.

O'Rourke, Kevin and Williamson, Jeffrey, *Globalization and History: The Evolution of a Nineteenth-Century Atlantic Economy*, Cambridge, MA, MIT Press, 1999.

Oxford History of the British Empire Vol. II, *The Eighteenth Century* (eds P.J. Marshall and Alaine Low), Oxford, Oxford University Press, 1998. Vol. III, *The Nineteenth Century* (ed. Andrew Porter), Oxford, Oxford University Press, 1999. Vol. IV, *The Twentieth Century* (eds. Judith M. Brown and Wm Roger Louis), Oxford, Oxford University Press, 1999.

Panikkar, K.M., *Asia and Western Dominance*, London, Allen and Unwin, 1953.

Parker, Geoffrey, *The Grand Strategy of Philip II*, New Haven, Yale University Press, 1998.

Parris, Henry, 'The Origins of the Permanent Civil Service 1780–1830', *Public Administration*, Vol. 46, 1968, pp. 143–66.

Perham, Margery, *Lugard, the years of authority 1898–1945*, London, Collins, 1960.

Peyrefitte, Alain, *The Collision of Two Civilisations*, London, HarperCollins, 1993.

Plumb, J.H., *England in the Eighteenth Century*, London, Penguin, 1990.

Pocock, Tom, *Battle for Empire: The very first World War*, London, Michael O'Mara, 1998.

Porter, Bernard, *Critics of Empire: British Radical Attitudes to Colonialism in Africa 1895–1914*, London, Macmillan, 1968.

Porter, Roy, *The Greatest Benefit to Mankind*, London, Fontana Press, 1999.

Priestley, Herbert I., *France Overseas: A study of modern imperialism*, New York, Appleton-Century, 1938.

Ray, Rajat Kanta, 'Indian Society and the Establishment of British Supremacy', in *Oxford History of the British Empire*, Vol. II (eds Marshall and Low), op. cit.

Reischauer, E.O. and Craig, A.M., *Japan; Tradition and Transformation*, Cambridge, MA, Havard University Press, 1989.

Renan, Ernest, *Oeuvres complètes de Ernest Renan*, Vol. 1 (1882), Paris, Calmann-Levy, 1947.

Risso, Patricia, *Merchants and Faith; Muslim Commerce and Culture in the Indian Ocean*, Boulder, CO, Westview Press, 1995.

Robinson, Ronald and Gallagher, John, 'The Imperialism of Free Trade', *Economic History Review*, 1953–4.

Robinson, Ronald and Gallagher, John, *Africa and the Victorians: The official mind of imperialism*, London, Macmillan, 1961.

Romein, J., *The Asian Century. A history of modern nationalism in Asia*, London, Allen and Unwin, 1962.

Rowbotham, Arnold Horrex, *Missionary and Mandarin: The Jesuits at the Court of China*, Berkeley, CA, University of California Press, 1942.

Rumbold, Sir Algernon, *Watershed in India 1914–1922*, London, Athlone Press, 1979.

Samuel, Raphael (ed.), *Patriotism: The Making and Unmaking of British National Identity*, 3 vols, London, Routledge, 1988.

Satre, Jean-Paul, *War Diaries: Notebooks from a phoney war, November 1939–March 1940*, trans. Quintin Hoare, London, Verso, 1964.

Schama, Simon, *Patriots and Liberators: Revolution in the Netherlands, 1780–1813*, New York, Alfred Knopf, 1977.

Schumpeter, Joseph A., *Imperialism and Social Classes*, New York, Augustus M. Kelley, 1951.

Schumpeter, Joseph, *Capitalism, Socialism and Democracy* (10th impression), London, Unwin University Books, 1965.

Schwarz, A., *A Nation in Waiting: Indonesia in the 1990s*, London, Allen and Unwin 1994.

Seeley, J.R., *The Expansion of England* (2nd edn), London, Macmillan, 1920.

Semmel, Bernard, *The Rise of Free Trade Imperialism*, Cambridge, Cambridge University Press, 1970.

Shaw, A.G.L., *The Story of Australia*, London, Faber and Faber, 1962.

Shleifer, Andrei and Vishny, Robert, *The Grabbing Hand: Government Pathologies and their Cures*, Cambridge, MA, Harvard University Press, 1999.

Sieyès, Emmanuel Joseph, Count, *Qu'est-ce que le Tiers-États?*, Paris, Messidor, 1799 (English trans. M. Blondel, London, Pall Mall Press, 1963).

Sjahrir, Soetan, *Out of Exile; based upon letters*, trans. with an introduction by Charles Wolf Jr, New York, John Day, 1949.

Smith, Adam, *Wealth of Nations* (2 vols, London, 1776) new rev. edn (ed. J.S. Nicholson) London, Nelson, 1884.

Spate, Oscar, *The Spanish Lake*, Minneapolis, University of Minnesota Press, 1979.

Stalin, Joseph, *Marxism and the National and Colonial Question* (ed. A. Feinberg), London, Martin Lawrence, 1936.

Sternhell, Zeev, *The Founding Myths of Israel: Nationalism, Socialism and the Making of the Jewish State*, Princeton, Princeton University Press, 1997.

Stokes, E., *The English Utilitarians and India*, Oxford, Clarendon Press, 1959.

Suntharalingam, R., *Indian Nationalism: An Historical Analysis*, New Delhi, Vikas Publishing House, 1983.

Tagore, Radindranath, *Towards Universal Man*, London, Asia Publishing House, 1961.

Talmon, J.L., *The Origins of Totalitarian Democracy*, London, Secker and Warburg, 1952.

Tawney, R.H., *Equality* (4th rev. edn), London, Unwin, 1952.

Taylor, A.J.P., *The Struggle for Mastery in Europe 1848–1918*, Oxford, Clarendon Press, 1954.

Teng, Ssu-yu and Fairbank, John K., *China's Response to the West 1839–1923*, Cambridge, MA, Harvard University Press, 1954.

'T Hart, Marjolein, Jonker, Joost and van Zanden, Jan Luiten (eds), *A Financial History of the Netherlands*, Cambridge, Cambridge University Press, 1997.

Thomas, Brinley, *International migration and economic development*, Paris, UNESCO, 1961.

Thomas, Hugh, *The Slave Trade: the History of the Atlantic Slave Trade*, New York, Simon and Schuster, 1997.

Thornton, A.P., *The Imperial Idea and its Enemies: a study in British power*, London Macmillan, 1959.

Todorov, T., *La Conquête de l'Amérique*, Paris, Seuil, 1982.

Tomlinson, Brian Roger, *The Indian National Congress and the Raj 1929–1942*, London, Macmillan, 1976.

Tomlinson, Brian Roger, *The Political Economy of the Raj 1914–47: The Economics of Decolonisation in India*, London, Macmillan, 1979.

Tomlinson, Brian Roger, *The Economy of Modern India 1860–1970*, Cambridge, Cambridge University Press, 1993.

Turgot, A.R.J., *Oeuvres de Turgot et documents le concernant*, 5 vols, Paris, 1913–23.

Van Leur, Jacob Cornelis, *Indonesian Trade and Society*, trans. James C. Holmes and A. van Marle, The Hague, Van Hoeve, 1955.

Veblen, Thorstein, *An Inquiry into the Nature of Peace and the Terms of its Perpetuation* (1917), New York, Kelley, 1964.

Vlekke, B.H.M., *The Story of the Dutch East Indies*, Cambridge, MA, Harvard University Press, 1946.

Waldron, Arthur, *The Great Wall of China: From History to Myth*, Cambridge, Cambridge University Press, 1992.

Walzer, Michael, *Just and Unjust Wars*, New York, Basic Books, 1977.

Watson, George, *The Lost Literature of Socialism*, Cambridge, Lutterworth Press, 1998.

Williamson, J.A., *Sir John Hawkins, the Time and the Man*, Oxford, Clarendon Press, 1927.

Wilson, Charles, *Queen Elizabeth and the Revolt of the Netherlands*, London, Macmillan, 1970.

Wilson, G.H., 'Trade, Society and the State', in *Cambridge Economic History of Europe* (eds Habakkuk and Postan), Vol. IV, *The Economy of Expanding Europe in the Sixteenth and Seventeenth Centuries*, op. cit.

Wolfe, Martin (ed.), *The Economic Causes of Imperialism*, New York, Wiley, 1972.

Woodruff, Philip, *The Men Who Ruled India*, I: *The Founders*, II: *The Guardians*, London, Jonathan Cape, 1953, 1954.

World Bank, *East Asian Miracle: Economic Growth and Pubic Policy*, New York, Oxford University Press, 1993.

Index